The Recovery of
Internationally Abducted Children

The Recovery of Internationally Abducted Children

A Comprehensive Guide

by

MAUREEN DABBAGH

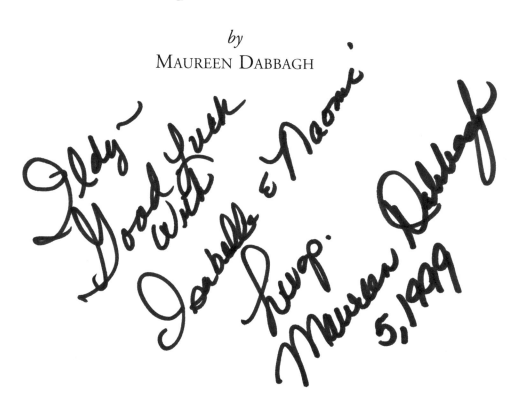

McFarland & Company, Inc., Publishers

Jefferson, North Carolina, and London

British Library Cataloguing-in-Publication data are available

Library of Congress Cataloguing-in-Publication Data

Dabbagh, Maureen, 1958–
    The recovery of internationally abducted children: a
comprehensive guide / by Maureen Dabbagh.
        p.   cm.
    Includes index.
    ISBN 0-7864-0289-X (sewn softcover : 50# alkaline paper) ∞
    1. Kidnapping, Parental — United States — Prevention.
    2. Kidnapping, Parental — International cooperation.   3. Conflict
of laws — Custody of children.   4. Children (International law)
    I. Title.
    HV6598.D33   1997
    362.88 — dc21   97-14081
                                                                 CIP

Manufactured in the United States of America

McFarland & Company, Inc., Publishers
  Box 611, Jefferson, North Carolina 28640

I dedicate this book to Stevie D.

Contents

Acknowledgments

Many hours of research went into compiling the information presented in this book. Although the book could very easily have been twice as long, my aim was to provide searching parents with the most important and useful information without burdening them with details that in time of crisis might serve only to frustrate and confuse.

This work would not have been possible without the wise direction and generous assistance of numerous individuals. I would like to express my deep appreciation to the following agencies, in the hope that it might serve as my personal acknowledgment to all who shared their time, knowledge, and experience with me. To the National Center for Missing and Exploited Children, the United States State Department, and the Syrian Embassy in Washington, D.C., as well as the United States embassies in Syria and Saudi Arabia, my thanks.

I would especially like to thank Reid Robertson, Bill Thurman, and Ed Satterfield of the FBI; Mounir Al-Amoudi, Esq.; Sheila Shanahan, for her sensitive understanding of bicultural relationships; and Johnny Ramazini of the International Center for the Search and Recovery of Missing Children. Deepest thanks are also due my family, for their support and patience during the writing of this book; and my children, who are the light in the dark world of abduction that I have lived in for too many years.

Preface

In 1992, I entered the world of the left-behind parent. My two-year-old daughter, Nadia, was abducted by her father during the course of divorce and custody proceedings and taken to the Middle East. Although he had spoken his intentions repeatedly before he actually abducted Nadia, the courts viewed his threats with little concern. Because Nadia's father and I lived in two different states, the presiding judge had ordered that a temporary visitation schedule be implemented until a final custody determination could be reached. According to that schedule, Nadia was to be shuffled between Ohio and Florida on alternating monthly visits.

Unsupervised visitation, especially over long distances, is not recommended by the Justice Department in cases where a child is at high risk for international abduction. Unfortunately, the judge in my daughter's case was not educated in this area. Desperately, my attorney and I took aggressive action to persuade the courts to implement safeguards, such as supervised in-state visitation, in order to prevent any possible attempts to abduct Nadia. Our efforts were in vain, and Nadia was sent to her father for visitation. She never returned.

The years since Nadia's abduction have been an exercise in frustration, disappointment, and anger at a system that has been ill equipped to deal with this federal crime. The machinery of justice actually made my child's abduction possible.

Lack of information, education, and coordination between agencies responsible for assisting parents, such as local law enforcement, prosecutors, judges, missing children's agencies, the State Department, and lawyers, led me on an aggressive research mission. I learned that federal law requires certain agencies to assist parents whose children have been abducted and clearly defines that assistance. To my amazement, I learned that in nearly every respect, the handling of my daughter's case had violated procedures spelled out in the United States code.

It was months before any law enforcement agency would take a missing persons report on my child. This was a violation of federal law, which states that no waiting period will be implemented in listing a child as missing. I had lost valuable time, during which Nadia was held in Florida for three months before she was successfully abducted to the Middle East. It took the courts seven months to determine custody, despite a letter to the judge from Florida HRS stating that the temporary visitation order was not in my child's best interests, and recommending that a custody decision be made. It took almost two years after Nadia's abduction for a warrant to be issued against her father through the state of Florida for international parental kidnapping. Florida also filed the missing persons report, as my home state was ignorant of federal law concerning custody jurisdiction.

The time spent in accomplishing the above had not led me any closer to my child; in fact, the long delay allowed her father time to conceal Nadia's whereabouts completely. Though I was granted sole custody of Nadia a year after the original custody hearing, and her father was given no visitation privileges, I was still without my child.

Because my success to this point was a direct result of my determination to see that some sort of action was taken on Nadia's behalf, I had gained valuable knowledge about legal procedures and agency responsibilities. To prosecutors and other attorneys, I found myself presenting the law that was used to promote their involvement. I was educating the very professionals who were empowered to assist me.

My support system had grown from family and friends to a nationwide network of parents who, like myself, had found themselves unable to elicit the assistance of those with the power to help them. With these parents I began sharing what I had learned of the law. In time, cases of international parental abduction were being referred to me by various agencies. I was now a teacher. The need for the information I had compiled was overwhelming. I was constantly inundated with requests for specific information from parents and professionals alike. With those requests, this book was born.

It is important that searching parents share information with each other. Without the willingness of my predecessor to share her avenues of recovery with me, I would not have had any hope of success in my recovery efforts. To her, I am deeply grateful.

My child has been gone since 1992. Though I now know her whereabouts, I have neither seen her nor spoken to her. I continue my aggressive efforts, and I intend to bring her home.

I have found a wealth of support from our federal government. With governmental assistance I have been able not only to locate my child, but to successfully litigate in Islamic court. Nadia's abductor has been arrested and jailed for kidnapping in a Middle Eastern country. As efforts to recover Nadia continue, I have involved myself in recovery efforts for other children abroad. Occasional successes have led to a better understanding of and sensitivity to this growing problem. The information that I have gathered since the heartbreaking abduction of my own child has been funneled into a work that I hope will be of help to others, so that out of this most horrendous crime and my personal loss, some good might come.

Introduction

International parental kidnapping is a crime. It became a federal felony on December 2, 1993. This crime is described as child abuse. It may consist of removing a child from the United States, or retaining a child outside of the United States after a visit. Each year hundreds, possibly thousands, of children fall victim to this crime. Currently there are no accurate statistics to indicate the actual numbers of these children abroad.

A parental abduction may occur when a parent removes a child to another town, county, state, or country. If a child has been removed from one state to another state, this crime falls under the state's child-snatching or custodial interference laws and may or may not be a state felony. Removing or retaining a child outside of the United States escalates this crime to a federal felony level.

As the left-behind parent of an internationally abducted child, I have compiled this guide based on the knowledge I have gained through my efforts to recover my daughter. I have attempted to organize this information in a fashion that will prove useful for other searching parents.

Chapter 1 defines the crime of international parental abduction and associated terminology. It explores the emotional state of the left-behind parent and stresses the importance of arming oneself with knowledge, both of available resources and of political circumstances that might affect the situation.

For a parent who believes his or her child is at risk for abduction, supervised visitation is sometimes the only available protection. Chapter 2 is a brief look at supervised visitation and some relevant court cases.

There are several steps a parent should take as soon as he or she believes an abduction has occurred. These are discussed in Chapter 3, which leads the reader through the process of filing a missing persons report, contacting various authorities, and determining the whereabouts of the abductor and the child. Chapter 3 also discusses three possible approaches to the crime — as a criminal, civil, or diplomatic matter — and offers advice for pursuing each course. Chapter 4 takes the reader further into the search process and ends with a discussion of the repercussions of recovery.

Many agencies are available to help searching parents. In Chapter 5, the reader will find detailed information about the agencies likely to be involved in a recovery effort, such as the United States State Department, Interpol, and The Hague.

Parents searching for abducted children will benefit from knowing the laws that have been passed to help them. To provide easy access to this material, Chapter 6 reproduces the text of relevant legislation from the United States Code.

A word about the law: Most searching parents have at least been tempted to explore the possibility of re-abduction, as opposed to recovery through legal channels. Please be aware that re-abduction can be dangerous, disastrous, even deadly. No illegal attempt to recover a child will be condoned in this book, and no actions generally deemed illegal will be advised. This is not to say that I am not sympathetic. As a left-behind parent, I have considered such action myself. However, attempts at re-abduction are truly not good for a child. Despite what experience may have led you to believe, the law is on the side of the searching parent. Those who may say otherwise are likely unfamiliar with the provisions you will find in Chapter 6. Be their teacher, and let the law work for you.

This book contains a number of stories about parents who have successfully recovered their children, as well as parents still searching. All these stories are somewhat oversimplified, with details obscured, as a way of providing anonymity to the families as well as preventing a potential abductor from using this information in some way that facilitates an abduction. Readers should not assume that successful recoveries were as simple as they may sound.

This work would not be complete without a word about parents who abduct their children in an effort to safeguard them from danger. Usually these cases center around abuse. A child who is being abused by a parent may be abducted by the other parent in an attempt to safeguard that child from future abuse. The incidence of this practice appears to be increasing. It seems likely that the increase is a direct result of the domestic and family courts' inability to protect children, which forces parents to take matters into their own hands even when threatened with imprisonment.

Not all parents who abduct should be regarded as criminals. It is my opinion that when a child is abducted because a parent has no other means of insuring that child's safety, the court that failed to protect the child should be held criminally and civilly liable. Although the United States Constitution does not guarantee the civil rights of persons under the age of 18, a parent has the right to petition the courts for a child's safety. When this petition fails, abduction may be the result.

Because it is not uncommon for a parent to accuse another of abuse during custody proceedings, judges have become skeptical of this charge. Many judges have gone so far as to award custody to the abuser as a way of "punishing" a parent for using abuse as a basis for requesting custody. This has occurred even where evidence indicated that the child had indeed been abused. Immunity from civil liability should not protect those who actually "order" the abuse of children, and issue a decree which gives the abuser free access to his victim, and punishes the parent who attempts to safeguard the child.

In one harrowing case, a Virginia mother was extradited and incarcerated for abducting her very young daughter. The child was given to the father, who had legal custody. Although the mother stated that she abducted her child to prevent sexual abuse, the courts denied the mother access to the child as a condition of bail. This case is still pending. Medical reports indicate this child was sexually abused, yet no further physical examination of the child has been done after she was returned to her father.

Similar cases are occurring at an alarming rate. Because of the high incidence of divorce and custody actions in the United States, many courts are simply overflowing with cases. Little time or consideration is given to the individuals involved — especially the children — when a decree is issued. It has been repeatedly demonstrated that domestic court judges enable the abductions of children. Unqualified judgments appear to be epidemic. Whether a parent is petitioning the courts to prevent the international abduction of a child (to which the courts commonly respond by allowing unsupervised visitation to the potential abductor), or requesting custody in an effort to stop abuse of the child (to which the courts commonly respond by granting custody to the abuser), the courts are the first line of defense for the child, and usually the first place a child experiences injustice.

Making Your Voice Heard

When a parent is put to the test of protecting his or her young, love provides an awesome power. A parent who lost her child through the actions of a drunk driver started the organization known as MADD. John Walsh became actively involved in bringing criminals to justice after the loss of his son. Margaret Strickland became an author and child advocate after the loss of her grandchild. The stories of these heroes whose fights for children go on and on, prove the power of parents. If those in administrative and judicial positions cannot or will not protect the children, then it must be the parents that do.

The crime of international parental abduction is not going away. The world is getting smaller. Bicultural marriages continue to increase as travel brings people together from the distant corners of the earth. Sometimes, when the blind veil of love is lifted, these cultures clash irreconcilably. When that happens, it is the very product of that love that is at risk.

Public demand for qualified family court judges is a must. It is in the courtroom that many children are lost...lost because of the incompetence of the judges. A report prepared by the American Bar Association offers extensive recommendations for changes in the system, including continuing education for judges and lawyers. These recommendations are excerpted in Chapter 6.

If those in power do not heed the cries of the searching parents, and do not believe that the children are the future, take note. Parents should write to their senators, congressmen, and those to whom they have entrusted the welfare of their state. The voices of parents need to be heard. Even if you have never voted, written to a political official before, or gotten involved in any committee, write a letter. Write a letter for the children. Write a letter for the youngest, most helpless members of our society. Perhaps it will be your letter — or your life, or your love — that makes the difference.

How to Read
Citations to Documents

Throughout this book you will find citations to court or congressional records. Volumes of these records can generally be found in law or university libraries, though court records are published in regional series and not every series will be available in every library. In general, the bigger the library, the more access to records covering a greater area. A librarian can provide information regarding the availability of specific materials and can also direct you to the source of needed information. Once you locate the necessary volumes, it is a fairly simple matter to look up citations, provided you understand the abbreviations commonly used.

A typical citation to court records includes the names of the two parties involved (separated by "v." for "versus"), a volume number, an abbreviation signifying the series of court records (called a *Reporter*— for example, *Pacific Reporter* or *Southeastern Reporter*), and a page number. An example follows:

Soltanieh[a] v.[b] King[c] 826[d] P 2d[e] 1076[f]

[a]first party
[b]versus
[c]second party
[d]volume number
[e]abbreviation denoting regional reporter series; "P 2d" means *Pacific Reporter, second series*
[f]page number

Acts of Congress are recorded in the *U.S. Statutes at Large*. A citation includes a volume number, the abbreviation "Stat" for *Statutes at Large*, and a page number. For example:

94[a] Stat[b] 3566[c]

[a]volume number
[b]stands for *U.S. Statutes at Large*
[c]page number

Federal laws are recorded in the *United States Code*. They are grouped under "titles" (general subject areas, such as immigration or copyright), which are numbered. The titles are divided into sections and subsections, also numbered. Citations to the code read as follows:

42[a] USC[b] §5780[c]

[a]title number
[b]stands for *U.S. Code*
[c]section number

Federal laws are accompanied by a body of administrative regulations, which may be found in the *Code of Federal Regulations*. Like the United States Code, it is divided into titles and sections. A citation might read:

22[a] CFR[b] §51.70[c]

[a]title number
[b]stands for *Code of Federal Regulations*
[c]section number (numbers following the period represent subsections; this is section 51, subsection 70)

1

Understanding International Parental Abduction

ANNUAL ESTIMATES OF PARENTAL ABDUCTION (INCLUDING FAMILY MEMBERS) HAVE REACHED 350,000.

> Finkelhor, Hotaling, and Sediak, *Missing, Abducted, Runaway, and Thrownaway Children in America. First Report: Numbers and Characteristics.* (Washington, DC: United States Dept. of Justice, 1988).

Federal law defines international parental kidnapping as removing a child (anyone under the age of 16 years) from the United States, or retaining outside of the United States a child who had previously resided in the United States, with the purpose of preventing the other parent from lawful exercise of his or her parental rights such as visitation, joint custody, sole custody, or access. It is important to note that a left-behind parent does not have to have legal custody of the abducted child in order to qualify the abduction as a crime.

Many law enforcement agencies erroneously believe that international parental kidnapping is a civil matter and may refer a searching parent to civil processes. This may be the first obstacle that a parent faces in his or her efforts to locate and recover a child. In fact, the overall lack of education, information, and experience among local law enforcement agencies can actually assist an abductor by hindering the implementation of procedures required by law. This widespread ignorance exists also among lawyers, judges, prosecutors, FBI agents, and U.S. attorneys. This claim is not intended to embarrass or ridicule any of the above-mentioned professionals, but only to set before searching parents the reality of the obstacles that may befall them in their search for their children.

The Vocabulary of International Parental Abduction

International parental kidnapping is a unique crime, and those who battle against it have had to develop a unique vocabulary. It is important that the reader understand this terminology. The United States Justice Department may refer to this crime as kidnapping, as it appears in the name of the International Parental Kidnapping Crime Act of 1993. The State Department, Office of Citizens' Consular Services, Child Custody Division (henceforth referred to as simply the State Department), calls it international parental abduction. The Office of Juvenile Justice and Delinquency Prevention refers to this crime as international parental child abduction. State laws addressing parental abduction fall under "child-snatching" or "custodial interference" laws. To further add to the terminology, one missing-children organization called "American Children Held Hostage" defines this crime as a hostage situation. While the term "hostage" does not appear to have been used in any official legal or diplomatic definitions, it seems likely that the word may have been applied as an emotional response or personal view of the crime. Since this book attempts to address the crime in the language of law and diplomacy, the word "hostage" will not be used, but the other terms will be used interchangeably, since all reflect the crime of removing or retaining a child outside of the United States.

Terminology describing the return of a child and the reuniting of the child and parent is also varied. Unlike the terms for the crime itself, which really hold no significant differences, words in this case convey different shades of meaning and should be used with care. The word "recovery" suitably describes the finding of something that was lost, while the word "rescue" conjures up images of dramatic action in order to achieve recovery. "Re-abduction" holds still more significance because it describes a "counter-crime." Those involved in international parental abductions appear to select a term based on factors such as their approach to the recovery. An individual working in an official diplomatic capacity tends to use the word "recover." Law enforcement may use the word "find." Still, organizations that lend themselves to recovering children may describe recovery as re-abduction or rescue.

The correct use of terminology in this area is essential in communicating exactly the intentions a searching parent has in recovering his or her child. A parent who communicates an intention to re-abduct a child may encounter a lack of support from the State Department or U.S. embassies abroad. Just as parental abduction is a crime in the United States, it is a crime in almost every country. In that view, United States embassies abroad and the State Department will not do anything to facilitate a re-abduction.

In contrast, a parent who expresses an intent to recover a child through legal and diplomatic channels will meet with support from the United States government. That support may be active (assisting in the effort) or passive (allowing the parent to freely pursue such recoveries), but in either case the parent benefits.

The definition of international parental abduction includes cases where children have been detained outside of the United States while both parents are in the detaining country. It is not unusual for a foreign national parent to take his or her family on a "visit" home, then refuse to allow the children to return to the United States. Although an American parent may be able to leave a foreign country freely, that parent may be prohibited under the laws of that country from taking the children along. One does not just go to the airport and leave. Many countries require exit visas. Permission from the citizen parent may be required to remove a child — and, depending on the country, even an American wife — across national borders. In Muslim countries, the man usually gets the children if the decision is to be made between a Muslim father and an American mother of any faith, including Muslim. Some countries do not even allow American women to enter the court system to fight for custody. Saudi Arabia is one example. To my knowledge, only one American woman has ever been granted permission to have her case heard in a Saudi court. She was literally persecuted for her efforts to recover her children. This woman was not only denied custody, but was thrown into prison without reason. When at last she was allowed to visit her children, it was under the most humiliating of conditions. (She had to spend the night and sleep in the same bed as her ex-husband's new wife.)

A parent trapped in a foreign country with his or her children may well be considered a hostage. For such an individual, life may become a daily struggle for survival. Many such parents are forced into impossible decisions when they are offered the chance to leave provided the children stay behind. These are among the most desperate and heart-wrenching situations.

The lexicon of international parental abduction includes terms to describe the parents involved. The parent who has lost his or her child is referred to as the left-behind parent, searching parent, and victim parent. The parent who illegally removed a child is referred to as the abductor or kidnapper.

A final term to learn is "federal kidnapping warrant." This term refers to a warrant issued under the International Parental Kidnapping Crime Act of 1993. Be aware that no warrant can be issued unless the crime has actually taken place; it is not a preventative measure. At present, it is not a crime for a potential abductor to announce his intent to abduct a child.

International parental abduction is not isolated to the United States. Parents all over the world have had their children abducted. Some of those children have been brought illegally into the United States from other countries. While the United States recognizes the taking of one of its citizens as wrong, it also views a foreign national being abducted to the United States as wrong. The United States has addressed this problem by signing the Hague Convention on the Civil Aspects of International Child Abduction. This is a multinational agreement to locate and return children who have been unlawfully removed or detained with the purpose of preventing the other parent access to the child. The problem is worldwide and is becoming larger as the world grows smaller.

The Emotional Impact of Abduction on the Left-Behind Parent

Searching parents are often so overcome by grief, guilt, confusion, frustration and panic that they are unable to take charge of their search. In these cases, a supportive network of family and friends can be a great benefit. (Unfortunately, many times, the searching parent's own family can be the first to give up the search and advise the searching parent to do the same.) However, much depends on the individual parent, and each may take a different approach to the crisis. Some searching parents are able to turn all their intense emotions into an aggressive energy that they funnel into productive search efforts. Some start out strong, then slowly become exasperated by the system, failures and disappointments. Still others are so distraught that they are unable to hold down jobs, have successful relationships, or even begin to coordinate recovery efforts.

Unlike losing a child to death, abduction usually has no resolution for the searching parent until the child is either recovered or grown. Many searching parents put their lives on hold, becoming so absorbed in the recovery process that little else matters. Study of the dynamics involved in this tragedy is just beginning.

For the searching parent, the intense emotional strain is aggravated at almost every turn. Many searching parents harbor strong negative feelings not only toward the abductor, but also toward the system they feel has abandoned them or failed to protect them. This may include family and domestic court judges, lawyers, local police, state and federal officials, and even those in missing children's organizations. The searching parent is looking for someone to recover his or her child. It appears that long before searching parents recognize their own responsibility for coordinating recovery efforts, they assume that the only real way to recover their children is through illegal re-abduction attempts.

The media have presented international parental abduction as hopeless. Talk shows present grieving parents who testify that the State Department or U.S. embassy abroad failed to assist them in recovering their children, and searching parents who boast of success through the use of paramilitary personnel. More media attention to successful legal recoveries would show that recoveries through legal avenues are eminently possible, serving to educate those carrying out their own recovery efforts. Perhaps these stories are not explosive or exciting enough to warrant media time. However, without knowledge of these successes, future recoveries are made more difficult. The lack of information has continued to frustrate both parent and professional.

In truth, there are many more successful recoveries — legal and illegal — than the media would have us believe. Not every parent is willing to come forward with his or her story. It is not uncommon for searching parents to "disappear" once they have recovered their children. These parents are often fearful of re-abduction. While some will share their experiences with others who are searching, many simply want to take no chance of being found. This includes those whose recoveries were accomplished through legal channels.

Because the media often have given the impression that re-abduction is the only successful recovery method available, a great many searching parents immediately lose hope. The searching parent may not be in a position to pay for a re-abduction. Such rescues can easily cost well over $100,000. Perhaps these parents do not know how to contact someone who will do the job. Still others are told that their child is in a country in which re-abduction is so dangerous that no one will attempt it. With little more information than that, it is no wonder that searching parents give up.

Another obstacle is the frustration a searching parent immediately experiences when faced with a judicial and administrative system that is basically ignorant of the crime of international parental abduction. Parents often meet with resistance from the very officials empowered to assist them in recovering their children through legal means. It is no wonder that so many, many parents jump immediately into the idea of illegal re-abduction as a means of recovery.

Illegal re-abduction does not always mean hiring paramilitary personnel to recover a child. There are cases where re-abductions were accomplished by the parent alone. In many of these cases no violence ensued, the child was not traumatized, and the searching parent used skill and cunning to achieve recovery, often without the knowledge of any agency. Often times, these successes involve older abducted children who assisted in their own recoveries. Some individuals may define these re-abductions as independent recovery efforts, since most of the children were of the age to request removal from their abductors' care, the searching parents had legal custody of the children, and no force was used. Yet it should be noted that crimes may very well have been committed by the searching parents in the countries where the children were recovered.

For the emotionally crippled parent, stories of success serve as a source of hope and inspiration, regardless of their legal standing. A moral imperative appears to override any civil or criminal law, driving searching parents to recover their children by any possible means, many times with little regard to any law or to the consequences to themselves. Parental love is a fierce and powerful emotion that cannot be absolutely controlled by laws. Instinct overrides cultural dictates and sometimes common sense. For that reason, those offering recovery services to desperate searching parents find a very lucrative market, even when they employ illegal tactics.

Yet the natural urge toward re-abduction can be dangerous as well as unproductive. In truth, few children are successfully recovered through re-abductions. Individuals have been caught on foreign soil and imprisoned. Searching parents have been left financially devastated by failed re-abduction attempts. In the time it takes to coordinate an illegal re-abduction attempt, a searching parent can initiate legal and diplomatic action at a fraction of the cost, and without the fear of being caught doing something outside the law. Illegal re-abduction may involve unnecessary financial burdens, alliances with untrustworthy individuals, and the threat of criminal liability. The main reason re-abduction continues to appeal to parents despite these dangers is that, lacking knowledge of possible legal avenues, parents gravitate toward any media reference to their situation. This is called hope.

For searching parents who have recovered their children, sympathy towards other searching parents often conflicts with the need to protect their own interests. Many times, a desperate searching parent will attach him or herself to a parent who has successfully recovered a child. Searching parents do this for emotional support, yet legal recoveries involve the support of both the United States and the foreign country. What better support than that!

Parents and Politics

Searching parents soon discover the importance of politics in the recovery process. Many of these parents have no idea how the United States criminal justice system works, nor how international politics work. The searching parent will become educated simply by going through the necessary steps mentioned in this book to reach a final plan of action.

A searching parent will need to fight off the overwhelming desire to force United States agencies to do something. From the first hour of a child's disappearance, a parent must become a diplomat. Hysteria will not allow him or her to effectively absorb the necessary information needed to follow direction. The parent has no control over an agency's willingness to help or that agency's experience or knowledge in this field, but with diplomacy, he or she can establish good lines of communication that will allow for education and the effective exchange of ideas.

For example, the process of listing an abducted child as missing has for some reason been a major obstacle to searching parents, even though federal laws have been enacted to support the searching parent's need to involve the assistance of local police. Knowledge of these laws (see Chapter 6) gives a parent a powerful tool for working with local law enforcement agents who refuse or delay assistance to a parent. However, these materials should be used to educate, not to initiate legal debates.

Local law enforcement agents may find they need the assistance of the city or county attorney in determining their role in recovering an abducted child. Because international parental abduction crosses the lines of both civil and criminal law, those in law enforcement are often unsure where their responsibility begins or ends, and liability becomes a question. Searching parents must avoid making enemies of the individuals empowered to assist them. Using patience, compassion, and most of all, the law, a searching parent should work to educate those who are not aware of their responsibilities. This effort to educate can often times be a most arduous task in light of the fact that most searching parents are in desperate emotional states and may find it extremely difficult to concentrate on law and politics. Unfortunately, it is a task the searching parent is likely to encounter at every step in the process of recovery. Working within the constraints of local or international politics can be a very stressful exercise, but a child's future may well depend on this issue. Recovery efforts often have more to do with politics than with the law.

The *Lexicon Webster Dictionary* defines politics in part as "the plotting or scheming of those seeking personal power, glory, position, or the like."

Although the word "scheme" has the connotation of something being done illegally, the same dictionary defines it as "a plan of something to be done; a project."

A searching parent is not looking for power, glory or position, but for a human being. On the other hand, a searching parent may need the assistance of those who are in the position of power and glory. An internationally abducted child should have nothing to do with politics, but that is not the case. Directly or indirectly, a searching parent's efforts are affected by politics at every turn.

Yet parents must realize that politicians will not necessarily be willing or able to intervene directly in child abduction cases. Many parents of abducted children frantically write letters to their senators and representatives as well as other officials in an effort to gain political support in recovering their child. While some may be supportive, most parents will receive a form letter in response to their request for assistance. The letters that parents send to senators, congressmen, and even the president are routinely funneled back to the United States Department of State, Division of Children's Issues, and placed in the parent's case file. The form letter a parent receives from the politician most likely will state that someone is "looking into" the matter or that the request has been forwarded to the "appropriate" agency. No real action is taken as a rule. This is not to say that a handful of sympathetic officials don't work aggressively for parents, but they are few and far between.

Sometimes a politician can help without direct intervention. For example, Representative Owen Pickett of Virginia recently introduced a measure that will likely have an impact on cases involving abductors who are members of the military. Representative Pickett was inspired by a case in which the step-grandfather of a young boy abducted him to Costa Rica from the Tidewater area of Virginia. The abductor is American and so is the child. The abductor is also a retired navy commander and as such was eligible to collect retirement pay even though he was out of the country.

Under Pickett's provision, which was attached to the House's 1997 Defense Authorization Bill, military retirees who flee the country to avoid prosecution in criminal or civil court cases would forfeit their retirement pay. The provision is designed to deter retirees from taking the law into their own hands in custody cases.

The provision was adopted by the House by voice vote May 14, 1996, without any discussion.

World politics — the relationships between nations — can also have a profound influence on child abduction cases. For example, if the United

States is working on peace talks or economic relief within a specific region, those efforts will tend to have a positive effect on the searching parent's relationship with the authorities of that country. However, if the United States is at war with that country, has sent in military troops against the wishes of the current government, or has placed economic sanctions on that country, the effect is likely to be negative. While the idea of keeping up with world politics may sound intimidating, even overwhelming, the searching parent can usually become sufficiently informed by concentrating on the politics of the country where their child has been taken, unless that country is directly affected by United States politics in neighboring countries.

World politics can exert a very positive influence on a parent's search. For example, in the mid–'90s, United States secretary of state Warren Christopher traveled to Saudi Arabia and to Syria for talks to improve the two countries' diplomatic relations. A parent then searching for a child taken to Syria found that this trip brought a great deal of strength, validity, and respect to her case. Although Mr. Christopher did not get involved in the case, simply his presence in the country and the fact that his name appeared on an authentication document brought a great deal of positive attention to the searching parent's plight. Doors suddenly began to open for this parent in Syria. A great deal of effort was put forth to locate the child. So profound was the effect of politics on this case that Syria issued a warrant for the abductor on the charge of kidnapping. Mr. Christopher may never know what a wonderful influence his presence had in Syria.

2

Preventing Abduction Through Court-Ordered Safeguards

ALMOST HALF OF PARENTAL ABDUCTIONS WERE THREATENED IN ADVANCE.

Hegar, R.L., and Greif, G.L., "Abduction of Children by Parents: A Survey of the Problem," *Social Work 36* (1991), pp. 421–426.

Supervised visitation as ordered by a court is often all that stands between a child and a parent planning international abduction or re-abduction. Since most judges are ignorant of parental abduction and the laws that have been enacted to prevent it, the searching parent may have to educate his or her attorney prior to standing before the judge. It is the attorney's duty to represent the client to the best of his or her ability. If the lawyer is ignorant about international parental abduction, then the parent must make available the resources that will assist that attorney in protecting a child. It may be an uphill battle. Fortunately, the law is on the side of the parent.

The American Bar Association Center on Children and the Law has conducted a study of risk factors in parental kidnappings. Dr. Linda Girdner is the director of these studies and has participated in previous studies involving other aspects of parental abduction. Her work is a great legal resource for a parent and an attorney. (Dr. Girdner can be reached at [202] 662-1720.) According to preliminary findings, a child who has been previously abducted or whose parent has threatened abduction is at high risk. For such a child, the court should order supervised visitation.

Although parents have requested supervised visitation and even denial of visitation to abductors or potential abductors, judges often times choose to ignore the request. This is quite common, and the predictable outcome is a parent's nightmare come true. Judges may feel they are not empowered to take action. Again, the ignorance of the courts has made countless abductions possible.

21

Consider the example of a Michigan father married to a German national. This father had reason to believe his estranged wife would remove their young son from the United States, having discovered that she had obtained a passport for the child. The father requested that the court order supervised visitation to the mother in an effort to prevent the abduction. The court did not grant the father's request, and the child was immediately abducted. The judge did, however, grant the father's request to supervised visitation *after* the child was abducted. The order was to be retroactive to the day before the child's last court-ordered visitation with his abductor.

In another case, an Ohio mother sought custody of her daughter against the Syrian national father who had repeatedly threatened to take the child to Syria. The courts were warned on numerous occasions of the father's threats. The mother's story appeared on the front page of the local newspaper. The judge ordered the father to take the child to his state of Florida for a one-month unsupervised visit, threatening the mother with contempt and jail should visitation not proceed. The mother never saw the child again.

It is important that a searching parent continue to plead his or her case for custody in domestic and family courts even if the child has been abducted. It is necessary for the searching parent to have legal sole custody (although it is not required in order to apply to The Hague for assistance or request an international parental kidnapping warrant against the abductor). Legal custody protects the child in the event of a recovery. Also, many organizations will not assist a parent who does not have a proof of legal custody of an abducted child.

Custody is not the only order a searching parent should secure. The law provides that an abductor can lose his or her rights to visitation or be granted only supervised visitation, or that visitation can be held at abeyance. A searching parent needs to build the safest legal environment for the child. If the judge has ordered that a high-risk child be supervised during visits with the abductor or potential abductor, it should not be determined that a family member will supervise the visits. This can lead to conflicts which may hinder the effectiveness of the order. Family members may be reluctant to supervise the visits or the abductor may intimidate the family member. The child may not be any safer than if the visits were unsupervised.

Individuals and agencies are available to supervise visits. A social worker or family clergyman might be used. However, it is important to understand that some individuals may not want to become involved. Finding the right person to supervise a visit can lead to a great deal of anxiety, not only for the parent trying to safeguard the child, but also for the child, who can pick up on the fear and frustration that visitation brings. This problem is being addressed by a very unique group of individuals.

Recent legislation authorized funding for supervised visitation centers as part of a crime bill introduced by Senator Wellstone. It is a version of the "Child Safety Act," S. 870. Supervised visitation centers offer parents a safe place in which supervised visitation can take place. These centers are available in many locations. A good source for information on supervised visitation is

Supervised Visitation Network
1101 N. 4th Ave.
Tucson, Arizona 85705
Tel: 602-745-9951 or 561-355-2157
Fax: 561-355-3175

If a supervised visitation center can offer a parent a safe place for visitation, that center should be written into the court order as the location where visitation will occur. Robert B. Straus, a leader in the supervised visitation network, recommends that situations which require supervision for safe access include abduction risk. (See *Family Law Quarterly*, Vol. 29, no. 2 summer, 1995.)

If a court refuses to initiate or order protective safeguards for a child, the burden of protection falls on the attorney and protecting parent, often times working against the most determined judge. Parent and attorney should contact the passport office and request that a passport not be issued for the child. If the child has a passport, the court can order that the child's passport, as well as the potential abductor's passport, be held during visitation. This should not be depended on to prevent an abduction.

Under no circumstance should a judge order a high-risk child to travel to another state for unsupervised visitation. This has been done many times, and the outcome is tragic. Remember, children have died at the hands of their abductors. This is not just a civil problem, this is a federal felony. Restraining orders should not be depended on either. A good judge who is knowledgeable in this area of the law will fight to protect a child and will award every safeguard the courts can offer. Safeguards include supervised visitation for the abductor or potential abductor, blocks on the child's passport, copies of the abductor or potential abductor's United States and foreign passport to be held on file, restraining orders which prevent the child from being removed from the state or country or deny access to the child, and orders that declare the protecting parent the child's legal guardian. Case law supports all of the above should a judge be concerned about infringing on an abductor's or potential abductor's rights. A court can also order the abductor's or potential abductor's passport and visa held and not released except by court order. Another safeguard is an order requiring the abductor or potential abductor to post a bond. Both these actions were taken in Soltanieh v. King, 826 P.2d 1076 (Utah App. 1992). Also see, Compare in re Joseph D., 19 Cal. App. 4th 678 (1193).

Other cases in which a parent was required to post bond to safeguard visitation include Al-Zouhayli v. Al-Zouhayli, 486 N.W. 2d 10 (Minn. App. 1992); Rayford v. Rayford, 456 So. 2d 833 (Ala. Civ. App. 1984); Bullard v. Bullard, 647 P.2d (Haw, Ct. App. 1982); and Biggers v. Biggers, 650 P.2d 692 (Idaho 1982). Cases in which restraining orders against the removal of a child include People v. Beach, 194 Cal. App. 3d 955, 240 Cal. Rptr. 50 (1987) and Mitchell v. Mitchell, 311 S.E. 2d 456 (Ga. 1984).

Appendix A of this book reproduces a United States State Department publication about international parental abduction. The first part of that publication, "How to Guard Against International Child Abduction," offers further suggestions for parents who believe their children may fall victim to this terrible crime.

3

Contacting Authorities
and Making a Plan

DOMESTIC VIOLENCE WAS PRESENT IN 54% OF ABDUCTED
CHILDREN'S HOMES PRIOR TO THE CHILD'S ABDUCTION.

Greif, G.L., and Hegar, R.L., "Parents Whose Children Are
Abducted by the Other Parent: Implications for Treatment," *American
Journal of Family Therapy 19* (1991), pp. 215–225.

To a left-behind parent, efforts to seek assistance in locating a child may quickly appear fruitless. In a time of crisis, this may further frustrate and anger an already emotionally distraught parent. Sadly, much of this frustration is caused by simple ignorance of what United States agencies can and cannot do. Misconceptions continually lead to unsuccessful attempts by parents to utilize the agencies empowered to assist them.

There are several facts which may surprise most searching parents, but which are vital to a successful recovery:

• First, *there exists no United States government agency which can or will go into another country and take possession of an abducted child and return that child to the left-behind parent.*

• Second, *it is up to the left-behind parent to coordinate a child's recovery.*

• Third, *it is up to the left-behind parent to find out what an agency can do and to utilize those resources.*

There is no course available on how to recover an internationally abducted child, and no easy way to learn. A parent may spend months in research before he or she can coordinate a constructive recovery effort. There is no short cut and no substitute for gaining information. The need for information is critical not only to parents, but to those involved in the judicial and law enforcement aspects of this crime.

Once a parent takes charge of a child's recovery, the impossible can become the possible. Children may be successfully recovered even if they have been gone for years. The beginning point of a recovery effort depends on how long ago the child was abducted and how much is known about his or her location. In may cases the whereabouts of a child are not known; therefore, determining whereabouts is an early step for many left-behind parents. On the other hand, a parent who already knows the child's location may need only to begin recovery efforts in the appropriate country. There are examples of how a searching parent must determine where he or she stands in the recovery process in order to effectively pursue a recovery. Another example is the custody question. Although custody is not an issue in requesting an international parental kidnapping warrant against the abductor, it may be if the searching parent intends to enter a foreign court to request return of the child. If custody has already been given to the abductor, the searching parent may re-enter the court and again request custody. Custody is also important because some agencies will not assist a parent who does not have legal custody. In Hague cases, a searching parent must have legal custody in order to request return of the child. Custody is not necessary if visitation rights are requested.

If a parent believes his or her child has been abducted abroad, *the very first thing that parent should do is call the local law enforcement agency to report the crime and file a missing persons report on the child*. How to file that report is described in the next section of this chapter, as well as how to counter objections and obstacles that may be encountered at the local law enforcement level. Following that section are instructions for contacting other agencies. Proceeding through these steps brings the searching parent to a point where he or she can decide how to approach the overall recovery effort — whether as a criminal, civil, or diplomatic matter. Elements unique to each case will determine whether alternative approaches are needed in overcoming obstacles and locating the child.

For any recovery effort to succeed, it is vital that the searching parent resist the hope that "others" will somehow recover the child. There are no "others" who can accomplish the task. Various agencies are empowered to provide assistance, but *the burden of recovery belongs to the searching parent*. This fact cannot be emphasized enough, and the searching parent must accept it in order to move beyond the feelings of helplessness that are a normal reaction to this terrible crime.

Two separate issues tend to dominate and motivate a searching parent. The first is the desire to recover the child; the second is to see that some sort of punishment is handed out to the abductor by proper authorities.

There are times when the second seems more motivating than the first in many cases. However, the searching parent must realize that prosecutions and convictions are rare in cases of international parental abduction. Furthermore, agencies empowered to assist the parent may not be sympathetic should they determine that the searching parent is more interested in penalizing the abductor than in recovering their child. In truth, of course, a searching parent cannot help wishing for both. There is a deep need for the same legal and judicial system that failed to prevent an abduction to fulfill its commitment to justice. That fulfillment would renew parents' trust in the system and give searching parents hope. For now, however, left-behind parents should make an effort to concentrate on recovering their abducted children, beginning with the steps described below.

Step One: Local Police

Immediately or as soon as possible after an abduction becomes evident, a searching parent should file a missing persons report on the child. This can be done through the local law enforcement office of the child's home city or country. It may be handled by either the police department or the sheriff's department, depending on where the child resides. When a parent requests that a child be listed as missing, a report will be taken and information, including a physical description of the child and the abductor, will be requested. The parent may be asked to provide photographs of both. (If few clear, current photos exist, the best prints can be taken to an office supply store or print shop for color copying. This is inexpensive, fast, and a fairly good quality of reproduction.) If local law enforcement officers refuse to list a child as missing, or request a delay, the searching parent should try to educate the local agency in the laws described below. It is imperative that a child be listed as missing immediately in order for the searching parent to go to the next step. Failure to have a child listed as missing may not only cause delays in a child's recovery, but will prevent a parent from gaining access to valuable resources and assistance.

Below are the most common problems that searching parents have faced in attempting to enlist the assistance of local law enforcement, along with the legal notes to help in combating ignorance, apathy, and lack of cooperation.

Local law enforcement refuses to list child as missing until child has been gone for a specified period of time, or until searching parent can "prove the child's whereabouts."

This is a violation of the **National Child Search Assistance Act of 1990**, Public law 101-647, 42 U.S.C. ss 5780. No law enforcement agency can require a "waiting period" before listing a child as missing. It must be done immediately.

The **Missing Children Act of 1982**, Public Law 97-292, 28 U.S.C. ss 534(a), encourages and promotes the involvement of law enforcement agencies in locating missing children. Although the local sheriff obviously cannot hop on a plane to Jordan to recover a child, this law does encourage involvement within specified duty areas.

Local law enforcement agency refuses to list child as missing, stating it does not have "jurisdiction." (The child was taken from another state, child was not a resident of state, etc.)

The **Uniform Child Custody Jurisdiction Act (UCCJA)** defines "jurisdiction" in custody cases. Jurisdiction can be defined any one of four ways:

1. A state has jurisdiction if the child resides in that state. If a custody hearing is ongoing in the state where the child lives, subject matter jurisdiction has already been established, unless another state abroad has established it.

2. A state has jurisdiction if the child has "significant connections," for example it is where the child attends school, has family, etc.

3. A state can have "emergency jurisdiction." In an emergency, a state can act on behalf of the child.

4. If a state refuses to recognize jurisdiction, another state can step in for the best interest of the child.

The **Parental Kidnapping Prevention Act (PKPA)**, 28 U.S.C. ss 1738A, is a federal law intended to settle disputes between states claiming jurisdiction. It gives priority to the child's "home state" (state of residence) when another state maintains a "significant connections" position.

Local law enforcement refuses to list child as missing because the searching parent does not have legal custody of the abducted child.

The **International Parental Kidnapping Crime Act of 1993** does not allow for this reason. According to this federal law, a searching parent who has been denied access to his or her child, whether by a violation of custody, sole custody, visitation, etc., has grounds for a complaint. The abductor is in violation regardless of custody status. *Custody status is not relevant for denial of a searching parent's request to list a child as missing.*

Local law enforcement refuses to list child, stating that the situation is a civil matter and must be taken up with civil courts.

The **International Parental Kidnapping Crime Act of 1993** made international parental abduction a federal felony, taking the matter into the criminal arena.

If attempts to educate law enforcement agents using the above-mentioned laws prove unsuccessful, perhaps a more drastic approach should be initiated. A searching parent can contact the county prosecutor's office, United States attorney's office, the National Center for Missing and Exploited Children, and the Department of State for assistance. If a parent still has no relief, the case of Scozzari v. City of Newport Beach may offer a solution. When police delayed in listing his child as missing, Mr. Scozzari raised a states tort claim for failure to act and sued the city of Newport Beach, California. This was a precedent-setting case as no individual had ever raised such a claim in a parental abduction case. (Mr. Scozzari was an attorney.) He was awarded 1.3 million dollars. Transcripts of the hearing are available. (Scozzari v. City of Newport Beach, unpublished, [Ca. Ct. App. 4 Dist. 1991].) The decision was, however, overturned on appeal. Mr. Scozzari is now deceased.

Step Two: National Crime Information Center (NCIC)

Once a child has been listed as missing, a searching parent should request that the local law enforcement agency enter the child into NCIC. This national computer link-up of information allows law enforcement agencies all over the country to have access to information concerning a child. Although local law enforcement agencies can enter a child (unless it is against state law), the FBI is bound by federal law to do so. (**Missing Children Act of 1982,** Public Law 97-292, 28 U.S.C.) Once the child is entered, the searching parent should have the child's NCIC number, as it may be requested by other agencies, such as the National Center for Missing and Exploited Children.

Step Three: National Center for Missing and Exploited Children (NCMEC)

Although there may be a difference of opinion as to whether a searching parent should next notify the National Center for Missing and Exploited Children or the United States State Department, the NCMEC will take a missing child application, provide pamphlets on parental abduction, and refer the searching parent to the State Department. Whether before or after speaking to the State Department, the searching parent should notify the NCMEC. Having your child's case on file can establish a great resource later on. While the NCMEC has access to NCIC, the State Department does not. Access to NCIC is critical during recovery efforts.

The NCMEC will send the searching parent application forms to register the child as missing with the agency. There is no cost to the parent. (Some missing children's organizations, such as Child Find, Inc., require an application fee.) These forms should not be ignored, nor should the idea of registering a child with the NCMEC. This organization can be of valuable assistance, providing unique and necessary services as the searching parent gets more deeply involved in the recovery process.

See Chapter 5 for more information on NCMEC.

Step Four: State Department

The United States Department of State has a division devoted to assisting parents whose children have been abducted to foreign countries. The division is referred to officially as the United States Central Authority, but it is the Division of Children's Issues that receives complaints concerning abducted children. This division will take an application on a missing child and provide the searching parent with direction, information, literature, and an understanding of what he or she may face. The State Department is the highest diplomatic organization in the United States that assists and works with the victims of international parental abductions. Many searching parents assume that the State Department is empowered to physically recover a child who has been taken abroad. This is not true. The State Department works within the confines of duty limitations just as the local sheriff does. The State Department works with a searching parent. If a searching parent does not take the initiative to proceed with the recovery of his or her child, the searching parent has tied the State Department's hands.

As the coordinator of the child's recovery, a searching parent must understand that it is his or her responsibility to find out what an organization can do, then utilize that recourse in the recovery effort. Misconceptions about an agency's role often times lead a searching parent into frustration, depression and anger. Commonly, when a parent reaches this point in the recovery effort, he or she tends to want the State Department to take over. However, a searching parent must work with the State Department just as he or she worked with the previous agencies: by providing information, and by learning to use whatever the organization can offer in the way of information, assistance and guidance.

The State Department will send a searching parent forms to fill out in order to gather information on the abducted child. These should be filled out completely and returned as soon as possible to the worker assigned to the case.

A searching parent should read all materials sent by the State Department as well as anything sent by any other agency. These materials help the parent to understand each organization's role and determine whether one agency might be better suited than another to the particular case.

See Chapter 5 for more information on the State Department.

Determining Whether an Abductor Has Left the United States

Because the fact of international abduction must be established in order to chart the course of a recovery effort, a searching parent should work in conjunction with authorities to determine whether an abductor has left the country. Here are a few possible avenues to explore:

1. The abductor's employment records can provide useful information. Ask work associates about his or her last day at work. Did he or she leave a forwarding address? Who was the benefactor on his or her insurance? Ask teachers or child care workers when the abducted child spent his or her last day at school, preschool, or daycare. Question neighbors, friends and relatives of the abductor. Information requiring a subpoena may be obtained by an FBI agent. The searching parent will have to provide the agent with the names, addresses and telephone numbers of information sources such as the abductor's employer.

2. If the abductor had a car, check airport parking lots for the vehicle. The local police may assist a searching parent with this, but they will need to know the make, model and year of the car, the license plate number if

available, and any distinguishing features of the car such as bumper stickers or dented fenders. In most airport parking lots, a vehicle check is done daily. Any cars that are left for long periods of time may be reported to the authorities. The airport may have a date when the car was first left at the airport, or a parking stub may be left in the car to indicate a possible departure date. If the abductor's car has been left at an unknown airport, request that law enforcement include information on the car in their NCIC report.

3. The FBI may be able to determine what time the abductor left the country through immigration, customs, or airport records. The searching parent may request that an FBI agent obtain this information.

4. Airline manifests may include the name of the abductor and the child. The FBI may obtain those records in an effort to follow the abductor's trail.

5. Credit and banking information on the abductor can provide information as to when he left the country. If an abductor requested cash advances or made significant bank withdrawals prior to leaving the country, these would show up on his statements. This information is not available to a parent because the abductor's credit history is protected by the right of privacy unless the searching parent is also on the account. A plane ticket purchased on a credit card can provide a wealth of information.

6. Check the abductor's mailbox. Opening another person's mail is illegal, so the postmaster and the FBI should be consulted if you wish to do so. If they have a problem with you opening mail on your own, request their assistance. Among the most useful mail is a telephone bill, which may include long distance calls and the phone number to a foreign location, possibly the intended destination of the abductor. The postmaster can put a mail trace on the abductor's mail at a searching parent's request.

7. If an abductor is in the United States military or National Guard, or is retired from the military, a searching parent may find additional resources available. Although this crime is still prosecuted the same way as a civilian abduction, the military may be able to provide the searching parent and supporting organizations and agencies with information on the abductor.

Information on the abductor ranging from where his pension check is sent (if retired) to his last duty assignment location can be made available, along with other information. To request information about the abductor, a searching parent can contact the appropriate authority listed below. If information cannot be released to the parent, the parent should ask to whom the information can be released — FBI, State Department, or other agency.

The parent should then ask the appropriate agency to obtain the information on the parent's behalf.

United States Air Force and Air Force Reserve
Air Force Military Personnel Center
Attention: Worldwide Locator
Randolph Air Force Base
San Antonio TX 78150
Telephone: (512) 652-5774 or (512) 652-5775

United States Army
Worldwide Locator Service
U.S. Army Personnel Service Support Center
Fort Benjamin Harrison IN 46249
Telephone: (317) 542-4211

United States Coast Guard
Coast Guard Locator Service
Room 4502 — Enlisted and Reserve Personnel
Room 4208 — Officers
2100 2nd St. S.W.
Washington DC 20593
Telephone: (202) 267-1615 — Enlisted Personnel
          (202) 267-1667 — Officers

United States Marine Corps and Marine Corps Reserve
Commandant of the Marine Corps — MMRB —10
Headquarters, Marine Corps
Attention: Worldwide Locator Service
Washington DC 20380
Telephone: (202) 694-1624, 694-1861, 694-1610, or 694-1913

United States Navy and Naval Reserve
Naval Military Personnel Command N036
Navy Worldwide Locator Service
Washington DC 20370
Telephone: (202) 694-3155, 694-9221, or 694-5011

Determining a Child's Location

Pinpointing a child's location can be one of the most difficult and frustrating tasks a searching parent encounters. Fortunately, there are resources available to assist the parent. In countries where a U.S. embassy is present, the State Department can request a whereabouts and welfare check on a child. A searching parent must make this request as the check is not automatically done when a child is reported missing. The embassy can also request the assistance of various foreign government officials, such as the immigration minister, in an effort to confirm whether entrance visas have been issued to the abductor and the child. Success in finding this information depends on the U.S. embassy abroad and the host country.

The most logical place to begin looking is the abductor's country of origin or the country to which he has significant connections. A searching parent can attempt to contact a member of the abductor's family in the country of origin even without a known telephone number. Director assistance may provide the necessary information. Old telephone bills are another possibility. If the abductor has specialized training in a specific vocational area, it would be prudent to contact likely places of employment. For example, if an abductor were a hematologist, then the most obvious place to begin searching would be hospitals in the region where the abductor is believed to be located. A listing should be available through the U.S. embassy, an area Chamber of Commerce, or directory assistance. This is a long and grueling process, but it has proved successful.

To find out the address of an abductor, a parent must rely on his or her imagination. The addresses of relatives may be beneficial because the abductor may not have a home immediately upon arrival in the country and may be staying with family. Information on the abductor's family and their addresses may be traceable through old telephone bills, letters, insurance policies (family members may be beneficiaries), and loan agreements (family members may be co-signers).Some countries, like Saudi Arabia, have no house numbers, and mail is not delivered to the home. Post office boxes are used. In this case, a worldwide delivery service may be able to provide a home address, which is required to deliver a package. If a telephone number is provided to the delivery service, they will call the intended recipient for directions to the home. The sender can request a return receipt with the abductor's address. The following international delivery services may be of assistance in this fashion:

Airborne: 1-800-426-2323
DHL: 1-800-225-5345
Emery Worldwide: 1-800-443-6379
Federal Express: 1-800-238-5355
International Bonded Couriers: 1-800-322-3067
Quick Pak Worldwide: 1-800-638-7237

The Federal Parent Locator service may disclose the whereabouts of an abductor still in the United States. Although a searching parent does not have direct access to this resource, law enforcement authorities do. This service has been made available through federal law.

If the abductor was on public assistance at the time of the abduction, those records can be accessed by authorities to determine if the abductor is still receiving benefits and where those benefits are being mailed.

Finally, do not overlook the possibility of contacting former spouses of the abductor, or even a current spouse. They have been known to help a searching parent.

Approaches to Recovery

There are several ways a searching parent can approach a recovery effort. All have proved effective in the right situation, but it is important to choose an approach that matches the circumstances. For this reason, the choice must be well thought out. Many variables influence the direction a parent can take to facilitate a successful recovery. The child's sex and age, the country to which the child was taken, and the relationship between the United States and that country are only a few of the details a searching parent must take into account. Pursuing more than one avenue can enhance the chances for recovery, provided the searching parent is careful to avoid approaches that conflict (for example, one should not pursue the abduction as a criminal case and still apply to The Hague for a diplomatic effort). Read the following sections carefully to prevent such mistakes.

CRIMINAL LAW APPROACH

A recovery effort pursued through the criminal justice system involves obtaining a federal warrant for the abductor and may include action through foreign criminal law. Currently, if found guilty of international parental kidnapping (which falls under the International Parental Kidnapping Crime Act of 1993), an abductor could face three years in jail and a fine. A UFAP warrant (unlawful flight to avoid prosecution) can be issued by request of a state prosecutor if an abductor is charged under a state felony offense. (Fugitive Felon Act, 18 U.S.C. 1073.) this possible state action is of consequence if a child has been abducted prior to December 1993 because abductions occurring prior to that date may not quality for recognition under the International Parental Kidnapping Crime Act of 1993.

A searching parent considering the criminal law approach should think about elements of the case that might predict success or failure. If an abductor is residing in a country with which the United States has no extradition treaty, a warrant may not prompt the arrest of the abductor. Also, the arrest of the abductor does not automatically mean a child will be returned to the searching parent. Even if an extradition treaty exists, international parental kidnapping may not be viewed as an extraditable crime in that country. The State Department can assist a searching parent by providing information on the likely success of this approach in a particular country.

European countries that enjoy a strong diplomatic relationship with the United States would be choice countries for this approach. However, these countries would also be good candidates for diplomatic efforts through The Hague. *A searching parent should be cautious not to bring criminal action if he or she intends to apply to The Hague, or has already applied and is awaiting results.* Combining both approaches may well cost the searching parent benefit of either.

Warrants have been successfully used in Middle Eastern countries. Although the United States has no extradition treaty with these countries, parents taking their cases to court to request custody have found a UFAP warrant or international parental kidnapping warrant to be a most influential tool. A warrant can influence a case by bringing prejudice against the abductor. Again, this depends on the country and the age and sex of a child as well as the reputation of the lawyer and the influence of the abductor or the abductor's family.

Warrants have also been used to arrest abductors in countries that recognize United States law. One mother obtained a federal warrant and coordinated her efforts with those of foreign local law enforcement (Scotland Yard) and was able to have the abductor arrested. This mother successfully recovered her child.

The reader should be aware that criminal pursuit of an abductor may also be achieved through criminal warrants obtained against the abductor in his or her country. This can be advantageous in many ways, particularly if the abductor is in a country other than the country of origin. For example, if an abductor is from Syria and took the child into Saudi Arabia, it is possible for Syria to request extradition of the abductor, provided the abductor has been charged with a crime and a warrant issued from Syria for his or her arrest. Extradition is provided for by the Arab treaties between Middle Eastern countries. It is very advantageous in countries where the United States has no extradition treaties. Also, unlike United States law, these treaties provide that a child's return can be requested. (United States extradition does not allow for the return of the abducted child, only the abductor.)

Action taken by the United States against an abductor abroad begins with issuing a federal warrant. While some jurisdictions are issuing both UFAP and international parental kidnapping warrants simultaneously, others issue only an international parental kidnapping warrant.

Once the warrant is issued, the FBI agent involved can send that information to Interpol with a request to distribute the information worldwide. If the abductor's or child's location is known, that information can be updated and directed to the Interpol office of the appropriate country. Red-flagging a wanted abductor in Interpol diffusions is not routine but is done and may bring about much more attention from foreign authorities than lower-priority flags. Presently, a missing child receives a yellow code — relatively low in view of the fact that criminal action is directed to non–Hague countries, which are probably also countries with no extradition treaty with the United States. Since the primary goal is to recover the child, not to extradite the abductor (whose extradition does not provide that a missing child be returned), communication on the child should include a red flag.

Once Interpol has sent out diffusions alerting area law enforcement of United States interest in both the abductor and the child, a request to the United States legate for support should be made. This can be done through the FBI. The legate may or may not have an office in the country where a child is being held. If there is no office in the country, chances are that country is handled by a legate who covers a multi-jurisdictional area and travels through that country. The legal department of Interpol and the legate can facilitate communication with law enforcement authorities on a non-Hague country to return a child. Requests should be made that the foreign authority pick up the abductor and the child. Once in hand, the child should be turned over to the legal custodial parent at once. In case the parent is not present when the child is recovered, arrangements for the handling of the child should be made in advance.

Making these arrangements can be complicated. United States embassies abroad cannot take an American child into custody. Their diplomatic function does not allow them to act in the capacity of a social services organization. Some countries may have a social services organization that will take a child into temporary custody until the legal custodial parent can take physical possession of a child. Interpol, the FBI, and other law enforcement agencies are not responsible for taking a child into custody pending reunification with the legal custodial parent, nor are they equipped to do so. With this in mind, it may be best to seek a trusted outside source. Religious organizations may be contacted by the U.S. embassy abroad in order to arrange temporary care for a child. It is possible that the embassy can facilitate temporary custody through a private family authorized to act as temporary foster parents. This arrangement need not last long; it should not take more than 72 hours for a parent to travel anywhere to recover a child.

However, a searching parent should not be dependent on the embassy to act in this capacity as it is not an official embassy duty. A parent needs to make every effort to take possession of the child as soon as the child has been released. The parent may have to obtain a passport for the child in order for that child to travel back to the U.S. While this is easily accomplished at an American embassy, the parent must be present to apply for the new passport in order to sign for a minor child. Only a parent or legal guardian can obtain a passport for a child. Also, a parent should know visa requirements in advance.

A child taken out of a Middle Eastern country usually needs the father's permission before an exit visa is issued for that child to travel. If the child is to travel with the mother, failure to have an exit visa or permission from the father can result in the child being denied exit by immigration officials. Although American embassies may be able to assist a parent in obtaining an exit visa, it is the country of departure that issues it. If a parent has legally taken possession of a child there should be no problem in leaving the country. There are some instances where a parent can obtain legal custody in a country and still be restrained from removing that child from the country. That is the case both in the U.S. and abroad.

For the searching parent who decides to pursue recovery through the criminal justice system, the following list of relevant agencies and the services they provide may prove useful:

U.S. Domestic/Family Court Judge— issues custody order

Local Law Enforcement— takes missing persons report on child and complaint against abductor; enters information into NCIC

County/State or Federal Prosecutor— receives request for criminal investigation against accused abductor; may obtain warrant

FBI— conducts investigation on accused abductor; may obtain warrant

Interpol— issues worldwide alert for child and abductor

State Department— lists child as "officially" abducted abroad, conducts welfare and whereabouts checks through U.S. embassy abroad

Justice Department— authenticates warrants for use abroad

Office of Authentication— authenticates documents and records for use abroad

Passport Office— provides passport information on child and abductor

To implement criminal action in the country where the abductor is residing, involvement of foreign law enforcement, attorneys, courts or legal aid may be used in conjunction with the work of the United States authorities listed above.

CIVIL LAW APPROACH

In pursuing a recovery through civil law, a parent takes his or her case to the foreign courts. Parents may request that their United States custody be recognized by the foreign court, that the foreign court grant them custody, and that criminal charges be pressed against the abductor. As with any other approach, a parent choosing the avenue of civil law must have a good understanding of the situation.

Parents have entered into foreign courts and have had their United States custody recognized. One mother was able to do this in Syria, but many factors worked in her favor. The child was very young, and female. Also, the mother had a warrant from the United States for the abductor's arrest. Under Syrian law, the mother qualified for custody; thus not only was her United States custody decree recognized, but Syrian law enforcement agencies located the child and delivered her to her mother over the angry protests of the father.

While not all countries will allow a foreign parent to enter their courts for custody disputes, most will. However, anyone considering civil action in a foreign court needs to have an understanding not only of the cultural views of such action, but the legal and even religious opinions. Saudi Arabia is one example of a country where the culture makes civil action very difficult for Americans. For example, one American mother was allowed to enter the Saudi courts. It was a terrible experience for the searching mother. She had to represent herself, as no Saudi attorney would take her case. The mother was allowed several visits to her children, but they were under the most difficult of circumstances. This mother never got her children, who are now grown.

If a searching parent opts to take a custody case into a foreign court, the parent may obtain a list of attorneys from the State Department. Parents may also qualify for legal aid. Documents may require authentication and the parent may have to travel abroad. Depending on many factors, a searching parent may not be required to travel to a foreign country to have his or her case presented in court. In order to request that a foreign court recognize a searching parent's rights to custody, legal custody should be secured in the United States first. Any supporting documentation which reinforces the searching parent's right to custody may only strengthen the case abroad.

A United States custody decree is not the only document that gives the searching parent an advantage in requesting custody or recognition of a custody in a foreign court. United States warrants for the abductor's arrest, as well as Interpol communications can also have a positive influence. Obtaining a copy of an Interpol communication may be done through the FBI agent who is investigating the child's kidnapping. The FBI agent will probably need the approval of Interpol to release this information. These communications should include the abductor's name, passport status, and nationality; a physical description of the abductor; and all information relevant to the abductor and child.

Again, it is the searching parent who will coordinate the child's recovery, by supporting the attorney abroad with information, documents and assistance. A searching parent should never assume that the lawyer is taking care of everything. No one knows a case better than the searching parent. The attorney knows foreign law. The combined knowledge and cooperation of parent and attorney is necessary in facilitating the return of a child. Once custody is granted by a foreign court, law enforcement may be requested to assist in the physical return of a child.

To facilitate recovery through the civil process, the following list of relevant agencies and the services they provide may prove useful:

Domestic/Family Court Judge— issues custody order
Local Law Enforcement— takes missing persons report on child and enters information into NCIC
NCMEC— lists child as missing
State Department— lists child as "officially" abducted abroad; provides list of foreign attorneys
foreign attorney— presents case to foreign court
Department of Authentication— authenticates documents for use in foreign courts

A parent may wish to combine both criminal and civil approaches for a stronger case. However, *a parent should not pursue the case as a criminal matter while working towards a solution with The Hague.*

DIPLOMATIC APPROACH

In pursuing a diplomatic approach, a searching parent employs recovery efforts that depend solely upon cooperation between government agencies, non-government organizations, and possibly the abductor. The Hague Convention on the Civil Aspects of International Child Abduction is a most effective diplomatic option under this approach. The Hague Convention represents the efforts of about forty countries united to promote the best interest of the abducted child. The United States became a member of The Hague in 1988.

A searching parent wishing to pursue the diplomatic approach may do so through the State Department. The State Department will work in conjunction with another member country for the safe return of a child. The Hague is not a law enforcement organization; however, they do recognize the orders of the local and foreign courts in custody matters.

Other diplomatic avenues may consist of a searching parent working directly with a foreign embassy and the authorities of the foreign country where a child is being held. If a country is not a member of The Hague, the U.S. embassy abroad may attempt to facilitate diplomatic efforts on the searching parent's behalf through the foreign minister. The embassy may assist in an effort to locate a child and discover the child's welfare. However, the U.S. embassy abroad is not an investigative or police organization and cannot use its diplomatic status to facilitate the investigation of an abductor, unless such an investigation is directly required in order to establish a child's whereabouts and welfare.

Countries have joined in this effort to work towards a worldwide solution in recovering internationally abducted children. The United States implemented the International Child Abduction Remedies Act (ICARA) to put into force the Hague Convention on the Civil Aspects of International Child Abduction. Both the Hague Convention on the Civil Aspects of International Child Abduction and the International Child Abduction Remedies Act are included in this writing. The following is a breakdown of the language and features of these acts. Mr. Adair Dyer, First Secretary of the Netherlands, is the Hague treaty's primary author.

As provided for in the International Child Abduction Remedies Act, a searching parent wishing to apply to The Hague for assistance in recovering a child, or for visitation rights with the child, can make application through the United States Central Authority, which is the office of Citizen's Consular Services, Division of Children's Issues, Department of State, Room 4817, Washington DC 20520. The Division of Children's Issues will send the searching parent an application. There is no fee for making application to The Hague. The Division of Children's Issues of the State Department does not charge for its services.

Once a searching parent has filled out the application, it must be returned to the State Department. It is important to fill out the application as completely as possible, providing all information as requested. Once the application is returned to the State Department, it will be forwarded to the Central Authority in the country the child is in. If the child is in a country that is not a member of The Hague, or was not a member at the time the child was taken there, the application cannot be made to that country. However, a searching parent may want to discuss making application to a country which is a member of The Hague, even though the child is not in that country, if that country has influence on the country the child is in.

When the Central Authority of the country where the child is being held receives an application for assistance, its sole objective is to secure the return of the child or establish visitation as defined in the Hague Convention. That Central Authority has six weeks from the time proceedings begin to decide whether it will assist the applicant. After six weeks, the searching parent or the State Department can request a statement explaining the reason for any delay.

Some of the considerations that go into a decision to accept a case are discussed in the Hague Convention and are summarized briefly below:

• Application to The Hague should be made within a year of the child's abduction; however, there may be exceptions.

• If it is determined that a child is "settled" in his or her new environment, request for the child's return may be denied.

• If the child is no longer in the country to which application for assistance has been made, the requested country can either dismiss the application or stay the proceedings.

• A child may not be returned to the searching parent if it is determined that his return would expose him to physical or psychological harm or put the child in an intolerable situation.

• A child may not be returned to the searching parent if the child is considered mature enough to know what he or she wants and does not wish to return to the searching parent.

• A child may not be returned to the searching parent if the searching parent gave consent for the child to be taken or if the searching parent did not have legal custody at the time the child was taken, or there was no restraining order preventing the removal of the child from the country.

If neither the searching parent nor the abductor had legal custody at the time the child was abducted, as in the case of pre-decree abductions, the country where the child is being held may request that the searching parent provide some sort of documentation from authorities to show that the child was wrongfully removed. The country in which the child is being held may assist the searching parent in obtaining this documentation when applicable.

The Hague works to return a child through peaceful and cooperative efforts among the parties involved. A searching parent does not have to have relevant documents authenticated as is necessary when appealing to a foreign court when applying for assistance. The authority in the country to which the child has been taken may direct the abductor to pay the costs of returning the child (travel, expenses incurred in locating the child, legal fees, etc.) should it be determined that the child is to be returned to the searching parent. Also, a searching parent does not have to have legal custody of a child to apply for assistance under The Hague should they wish to exercise visitation.

The following countries are Hague members:

Argentina	Ireland
Australia	Israel
Austria	Italy
Bahamas	Luxembourg
Belize	Mauritius
Bosnia-Herzegovina	Mexico
Burkina Faso	Monaco
Canada	Netherlands
Chile	New Zealand
Croatia	Norway
Denmark	Panama
Ecuador	Portugal
Finland	Poland
Former Yugoslav Republic of Macedonia	Romania
France	Spain
Germany	Sweden
Greece	Switzerland
Honduras	United Kingdom
Hungary	United States
	Zimbabwe

For information concerning the addition of other countries, contact the United States Central Authority (U.S. Department of State).

Those wishing to apply for assistance under The Hague are encouraged not to pursue criminal legal action against the abductor prior to or during Hague assistance. For more information regarding The Hague contact:

The Hague Conference on Private International Law
Permanent Bureau
6, Scheveningseweg
2517 Kt The Hague, Netherlands
Telephone [31]-(70)-363-33-03
Fax [31]-(70)-360-48-67
Attention: Adair Dyer, Secretary General

Although a searching parent may make application for assistance through the State Department, the searching parent may need legal representation in the United States and abroad. It is possible that legal aid is available to the searching parent both in the United States and abroad. Few United States attorneys are familiar with the Hague Convention, but a parent can obtain a referral for an attorney who practices either international law or marital and family law. Below are a few possible contacts.

American Academy of Matrimonial Lawyers
150 N. Michigan Ave., Suite 2040
Chicago IL 60601
Telephone: (312) 263-6477
Fax: (312) 263-7682

The American Bar Association
Section of Family Law
750 N. Lake Shore Dr.
Chicago IL 60611
Telephone: (312) 988-5613
Fax: (312) 988-6281

International Academy of Matrimonial Lawyers
10 S. LaSalle St., Suite 2424
Chicago IL 60603-1906
Telephone: (312) 782-3020
Fax: (312) 782-2397

The following referrals have been compiled from the *North American Symposium on International Child Abduction: How to Handle International Child Abduction Cases.* (1993) Washington, D.C., Department of State. (Sponsored by the American Bar Association).

Robert D. Arenstein
Attorney at Law
295 Madison Avenue
New York NY 10017
Telephone: (212) 679-3999
Fax: (212) 370-5822

The Honorable Danny J. Boggs
United States Court of Appeals for the Sixth Circuit
Louisville KY 40202
Telephone: (502) 582-6492
Fax: (502) 582-6500

Carol S. Bruch
Professor of Law
University of California
Davis School of Law
Davis CA 95616-5201
Telephone: (916) 752-2535
Fax: (916) 752-4704

Leonard Dubin
Attorney at Law
1200 Four Penn Center Plaza
Philadelphia PA 19103
Telephone: (215) 569-5602
Fax: (215) 569-5555

William M. Hilton
Certified Family Law Specialist
Box 269
Santa Clara CA 95052
Telephone: (408) 246-8511
Fax: (408) 246-0114

Marilyn Feuchs Marker
Smith, Helms, Mulliss & Moore
Attorneys at Law
P.O. Box 21927
Greensboro NC 27420
Telephone: (910) 378-5451
Fax: (910) 379-9558

G. L. Nissenbaum
Nissenbaum Law Firm
211 Congress St. NW-400
Boston MA 02110-2410
Telephone: (617) 542-2220
Fax: (617) 542-3879

Edward S. Snyder
280 Corporate Center
5 Becker Farm Road
Roseland NJ 07068
Telephone: (201) 740-0500
Fax: (201) 740-1407

HIRING PRIVATE SUPPORT

A searching parent should use caution when hiring private individuals or companies to recover a child abducted to a foreign country. Very few such organizations offer the searching parent a resource that cannot be obtained through a public agency. However, a few do provide unique services and operate as legitimate businesses, that is, openly and legally. They do not plot covert re-abduction attempts. They operate by gathering information, serving as cultural and diplomatic liaisons, and filling the gaps other organizations cannot fill.

A parent wishing to utilize the services of such an organization should ask for a company profile and have a full understanding of the company's methods of operation. While the right company can offer great support for recovery efforts, most offer only illegal, dangerous, expensive methods. For the parent desperate to recover a child, hiring a company that proposes to accomplish the task "in any way necessary" is a powerful temptation, but one that must be avoided.

International parental abduction has been a felony for only a few short years. Companies that address this crime and have any amount of integrity should have been in operation prior to this time. The company should not derive its sole income from this type of case, and the company should have the necessary resources and working knowledge of the law to approach and accept such a case. To determine whether a company utilizes legal and diplomatic approaches towards recovery while working with other authorities, a searching parent should question the company extensively prior to agreeing to any business arrangement.

A searching parent needs to determine whether the company can offer assistance in overcoming language barriers and legal differences between countries. Also, can the company promote and offer cultural understanding and offer information on the scope of international abductions and all they encompass? These questions alone will easily filter out the majority of private companies that offer their services towards recovery. What should remain are companies that offer legal avenues to problem solving, have international connections, and have successfully recovered children through the cooperative efforts of both legal and diplomatic organizations. These are few and far between, but they can assist a parent greatly; often they are the last link in coordinating a successful recovery.

Unlike government and diplomatic organizations, these private companies do not work for free; however, there is no excuse for the fees some charge of $50,000 or more. An estimate should be provided before any work is done, and an actual accounting should be provided once service is complete. Charges may include airfare, long distance telephone charges, hotel expenses, and professional fees.

These companies should work towards supporting a parent's efforts towards recovery. Parents should use extreme caution in hiring private detectives to find a child. Not only can fees financially cripple a parent, but the level of success many achieve could easily have been achieved through law enforcement and government agencies at no charge to the parent:

THE QUESTION OF RE-ABDUCTION

A most sensitive issue is the re-abduction of a child by individuals or groups for hire. Although children have been recovered through this method, it is not only illegal, but dangerous to the parent, the child, and everyone else involved. The danger may run from imprisonment to death. Any parent even considering this approach must take a hard, realist look at the consequences of such action.

Many individuals are suddenly claiming to be experts in re-abduction. A closer look may show that some of these individuals have never before attempted a re-abduction. Many have never even been to the country where the re-abduction is to occur and may know nothing of the language, the geographics, or the foreign laws involved. Yet they are quick to accept the task and even quicker to quote their price, noting there is no guarantee. Searching parents often fall victim to these people.

Perhaps these individuals are not deliberately conning the grieving parents. Perhaps they jump into the situation so quickly that they themselves are not aware of the risks. Once the risks become apparent, they may get cold feet, but in such cases most of them are too proud to back out. They simply pretend to attempt a recovery, then collect their pay. Searching parents are devastated by such failed "attempts," which usually leave them financially drained and emotionally shattered.

Re-abductors may brag about previous careers in the military or government. Searching parents should not be impressed by those who claim former experience in the CIA, Delta Force, or Navy Seals. (Maybe the previous employment with the CIA was as a janitor!) Little concern for the child may exist, and a great deal of discussion on money may dominate all conversations.

A parent who gets involved in a re-abduction attempt *will not* have the assistance or support of the State Department or the U.S. embassy abroad. In fact, if either agency becomes aware of a re-abduction attempt, the agency may inform the abductor of the searching parent's intentions. It is said that innocent embassy employees have been fired as a peace offering to the host country where a re-abduction has taken place. Also, the State Department has issued formal apologies to foreign governments for successful re-abductions. With all this in mind, a searching parent would be very unwise to try this illegal act. Yet the stakes get even higher.

When an American citizen is arrested for re-abducting a child in a foreign country, the U.S. embassy can only do so much on his or her behalf. An American who enters another country is responsible for obeying the laws of that country. If the re-abductor does not have legal custody of the child, it is possible that he or she may have to return the child to the country where the re-abduction took place. Criminal charges may be brought against a re-abductor. People have been caught and imprisoned in foreign countries. This is the reality. Should a parent successfully re-abduct a child, the country from which the child was re-abducted may ask the United States to extradite the parent to face criminal charges.

An American mother successfully recovered her child from another country and returned to the U.S. Neither parent had bothered to obtain a legal custody order. In an effort to prevent the child from being re-abducted, the mother hid the child. The abductor returned to the U.S., obtained legal custody, and the mother not only lost the child, but was placed in a U.S. jail for violating the father's custody order.

In re-abduction attempts many methods have been employed. These methods range from subtle trickery to violent snatchings. People have been bound and gagged. People have been killed. A child could easily be caught in the line of fire during a hasty and vicious re-abduction. The charges then are murder, and a child is lost forever.

A less dramatic but extremely important concern is the child's emotional welfare. A child who has already experienced a sudden and probably traumatic separation from a parent may be re-abducted just as he or she is beginning to adjust. The care a child receives from both the searching parent and the abducting parent will influence his or her state of mind. The scars of separation can last a lifetime.

One actual case illustrates some of the problems inherent in the question of re-abduction. A young boy who was abducted became suicidal. Still in the hands of his abductor after four years despite numerous attempts to recover him, he had lost hope. Legal channels were not an option in this case. Diplomatic channels had failed. This child's life was at risk from severe and prolonged abuse. He wanted to come home. His only way was a re-abduction attempt. United States authorities could not and would not assist. The foreign government would not. This child would have probably died at the hands of his abuser before he reached the age of eighteen had he not been successfully re-abducted.

Although this story may sound like a very good justification for re-abduction, it was told to make a different point. The reason so many doors for legal recovery were closed on this child was that another child in the town where he lived was successfully re-abducted by another foreign parent. Security heightened, and sympathy for searching parents all but disappeared.

In considering any recovery attempt, the first concern should be the child's welfare. The second should be the opening of as many doors as possible to the recovery of all children.

Coordinating Resources: A Sample Case

Once a searching parent has decided how to approach the recovery of a child, there are many details to be attended to. This section deals with the specifics of the previous avenues of recovery mentioned, and the possible obstacles, as well as possible methods of overcoming those obstacles. It is important that a searching parent have a good understanding of why he or she chose a specific approach and what chance of success that approach offers in his or her situation. Furthermore, even though an approach has been selected, the parent must still coordinate the recovery effort to custom-fit the situation.

In this regard a searching parent will learn to be not only resourceful, but creative. Parents have been able to use their imaginations in facilitating the most wonderful successes, *all within the law*. Staying within the law is important. A searching parent who deviates from legal and diplomatic channels may very well be left without resources or support.

The following sample case may help to demonstrate how resources may be successfully coordinated. The success in this case depended on the searching parent's knowledge of the abductor, investigative skills, and use of the foreign legal system.

The searching parent had sole custody of a very young female child. The child was taken to a Middle Eastern country whose laws would normally award custody of such a child to the mother. To further enhance this American mother's case, the abducting father had failed to register the marriage, the child's birth, or the divorce in his native country. Initially the mother assumed the father had registered the child's birth, and she was pleasantly surprised to learn from her attorney's investigative work that she had been misled. It was now apparent that she held another advantage, since without registration, the Middle Eastern country did not recognize the child as one of its citizens in the strictest legal sense.

The mother now found many doors open for legal proceedings. Since the child's birth was not registered, the father could not obtain a passport for her from his country. That meant that the child was traveling on her United States passport, which would expire within a few months. By placing a block on the renewal of the child's passport, the mother was able to ensure that the child would not be moved to another country. At the same time, the courts of the country where the child had been taken recognized the child's United States citizenship. With that, the case was not considered a custody matter, but rather a "kidnapping." Since the father failed to "claim" the child legally, he possessed her "illegally." Since the father never registered himself as the child's father, he was viewed as not being the father, and thus he had taken possession of this small American child through criminal kidnapping.

At this point the mother was very successful in obtaining a warrant for the abductor's arrest on the grounds of kidnapping in a Middle Eastern country. This was actually easier and quicker for the parent than requesting a warrant for the arrest of the abductor in the United States. Unbelievable as it may sound, it is true.

The father was intentionally kept unaware of the mother's efforts as she worked with many organizations and government agencies from both countries to lay down paperwork that would put the abductor in "checkmate" should he attempt to flee with the child prior to the actual recovery. Obstacles were placed in the abductor's path, and the abductor was eventually jailed, through the following coordinated actions:

1. Mother blocked further issuance or renewal of child's passport.
2. Mother obtained United States custody of child and the order included no visitation for the father. The judgment also ordered the abducting father to return the child immediately.
3. Mother registered child's disappearance with police, and child was entered into NCIC.
4. Mother registered child with NCMEC and State Department.
5. Mother set up fund-raising booths at area shopping centers to finance child's recovery.
6. Mother obtained warrant for abductor under International Parental Kidnapping Crime Act of 1993. Warrant went out through Interpol and was raised to red-flag priority after an investigation by the FBI.
7. Mother obtained prominent attorney in the native country of the abductor and had all documents authenticated.
8. Because more than two years had passed since the child's abduction, mother requested and received age-enhancement photos of child through the National Center for the Missing and Exploited Children, which were distributed to the FBI, U.S. embassies abroad, and the State Department.
9. Foreign attorney petitioned the court to
   • Recognize mother's custody.
   • Issue warrants for abductor's arrest on charges of kidnapping.
   • Request return of child.
   • Order that abductor financially compensate mother for costs incurred in recovering child, plus pain and suffering.

The mother's custody was recognized, and a kidnapping warrant was issued against the abductor. He was arrested in his native country and jailed.

In the above case, many elements led to each level of the searching parent's success, and each step required a great amount of time before success was achieved. Sadly, these delays were caused by lack of cooperation from the searching parent's local law enforcement, the county prosecutor, and the domestic courts. The mother was much more successful at the federal level and in the foreign legal system.

A searching parent should not get mentally locked into problem-solving based on United States law. Foreign law can provide surprising advantages to the searching parent. Facts that seem unimportant in the United States may be extremely important in another country. For example, while a child's age or sex may not be significant in a United States court, it can very well mean automatic custody to one parent or the other in another country, regardless of other factors. This can be an advantage to a searching parent who has a child in a Muslim country. Many Muslim countries hold the religious training of a child to the father's responsibility. With that, a child who has reached a certain age goes to the father. The sex of the child may determine what age a child goes to the father. In Saudi Arabia, a female goes to the father at age seven; in Syria (although Syria is not considered an Islamic state), a female goes to the father at age twelve. Recognition of this particular law has afforded American mothers the right to custody of young daughters abroad.

While United States courts may consider such factors as a parent's ability to financially support a child, the parent's standing in the community, the background of the parent, and the emotional and mental stability of each parent, they do not consider religion a factor in determining custody; nor is the child's age usually taken into consideration. Conversely, in obtaining a foreign custody decree, a parent may never be asked about occupation, income, family background, or standing in the community, but the child's age and sex and the parent's religion may all be of concern to the court. Of concern, too, may be a woman's marital status. A woman who remarries may forfeit the right to custody. Searching mothers who have remarried may want to consider the impact that knowledge of their marital status might have on the courts.

When religious affiliation places a searching parent at a disadvantage, a parent may find even his or her faith challenged. Searching parents have converted to the abductor's religion. However, there is no guarantee this will satisfy a court. An example of religious prejudice is that a Muslim man has right to marry a Christian, but a Muslim woman does not. Also, Islamic countries recognize only two religions besides their own. Buddhism and Hinduism are not recognized religions. While the Jewish faith is recognized, tension between the two certainly cancels out any advantage of that recognition. From these few examples one can see the importance of understanding the culture, religion, and laws of the country where a child has been taken or the abductor's country of citizenship. While Canada,

Mexico, and most European countries may not present recovery obstacles in these areas, certainly many African and Middle Eastern countries do.

A final note: Though much careful consideration is required in the choice of an approach, it is also important that a searching parent make that choice as soon as possible. Many searching parents are reluctant to take action against abductors for fear they will anger the abductors and recovery of their children will be made more difficult. Each searching parent must weigh the decision carefully. Many searching parents do not implement aggressive recovery procedures until they feel almost hopeless. Unfortunately, a year or more may pass before some searching parents reach this point, costing the searching parent not only time, but possibly the child as well.

Summary: A Recipe for Recovery

1. The searching parent is the coordinator of all efforts to recover his or her child.

2. It is the searching parent who must find out what any agency — whether it be a law enforcement office, diplomatic station, legal firm, or nonprofit organization — can do within its own guidelines, and how to utilize that resource.

3. The searching parent must become knowledgeable in foreign custom and law in order to work within the legal confines of the foreign country for the child's return.

4. The searching parent should consider all options and choose an approach to recovery:
   - Recovery through diplomatic channels (i.e., The Hague).
   - Recovery through civil process (i.e., have the abductor deported to United States with the cancellation of U.S. passport; have searching parent's legal custody recognized or granted by foreign country).
   - Recovery through criminal process (i.e., have abductor extradited to United States, or charged in his own country for infractions such as passport violations or kidnapping.

4

Organizing the Search
and Following Through

MOTHERS ABDUCT THEIR CHILDREN SLIGHTLY MORE OFTEN
THAN FATHERS (47.5 PERCENT FATHERS, 52.2 PERCENT
MOTHERS).

Johnson, J., Sagatun, I.J., and Girdner, L., *Risk Factors for Family
Abductions: Preliminary Findings* (Washington DC: OJJDP, 1991).

Setting Up a War Room

Because of the volume of information that searching parent may be handling and the need for easy access to specific resources, it is important for a searching parent to have a place to work that affords convenience, and possibly privacy, so he or she can concentrate on the recovery effort. The work area or "war room" can be any space the parent can convert to an office — perhaps a spare bedroom or a corner of the kitchen. There should be room for office equipment and several other items that are more or less standard for the search process.

A large map of the country to which a child is believed to have been taken allows a searching parent to study the various geographical features. Perhaps a parent may need to know the distance between law enforcement offices, courthouses, the lawyer's office, and area hotels in order to expedite traveling time. Airports, the embassy, and various agencies need to be located in advance to facilitate traveling plans. Many foreign embassies in the United States offer maps to the major cities and well-known tourist attractions in their countries. Some of these city maps are very detailed, allowing a searching parent to easily determine the routes to various facilities. A map may also provide clues to a child's whereabouts should they be undetermined.

In dealing with international parental abduction, a searching parent may quickly accumulate large phone bills due to the necessity of long distance calling. To cut down on telephone calling costs as well as to facilitate rapid communication and document transfer, a fax machine can be one of the best investments a searching parent makes. Messages that take ten minutes to convey by phone can be reduced to two or three minutes if sent by fax. Furthermore, as a searching parent begins the coordination of a child's recovery, it may be necessary for the parent to communicate a single issue to several agencies at once. Since overseas mail can take up to two weeks to deliver, a fax greatly expedites that process. Private mail couriers and delivery services can charge $75.00 or more for a single page to be delivered in two to four days overseas, while the same page can be sent immediately and inexpensively by fax. However, be aware that authenticated documents cannot be sent by fax, and for such items a searching parent may want to consider a delivery service.

Fax machines are becoming less expensive and can be plugged into an existing phone outlet. There is no need to have an extra telephone line installed in the home. Literally hundreds of dollars can be saved in telephone charges each month. With these savings, a fax machine can pay for itself in a short time. More important is the ability of the fax machine to facilitate rapid communication. It should be noted that faxed documents fade. Critical information should be recopied on regular paper.

To keep important information and communications organized, a searching parent should establish some type of filing system that offers quick access to any document at a moment's notice. Documents such as the child's birth certificate and the parent's custody decree should be part of this system, along with such information as the abductor's social security number and the names, telephone numbers, and addresses of the abductor's family. As a parent receives information from organizations, it should be filed according to subject. Something that may initially seem unimportant can become surprisingly important later when an opportunity arises to use it, or a question needs an answer. Everything connected with a child's recovery should be located in the "war room," from legal documents and visa applications to special address books containing the telephone numbers (and fax numbers) of the individuals and agencies actively involved in the case. (Note: A parent may be able to obtain a telephone directory for the area in which the child is believed to be located.)

To hold down the cost of recovering a child, a parent should send letters when communication is not time-sensitive. A typewriter or computer can be an asset if handwriting is a problem. Of course, writing materials such as paper, envelopes, pens, and stamps should be available in the work area.

It is very important for a searching parent to log all efforts in recovering a child. Information concerning successful recoveries through legal and diplomatic channels appears to be rare. The more documented cases that exist, the more information searching parents will have for future recovery efforts. The State Department keeps track of recovery efforts. It is up to searching parents to keep the State Department informed of the steps they have taken and their success. This allows the information to be passed on to another searching parent who may have a similar case or be confronting a similar obstacle. The State Department will not give out a searching parent's name or detailed information on recovery efforts, so a parent need not fear that his or her identity will become known in the transfer of information. Problem-solving efforts in international parental abduction are in their infancy; so are laws and policy. Although a searching parent may be reluctant to share the secrets of his or her success, doing so may bring another child home.

There may be times when a searching parent receives multiple communications, followed by periods of silence. It is these silent times that may be the most difficult. During such periods a searching parent should take advantage of the opportunity to study how the case has progressed, and analyze both effective and ineffective efforts.

Collecting Documentation

Gathering necessary documents and information should be an ongoing part of the recovery process. A searching parent should obtain and carefully file the following:

1. The *social security number* of an abductor which can be accessed through the Federal Parent Locator service or through such records as old tax returns and pay stubs. Possibly the abductor's social security number may be his health insurance number and may be present on old claims, medical bills, etc. The child's social security number should also be kept on file.

2. If the abductor is a foreign national, a *civil registration number* may appear on passport or immigration documents. A foreign attorney may be of assistance or an American Embassy abroad. It is possible that the State Department may request this information from the American Embassy abroad. If the parents of an abducted child have been divorced or entered into a family court system, it is possible that the attorneys involved have

both the social security number and the civil registration number of the abductor.

3. *Passport information.* If the abductor has a United States passport, the State Department may be able to access information from the U.S. Passport Office. If the abductor is carrying a foreign passport, it may be more difficult to obtain a copy. A foreign authority will probably not assist a parent in obtaining this information. To find out if the abductor obtained a United States passport for the child, again the State Department may be able to request the information from the Passport Office.

Passport information is very important for many reasons. For instance, a searching parent may wish to take the abducting parent to court in the foreign country. Some countries have a civil registration for their citizens. This civil registration contains information that may be quite beneficial to searching parent's legal counsel. In order to access this information, the civil registration number must be known. It appears on some passports, depending on the country.

Passport information can also assist a searching parent and the U.S. embassy abroad in requesting specific entry and exit visa information from a foreign minister. Again, the success depends on the country, the U.S. embassy abroad and the amount of information a searching parent can provide.

Passport information can also assist Interpol in determining when a foreign national left the United States. Again, there are many variables involved.

4. A *birth certificate* for an abducted child, which is usually easy to obtain. Since each state has varying methods for obtaining one, a searching parent may want to contact the hospital where the child was born and request information on obtaining the child's birth certificate. Although the courts of some countries do not recognize a child's United States birth certificate as proof of citizenship (anyone born on United States soil gets one), a searching parent should always have one for his or her records.

5. *School records.* These records easily determine when a child stopped attending school and thus can prove helpful if a parent is trying to determine when a child left the country. A parent has the right to request a child's school records. The same holds true for daycare records. A parent need only request the records from the school the child was enrolled in.

6. *Medical history* on a child. A parent is entitled to this information and can simply request a copy of the child's records from the doctor. Medical records on an abductor, however, are protected under the right of privacy.

The Cost of Recovery

The costs incurred in searching for a child can be great. Because each case is different, so is the cost. This section will offer some advice for distinguishing between wasteful and productive expenditures. Many searching parents have handed out thousands of dollars to individuals who claim they will return their children, only to be left disappointed and broke. Many parents have had to abandon their efforts in recovering their children simply because they could not afford to continue. This is not only heartbreaking, but scandalous. People who take financial advantage of searching parents should be ashamed of themselves. Yet their scams are apparently all too common.

Fortunately, an effective recovery does not have to be hampered by unbearable financial burdens. If approached discreetly, a parent from a modest income bracket can well utilize the funds he or she has available.

A searching parent should not have to pay any money to have a child listed with the local law enforcement agency. It is the agency's duty to list that child. Nor is there a charge for a child to be entered into the NCIC. There is no cost for listing a child as missing with the NCMEC, or the State Department, except the cost of a postage stamp to return the applications. In these early stages, if a searching parent has incurred any costs, they may be related to the long distance telephone calls sometimes needed to overcome obstacles in the above steps. The call to the State Department may be long distance depending on where the searching parent lives.

Should a searching parent decide to apply to The Hague for assistance, there is no application fee charged by the State Department. Postage and long distance telephone calls should be the only expenses a parent incurs in this step. If a parent is pursuing a criminal warrant against the abductor, again, long distance telephone calls and postage should be the only expenses. There is no charge to the searching parent for a warrant issued against an abductor. Costs may be incurred during the litigation stage of Hague efforts.

Flyers and posters of a missing child can be made by the NCMEC, as well as age-enhancement photos. There is no fee for any of these items; however, the NCMEC will not send a searching parent many copies. It is the responsibility of the searching parent to have copies made. There are many, many office supply stores and copy stores that will print flyers about missing children for free. A searching parent should call around to find a business that will donate its services. Other missing children's organizations offer professional flyers at no charge. The International Center for the Search and Recovery of Missing Children (listed in Appendix C) makes an excellent flyer, as well as Child Quest International, Inc.

The services of translators and interpreters can be very costly if a parent goes through an agency. An agency may provide its services free, but it will be up to the parent to uncover such a resource. Other possibilities are soliciting for an interpreter or translator from a local college or university, or hiring a foreign student at a reasonable cost. This can be done by placing an ad on the school's bulletin board or going through the student guidance office. Use some caution. This route may not afford a parent accurate or professional services. Also, the searching parent will have to be able to trust that the interpreter will keep all information confidential. Still another resource is the International Center for the Search and Recovery of Missing Children (listed in Appendix C). It offers a variety of translators and interpreters at no charge. Child Quest International also offers translation services free of charge.

It is important to note that a good foreign attorney does not have to speak the same language as the searching parent. This should not be a reason for not retaining an attorney who otherwise is outstanding in his field.

Attorney fees seem to devastate most searching parents, whether for the services of an attorney abroad or in the States. Legal aid societies exist not only in the States, but in foreign countries. These are worth pursuing and are discussed more in the section on attorneys.

Below is a brief list of costs that may be involved in searching for a child. In reviewing these charges, a searching parent should keep in mind that all these expenses can stretch out over a long period of time, perhaps enabling the searching parent to meet the financial obligation more easily.

Authentication fees	Up to $20.00 per document and postage
Visa	Approximately $10 to $25
United States passport	Approximately $65.00 for an adult, $50.00 for a child
Passport and visa photos	Approximately $10.00 per set of two (as low as $2.00 at a photo booth)
Fax machine	Varies
Travel expenses	A parent may not be required to travel abroad for court appearances. Physical recovery of the child will require a parent to travel.
Office supplies	Varies
Telephone charges	Varies
Attorney fees	A parent may quality for legal aid in the foreign country in which he or she wishes to pursue a legal solution. A searching parent may establish a payment plan with an attorney.

Passports

A searching parent who is planning to travel to a foreign country will need a passport. A visa may also be required. If the searching parent is planning to return to the United States with the child, the child will also need a passport. Passport applications are available at many large post offices, or they can be obtained through a passport office. An adult must apply in person. Once completed, the application, two passport photos and I.D. are submitted to the passport office. It may take up to six weeks before a passport is issued.

Passport photos can be obtained at many camera shops and photography studios, as well as from passport photo booths. The fee for a set of two passport photos currently averages about $10.00. A passport for an adult is good for ten years, while a child's passport is valid for five. Some travel agencies offer assistance and information regarding passports, photos and visas.

A visa will allow a traveler to pass into and out of a foreign country. While this process may be quite easy in some countries, it can be very difficult in others. It is wise for a searching parent to obtain information concerning travel requirements and customs well in advance of a planned trip. The State Department, the foreign embassy, and travel agents can be a great source of information and assistance. The State Department can also advise a searching parent of any restrictions to travel in specific countries. For example, an individual who has an Israeli visa on his or her passport may not be permitted into some Middle Eastern countries.

The United States passport office can offer very beneficial services to searching parents. A parent can request that issuance of a child's passport be denied. This will prevent an abductor from obtaining a passport for the child or renewing an existing passport. However, if the child has already been issued a passport, the passport office will not revoke it. If the child has a passport, a searching parent may want to keep its expiration date in mind in an effort to prevent its renewal. If a parent feels an abduction is likely, and the child already has a passport, the parent should request a block on further issuance. The courts can be petitioned to hold the already issued passport.

If a block is requested on a child's passport, a searching parent cannot request a duplicate passport unless the child has been located and is in the legal custody of the searching parent; current passport photos of the child and current I.D. are presented; and the searching parent has the child at the time the application for renewal is made. Inability to obtain a duplicate passport can be problematic but is not an insurmountable obstacle. For example, one mother was able to find a solution when she needed a copy of her child's passport to prove the child's citizenship for legal action abroad. (A birth certificate was not sufficient.) The abductor had the original passport, and the mother could not obtain a duplicate because she had had a block placed on reissuance. The passport office provided the mother with an authenticated copy of the child's original passport application along with a cover letter stating that the child was a United States citizen. This story shows how ready the State Department and passport office stand to assist a parent in overcoming any obstacles to recovery. If a searching parent has not had a block put on the child's passport, there should be no problem in requesting a duplicate. Many children have blocks placed on their passports in an attempt to prevent the abduction. Some 15,000 children have been entered into the passport "name check" system. This is of little value as a safeguard if a child already has a passport, since an abducting parent can still use the current passport. In such cases it is important to ask the United States courts to hold the child's passport and to issue an order restraining a child from being removed from the country.

The State Department cannot prevent an abductor from requesting a foreign passport for a child. If a parent believes that his or her child is in danger of abduction and that the potential abductor may try to secure a foreign passport for the child, the parent can contact the foreign embassy and request that one not be issued. There is no guarantee, however, that such a request will be honored; therefore this should not be viewed as an effective safeguard.

A block on a child's passport will insure that issuance from any U.S. embassy in the world, as well as from any passport office in the United States, will be denied. Although mistakes do occur, it is the intention of the passport office to work diligently to prevent errors and accidental issuance after a request for denial has been made through the proper channels.

If a searching parent is not prepared, a frustrating delay may occur when a parent recovers a child and requests a passport for the child from the U.S. embassy in the foreign country where the child was found. If the parent does not have the proper passport photos, the passport may be denied until they are obtained. If proper I.D. is not presented, the passport may be denied. It is the important responsibility of the searching parent to make sure that both the State Department and the U.S. embassy abroad are informed of the parent's intention to obtain a passport in advance in order to avoid painful delays.

Lack of information can cause real problems in a parent's attempts to recover a child. Guidelines and regulations can also break the hearts of government workers. In one case, an American child had been taken against her will by her father. The girl was fifteen years old and desperately wanted to be with her mother in the States. The mother was the legal guardian of the child. The father allowed no communication between the mother and the daughter. In desperation the teenager contacted the U.S. embassy and requested a new United States passport so that she could try to go home. The embassy denied the teenager's request, stating that the father was the child's legal guardian and to issue a passport would be breaking foreign law. This young lady was eventually recovered.

The passport office can revoke an abductor's United States passport. In order to pursue this option, a searching parent must request that the FBI or United States attorney's office send a copy of a warrant against the abductor (for UFAP or international parental kidnapping) to the State Department's Office of Citizenship Appeals and Legal Assistance ([202] 326-6168). This federal regulatory code is found in 22 C.F.R. 51.70, et seq. The passport office will review the request to determine whether the abductor's passport will be revoked. This can be an advantage to a searching parent.

In many countries, an individual without a valid passport is deported. If the abductor is deported to the United States because he or she does not have a valid passport after it has been revoked, a searching parent may have found a way to recover the child. However, a child may or may not be deported with the abducting parent.

If the abductor is a foreign national, the searching parent can request that the State Department prevent the abductor from reentering the United States. This procedure was made available by a reform in the U.S. Immigration and Naturalization Act (Title 8, USC) in June of 1991. In order to take this action, a searching parent must present a valid custody decree. For more information on this action, contact the Division of Children's Issues of the Overseas Citizens Services at (202) 647-2688.

Entrance visas are necessary to enter many countries. A visa may be stamped into a passport at the time a United States citizen enters a foreign country. Other countries require that a visa from the appropriate country or embassy be applied for in advance. A searching parent can write to the foreign embassy and request visa information and apply for a visa in person or through the mail. A parent may also request the assistance of a travel agency in acquiring a visa. There may be a fee connected with obtaining a visa, and passport photos may be requested with the visa application.

Exit visas can cause significant problems if a searching parent is not knowledgeable about the country to which he or she is traveling. An exit visa is permission to leave the country. Although many Americans may be surprised to learn that they would not necessarily have the freedom to leave when they wished it is an accepted way of life for many people around the world. For the searching parent who has recovered a child and is anxious to leave a foreign country, the delay or denial of an exit visa can be heartbreaking. An exit visa may be denied if a parent is leaving with a child, and proof that the child is traveling with the consent of the child's father may be requested. If the parent is unable to provide the requested information, permission for the child to leave the country may be denied. It is possible that authorities will investigate the legitimacy of the searching parent's claim to custody and prevent any attempt to remove the child from the foreign country. This is especially true in the Middle East. However, there are ways around these obstacles. A searching parent should never feel intimidated by the laws of a foreign government if the parent has not broken those laws. A searching parent should remember that a United States custody order is not always recognized by a foreign government. The State Department and the foreign embassy can advise a parent on visa requirements.

When applying for a visa, a searching parent will be asked if the travel is related to business, vacation, or some other matter. Common sense should be used when filling this out. For example, Saudi Arabia will not issue "tourist" visas. Saudi Arabia does issue visas for individuals who wish to make the religious pilgrimage to Mecca, and will allow a mother to enter the country if the abductor agrees to sponsor her entry. It is becoming easier for American mothers to obtain entrance visa's without the abductor's sponsorship through the Washington D.C. Embassy.

Another example also shows why a searching parent needs to investigate visa information thoroughly and pay special attention when filling out the application: A mother who has remarried and presents a passport with her new married name on it may not have the support of Middle Eastern countries even though the parent is working through legal channels. The reason for this is that most of these countries practice a forfeit of a mother's rights to her children if she remarries.

The U.S. Embassy abroad may be able to request that the host country not permit reentry into the country by an abductor who has left.

For more information on passport action, contact:

Office of Citizenship Appeals and Legal Assistance
Office of Passport Services
1425 K St. N.W. Room 300

Washington, DC 20522-1708
Telephone (292) 326-6168

Hiring and Working with a Foreign Attorney

A searching parent may need to hire a lawyer in a foreign country in order to achieve a child's recovery, whether through efforts initiated through The Hague, the civil courts or the criminal courts. An excellent attorney referral resource is the State Department, which provides lists of attorneys who will take American clients. The State Department will not recommend a specific attorney, so the choice will involve some research for the parent. Another excellent resource is a referral list from the foreign embassy.

The State Department Address is:

U.S. Central Authority
Office of Citizen's Consular Services
Division of Children's Issues
Department of State, Room 4817
Washington DC 20520
Telephone: (202) 647-2688

Another resource may be large international law firms, or the International Bar Association. A searching parent may contact them at:

International Bar Association
2 Harwood Place, Hanover Square
London WlR9HB, England
Telephone: [44] (71) 629-1206
Fax: [44] (71) 409-0456

Naturally, the same caution should be exercised when a parent chooses an attorney referred by this or any other source.

In retaining an attorney in a foreign country, a searching parent may be required to sign a "power of attorney" contract, allowing the foreign attorney to represent the client's interests abroad. If this is the case, the foreign embassy in the United States may have the required form for this contract. The contract may have to be witnessed and made legal by the foreign embassy. The contract may be in a foreign language unfamiliar to the searching parent. In many cases, the foreign embassy will assist a parent in preparing the document.

The foreign attorney may request that all documents used in legal proceedings be authenticated. Authenticated documents cannot be faxed to the attorney. The attorney must have the originals. They may be sent through a worldwide delivery service such as Federal Express or DHL. Information on authenticating documents is contained in the next section.

Many countries offer legal aid services to those who cannot afford to pay for an attorney. Legal aid programs are often administered by a country's Justice Department. A searching parent may wish to ask a foreign embassy in the United States about the availability of and requirements for these services. Also, the U.S. embassy abroad may be able to provide information on availability of legal aid in the country where the abducted child is believed to be held or the country where a searching parent intends to initiate legal proceedings.

If a searching parent does not qualify for legal aid, or if it is not available in a particular country, a parent may be able to make financial arrangements with the attorney who is handling the case. A parent may have to wire payment directly into a foreign bank for deposit. In this case, the searching parent will want to contact a bank in his or her area and inquire about overseas money transfer service. There may be a charge for the service. Charges vary, from modest to extremely high. A parent should never use a company such as Almost a Bank. Although they may be able to assist in transferring funds, they are extremely expensive.

It is not wise to pay a foreign attorney for his or her services in advance. Although a retainer or partial payment is expected and acceptable, paying a large sum of money in advance on the estimated cost of the services of an attorney is not good business practice. Just as anyone should in the United States, a searching parent should set a price with the attorney involved prior to the proceedings.

Choosing an attorney in a foreign country can be difficult if a searching parent has no way to assess an attorney's ability to handle a case. Although the State Department or U.S. embassy abroad can provide a searching parent with a list of available attorneys, it is the parent who must decide if a particular attorney is right for the case. Ideally, a searching parent will want someone with experience in cases of international parental abduction. Unfortunately, such attorneys are very few and far between. The U.S. embassy abroad may know whether a particular attorney has represented an American parent previously.

One of the most important factors in obtaining foreign counsel is the attorney's reputation, which oftentimes determines his or her success in a case. The searching parent will need every possible advantage, so it is worth investing time and money in finding a respected attorney. Believe it or not, a parent of even modest income may be able to afford the foreign equivalent of an F. Lee Bailey. In many countries the United States dollar is extremely valuable, and the services of attorneys may not command the high fees they do in the United States. Parents may be pleasantly surprised at what legal genius their money can buy abroad.

It may not be a surprise to a searching parent that the legal counsel he or she prefers does not speak English. Even the searching parent cannot speak the language of the attorney, this is nothing to panic about. A searching parent can obtain the services of a translator or interpreter. The foreign attorney may also have someone who can convey messages to the parent. A searching parent will always want to ask if the attorney can provide an interpreter or translator. The U.S. embassy abroad may also provide a parent with the names of individuals qualified to act in this capacity. Remember, it is essential that interpretation or translation be accurate. Just because someone speaks the language does not mean he or she can accurately convey communications between a parent and a lawyer.

In working with an attorney abroad, it may not be feasible or necessary for the searching parent to leave the United States. A fax machine can greatly enhance communication. Letters can often be translated more conveniently, and the parent can fill an attorney's request for documents at a moment's notice. Often it is helpful to transmit copies of documents by fax even if the original documents must arrive at a later date. Mail can take weeks to arrive overseas. In a legal case, time can be critical.

A fax machine also allows a searching parent to quickly coordinate the work of many organizations. Providing updated information to the State Department, U.S. and foreign embassies, law enforcement and legal representatives is the responsibility of the searching parent. For example, if a foreign attorney has located an abducted child and informed the searching parent, the parent must then notify the agencies involved.

Even if a searching parent is unable to hire an attorney who possesses the legal advantage in his or her country, the parent may wish to continue working with the attorney as a resource to enhance other efforts. For example, a foreign attorney may be able to locate a child, but not legally obtain custody for a searching parent. The attorney may also be able to disclose information that will enable the searching parent to initiate criminal charges against the abductor in his or her country of residence. Should this latter effort prove successful, it is possible that a searching parent can appeal to the court for a more favorable custody judgment based on the abductor's criminal history.

An abductor's criminal history may range from some civil infraction to a major criminal offense. Parents should always use the discretion and the advice of their attorney in deciding what information should be used concerning the abductor. It may prove to be a liability to the case. More information on using an abductor's criminal history will be found in the section entitled "Apprehending the Abductor."

Authenticating Documents

The purpose of having documents authenticated is to facilitate their use in legal action abroad. It is necessary to ensure that documents are authentic when they are submitted in a foreign jurisdiction. A searching parent who is planning to take a custody dispute to court in another country, or initiate any other legal actions, may need to have documents authenticated. Documents to be used in conjunction with Hague action may not require authentication. The State Department can instruct a searching parent on Hague requirements.

Authentication can be a grueling process. An attorney may be able to assist a parent, but parents who are on a tight budget may wish to obtain authentication themselves. Each document will undergo several processes before authentication is complete.

Documents that may need authentication include, but are not limited to, the child's birth certificate, the marriage license, the divorce decree, the custody decree, any restraining orders, any warrants for the abductor, and any other document foreign counsel requests. As the coordinator or the child's recovery, a searching parent must pay close attention to detail at every step of the recovery process. The parent should never assume that someone else is doing a particular task. Therefore, a parent who opts to handle the process of authentication may find a trip to Washington DC very fruitful. While authentication by mail can take weeks, it is possible to complete the process in person in just a matter of hours. If the parent wishes to obtain a visa from a foreign embassy, that can be accomplished on the same trip.

One mother who traveled to Washington for authentication of a federal warrant against the abductor reports that the final document was quite impressive, decorated with red ribbon, a gold seal, and the signature of

Attorney General Janet Reno. The foreign attorney who received this document was not only impressed, but was of the opinion that the parent personally knew Janet Reno and had a very important case. The truth of the matter is, the mother received a routine authentication.

The first step in authenticating documents is to make notarized copies of originals. A parent should keep all original documents and send notarized copies. There may be a small fee for notarization, which can be done by the clerk of court. Call the court where the legal documents originated for instruction and fees.

Once the documents have been notarized, they must be sent to the secretary of state in the state where the documents originated. Each state has its own seal, which will appear on the document along with the secretary of state's signature. Again, a small fee may be involved. Once that step is completed, the documents are ready for authentication.

All documents will be authenticated by the State Department, except warrants. Federal warrants must be authenticated by the Justice Department. Usually they will be UFAP or international parental kidnapping warrants. Once this has been completed, all documents must be "legalized" by the country in which they will be used. This can be done at the foreign embassy. (See Chapter Five for addresses of foreign embassies in the United States.) Again, there may be a fee involved.

Failure to have documents authenticated may result in refusal of the foreign court or country to recognize them. It is the responsibility of the searching parent to have documents authenticated. All documents must go through the proper steps for successful completion. Missing a step may result in denial of authentication.

Up to fifteen documents can be authenticated as one time. The current charge for authentication is $4.00 per document, payable by check or money order. The Authentication Office can forward your documents to the foreign embassy for legalization if you so request, and if a properly addressed, stamped envelope and fee are included. For more information, a pamphlet is available by writing to:

Authentication Services
Authentication Office
Department of State
2400 M St. N.W. Room 101
Washington, DC 20520
Telephone: (202) 647-5002

Those planning to visit this office in person should be aware that it is open only from 8:00 until noon, Monday through Friday.

Gathering Information

As discussed earlier, a searching parent has the responsibility of coordinating the recovery of his or her child. To that end, it is necessary for the searching parent to assume the role of detective. The parent may have some advantage in gathering information that the FBI does not. This may be especially important if a searching parent intends to take a custody case to a foreign court. A note of special interest here: If the abducting parent has violated the law of the country where he and the abducted child are residing, knowledge of that violation may facilitate a return of the child through court prejudice against the abductor. I cannot stress enough how advantageous this can be. Here is where a searching parent's determination and imagination can make all the difference in a successful recovery. The following section explores this concept in detail.

Apprehending the Abductor

Although a searching parent may have United States warrants for the arrest of an abductor, they may be of little use in actually apprehending the accused. Obstacles in extradition, knowledge of the abductor's whereabouts, and even the attitude of the authorities all play a large role in the success of capturing these criminals. Since few abductors are actually convicted, abductors probably do not live in fear of apprehension and conviction. If that were the case, international child abductions would not continue at their current alarming rate.

With few foreign courts evincing an interest in international abductions, sometimes a searching parent's best hope is to concentrate on ways the abductor might have broken the laws of his or her country — laws that have nothing to do with kidnapping. After all, if a foreign national will break the laws in the United States, it is not too great a stretch to believe that person lacks respect for law in general, and that he or she would break the laws of another country as well, if it seemed expedient to do so. Most abductors are not very clever; however, most Americans are not familiar with foreign law, and their ignorance is the abductor's strength. With that in mind, most abductors begin the process of abduction by lying to the other parent.

Stories of actual cases suggest that the same scenario is played out over and over with a great amount of success on the part of abductors. It is not unusual for an abductor to begin lying to the other parent long before a child is ever born. Usually these lies center around the abductor's importance, or the importance of his family, in his country of origin.* The abductor convinces the other parent that he has powerful connections in his country, so powerful that if someone were ever to pursue or bother him, he could simply have one of his "connections" take care of the problem. This pattern of likes appears to be very common. The language may be a little different, but the message is the same. Such fabrications later make the searching parent fearful of going to the abductor's country of origin to seek the abducted child. Many left-behind parents are completely convinced that abductors can simply have their names put on a list and they will immediately be picked up at the airport and harmed in some way. This belief has kept some searching parents from finding their children. However, the abductor may have lied or else greatly exaggerated the facts. Even if the abductor has a cousin who works for the minister of some governmental department, a parent should not be intimidated. A parent who is pursuing legal and diplomatic avenues to recovery should have little to fear.

The abductor's lifestyle in the United States can provide many clues about his importance in his country of origin. Is the abductor going or did he go to school in the United States? Who paid for that education? These are very important questions. Countries, such as Saudi Arabia, sponsor Saudi males abroad for an education and will also pay for it. Grades are not a big deal; neither is money. So a poor Saudi can come to the States, attend a university, live off his government, and convince unsuspecting Americans that he is from a wealthy, politically connected family. Most Americans swallow this hook, line and sinker.

Other ways foreigners achieve an education in the States is through family support. Even this does not guarantee that the foreigner is from a wealthy family. It may take a father, two uncles, and six cousins to pay for his education. This is not uncommon; nor is it unusual for the student to keep his financial position hidden for fear he will be considered lower than his American peers. A foreign student may be receiving school aid both from the United States and his country of origin. Foreign students who do not have their own apartments, drive nice cars, wear expensive clothes, and travel home at least once a year are probably like most college kids: broke.

---

*Because this scenario usually involves a foreign national father, the text in this section refers to the abductor as "he."

Once out of school, did the abductor work? Did he return home? Chances are he did not return home. Chances are he remained in America and either found a job in his field or went to work for family in the States. The key word here is work.

Many schools require that a foreign student provide collateral to guarantee payment of educational expenses. This collateral may be monies held in escrow, or the deed to property to prove an income source. This information may be in a foreign student's file. The FBI can access this information and find a complete background on an abductor. The idea is to determine whether the abductor has any real political resources or advantages in his country. However, it will take more than an educational background to make that determination.

The reader has been advised to concentrate on how an abductor might have violated the laws of a foreign country. The reason for this approach is that it will be foreign law that convicts the abductor of wrongdoing. With the sympathy of the foreign government, a searching parent may expect a great deal of assistance. Many foreign countries would rather punish a criminal within their own systems than have the United States do it. Reasons vary: the country may be embarrassed by the actions of the citizen, or perhaps officials want to make sure the criminal is punished and believe the courts of the United States will be too lenient. Many crimes carry a much more severe penalty in other countries, including kidnapping. (Note: Outside the United States, international parental kidnapping may be translated to simply "kidnapping.") International parental kidnapping is not a crime in many countries. Many countries do not believe a parent can kidnap his or her own child. Therefore, the abductor would have to be proved not the legally recognized parent of the child. Sound complicated? It really isn't, and it has been done successfully. Some countries require that a child's birth be registered. If a father who is a citizen of such a country fails to register a birth, the court may hold that he is not the father of the unregistered child. Because he is not the father, the child has been kidnapped. In short, there is a very high chance that an abducted child has been brought into or is residing in a foreign country in violation of that country's laws. A good attorney, particularly one from the country in question, who is familiar with immigration and resident laws can investigate and advise a parent if an abductor has violated the law. It may be that loopholes in a country's laws will allow an attorney to argue this position. This whole strategy is based on the fact that an abductor has no real power in his country. He really has no friend in high places that would do favors for him, especially favors like arresting Americans just for entering the country.

The next step is to determine if the abductor is the legally recognized parent in his country of origin *even if the child is not residing in that country or the United States.* In order to determine parental rights, a searching parent should hire a lawyer in the abductor's country of origin. With laws varying from country to country, it would be difficult to write a text covering all aspects of parental rights worldwide. However, the following information demonstrates how parental rights might successfully be determined.

The attorney may want to see documentation and request information on the abductor and the child. A smart attorney will do a background check on the abductor before agreeing to accept the case. No attorney wants to go up against the child of a most important person. The attorney will also want to investigate whether the foreign national registered his or her American marriage, child's birth, and divorce in his or her country. A registered child becomes the citizen of the abductor's country. Failure to register the child's birth may mean the abductor committed a crime in the civil law, and also that the child does not have citizenship in the abductor's country. Failure to register a marriage may also result in criminal civil charges against the abductor in his or her country.

If a marriage and birth of a child have not been registered by an abductor, it is probable that the foreign court will honor the American parent's United States custody order for the child, to the extent of offering assistance in physically retrieving the abducted child for the American parent. This has been done in the Middle East.

Even if the abductor has registered the marriage and the child's birth, a lawyer may be able to still obtain recognition of the American parent's right to custody. For example, in one case the courts recognized the American parent's right to custody and recovered the child for the searching mother because the foreign law held that the child's age and sex determined that the child should go to the mother. Again, this occurred in the Middle East. Although the abductor had not committed the crime of failing to register the marriage and the birth of the child, the law of foreign court still went against the abductor.

Whatever the situation as far as parental rights, it remains true that one of the most effective uses of a foreign attorney is to find garbage on the abductor—anything he or she did wrong in the country of origin. For example:

1. If a foreign national is receiving school financing through loans, grants, or scholarships from his or her country of origin, but is not attending school, the foreign embassy may be quite interested in knowing about this. The embassy may also provide the searching parent with a strong ally force in the foreign country.

2. It is not unusual for a foreign national male to be bound to serve in the military in his country of origin. Some foreign nationals try to avoid this by attending school in the United States. If an abductor came to the States to avoid compulsory military duty in his country, but does not actually attend school, he may be facing serious charges. A searching parent may request the foreign embassy to provide information on military requirements. If the abductor has not served his military duty, is not enrolled in school, and has not become a United States citizen, it may be possible to demonstrate that he is avoiding his obligation. Should it be determined that the abductor has committed a crime in his country of origin, it is possible that not only will his own government assist a searching parent in finding a child (out of gratitude), but the abductor may face criminal charges. Proving this particular crime may be a very grueling process, but in any case it is well worth the effort. It has proven successful.

3. A foreign national may be responsible to pay taxes in his or her country of origin for monies earned in the United States. Again, a searching parent can inquire about the abductor's status in this regard. Should there be a reason to believe an abductor has intentionally avoided paying income taxes to the country of origin, a searching parent can present income tax returns and W-2 forms as proof of income earned in the States. A searching parent will have to work through the foreign embassy or a foreign attorney. The IRS will not provide a searching parent with copies of an abductor's income tax return unless the searching parent filed jointly.

4. An abductor who is carrying passports from more than one country may be in very serious trouble. Even if an abductor has dual citizenship, the visa on his or her passport could land him in serious trouble. To get around this problem, the abductor may illegally use one passport from one country and the other for other travel. If proof of such a crime were given to authorities, the abductor could very well be arrested should he enter his country. In some countries, just having two passports without the knowledge of the authorities is a crime. Again, the searching parent will need to contact the foreign embassy or a foreign attorney for passport regulations.

5. If the abductor is in a Hague country and application to The Hague has produced no positive results, the searching parent may want to investigate whether that country will recognize a felony warrant for parental abduction and proceed through the legal avenues in an effort to have the abductor arrested in his country or extradited to the United States.

Success in any of these endeavors depends on the country and how aggressively the lawyer pursues the investigation. Many parents have learned that money talks; in fact, United States currency screams in many countries. A good lawyer can buy the keys to many closed doors. This may sound a bit frightening to Americans, but bribery is a long-established practice in many countries today. However, *it should be left in the hands of a good lawyer.* It becomes a bit of an art. A lawyer may prefer not to divulge to a client that half of his or her fee is going directly to bribes.

The more information a lawyer finds out about the abductor, the better the searching parent's case will be. Even though a searching parent may have United States custody of the child and have warrants for the arrest of the abductor, these facts may do no good except to support criminal charges against the abductor in his country.

To complicate the matter a little more, let us say the abductor takes a child to a country that is not a Hague country, does not enjoy a strong relationship with the United States, and is not the abductor's country of origin. It may or may not be advantageous for a searching parent to work within the confines of that country. Let us say that the child is in a most difficult country and recovery seems impossible. Then the searching parent must get the abductor out of that country and hope that the child comes, too.

It would be wonderful if the searching parent could simply call the abductor and request that they meet in some neutral location, such as London. That has been done successfully, but it is usually not the most promising option. The searching parent could have the abductor thrown out of the country he or she is in, or forced to leave for economic reasons. One mother had her husband fired from his job in the difficult country, and he had to return to his country of origin to find work. The mother then continued her efforts in the more sympathetic atmosphere of that country, and she and her child are now safely home. Another parent requested the assistance of the foreign consulate in removing the abductor from a country. The consulate agreed, and in less than two weeks the abductor and child were met by police in another country. Although it takes no lawyer to achieve what these parents have, the assistance of a lawyer was needed in one case once the child was in a more sympathetic country. Even in Hague countries, a parent may need to hire a good attorney.

The abducted child of unmarried parents may present some unique problems. It could be that the laws of that country provide that neither parent has custody of the child. Again, consult with a good foreign attorney. Find out the laws of that country. It may be that the recognition of a searching parent's rights rests solely on the civil and criminal law of the foreign country.

A word of caution: If a searching parent believes that an abducting parent is or has been involved in extremist political groups, great caution should be used. A searching parent should not be a loose cannon. Perhaps the abductor was or is affiliated with a political group whose intention is to overthrow a current government or to create chaos. While such information may initially appear advantageous to a searching parent, proof may be required before a searching parent will be believed, and proof may be dangerous to obtain. Again, use caution in the world of politics. One parent has actual videos of an abductor speaking about his involvement with the PLO while brandishing a gun before the camera. She made the choice not to go public with this information.

In apprehending an abductor in a foreign country a searching parent must work with the authorities of that country. Depending on the country, the parent may also coordinate law enforcement efforts in the United States to support those of the foreign authority. Sometimes a United States agency may be unable to supply information or documentation to a foreign authority but can supply that information to a searching parent, who then can present it to a foreign authority. For example, the FBI or state prosecutor may not send a copy of a warrant for an abductor directly to a searching parent's foreign attorney; however, either authority may make a copy available to the searching parent, who can forward it to the appropriate foreign authority. As the coordinator of the recovery effort, a searching parent will often be the mediator between United States and foreign authorities. In this position it is essential that the parent understand the workings of United States agencies and how they can support a searching parent's efforts through foreign legal avenues. (See Chapter Five for information on this subject.) A searching parent must remain in control of the case and work closely with all agencies involved.

It is impossible to overstate the potential for harm when a searching parent contemplates illegal action in recovering a child. Such action may serve not only to alienate United States resources, but also to cause a great deal of mistrust at home and abroad. Should a searching parent find that doors are constantly being closed, it could be that his or her recovery efforts have not been perceived as legal.

Recovery Stories

The following cases are presented as examples of recovery efforts. They are presented in the simplest form in order to protect those involved.

While these cases are presented in an effort to inform and educate, they are not necessarily offered as examples of how a parent should handle a recovery.

AUSTRALIA

NOTE: *Australia is a member of the Hague Convention and the following recovery may or may not have been made possible through that channel.*

An American mother divorced from her financially well off Iranian husband lost her children to international parental abduction. After she had recovered her children, the state of Ohio did not prosecute the abductor.

The children were subsequently abducted again. The abductor took the children to various countries, none his own. The children contacted the mother informing her of their whereabouts and their desire to return to the United States and be with her. Frustrated by the legal system, which had inspired little confidence in its ability to assist with recovery efforts, the mother decided to recover her children herself.

After learning her children were in Australia, the mother obtained a warrant against the abductor under the 1993 International Parental Kidnapping Crime Act. She then arranged to travel to Australia and to meet her children at a specific location. Once she had her children, the mother immediately boarded a flight back to the States. The recovery was a success.

This parent had a United States custody order, passports for her children, and a warrant. The warrant was to be used as "insurance" should the abductor find out about the recovery and attempt to prevent her and the children from returning to the United States.

Many factors contributed to the success of this mother's recovery effort. Among them:

1. Exit visas were not needed in advance.
2. The mother had United States passports for the children.
3. The children were not in the abductor's native country.
4. The mother had United States custody.
5. The mother had a warrant for the abductor.
6. The children assisted in their own recovery.
7. The abductor was unaware of the recovery effort.

GERMANY

An American father having sole legal custody of his young son was unable to prevent the child's abduction to Germany, which was his estranged spouse's country of origin. The father applied to The Hague with unsuccessful results.

The father then obtained a warrant for the arrest of the abductor under the 1993 International Parental Kidnapping Crime Act. With the assistance of the authorities in Germany, the child was found. Once confronted with the criminal charges, the mother voluntarily turned the child over to the father in an effort to avoid criminal prosecution. Recovery took about one year.

This case illustrates how legal approaches can be utilized when Hague approaches fail.

GREECE

A father from Cyprus abducted his young daughter during an unsupervised visit, sending word to the American mother that she would never see her daughter again.

The mother secured the services of a Greek attorney and filed for custody in Greece. The abductor then also filed for custody. Working with the United States officials and Greek authorities, the mother was able to locate her child. The abductor was arrested a few days later on a UFAP warrant at Kennedy International Airport, and incarcerated for not handing the child over to the mother. The abductor had hidden the child with his family in Greece.

The mother received custody in Greece and filed criminal charges against the abductor's family there. The abductor then revealed the whereabouts of the child, and a relative turned the child over.

JAPAN

An American parent had legal custody of a child abducted to Japan. The abducting parent was also American and worked as a lawyer in Japan. The searching parent obtained an international parental kidnapping warrant against the abductor. She was then able to have his U.S. passport revoked placing him in violation of Japanese immigration law. The abductor faced deportation to the U.S. where a warrant awaited him. (He also faced the possibility of losing his license to practice law.) The abductor voluntarily returned the children.

JORDAN

In a tragic case involving not only the abduction of two children, but the murder of their mother, a Jordanian father fled to his country after his crimes. The children's aunt filed for legal custody in the United States and was assisted by United States officials.

King Hussein of Jordan became actively involved in the case and worked with the United States officials in not only recovering the children, but also in prosecuting the abductor.

The abductor was an individual of some note because his brother was a brigadier general in the Jordanian army. This case illustrates the possibility of recovering a child despite an abductor's favored status. It also illustrates cooperation between two countries despite the absence of an extradition treaty. Jordan is not a member of the Hague Convention. The abductor was tried in Jordan.

The mother of these children was an American Muslim woman. She was estranged from her husband, and he strangled her for refusing to reconcile with him. Although Jordan usually grants custody of children to the father, this case inspired active participation on the highest levels to recover the children.

PAKISTAN

An American mother had United States custody of her two children. The Pakistani father took the children to Pakistan. The abductor returned to the United States without the children and was arrested on criminal contempt charges and ordered to serve sixteen months to four years in prison on Rikers Island. (The International Parental Kidnapping Crime Act only allows for up to three years in jail and a fine.)

The father has refused to turn the children over. They are living with relatives in Pakistan.

This case illustrates how an abductor can be apprehended without the return of the children. Pakistan is not a member of The Hague. This parent continues her search.

A very young American girl was abducted by her non-custodial father and taken to Syria, his country of origin. The American mother was unable to apply for assistance under The Hague as Syria is not a member country. Extradition treaties do not exist between Syria and the United States, so no United States warrant could be enforced. This mother turned to Syrian courts and was able to have her United States custody order recognized. Syrian authorities recovered her child and both are home safe.

This case illustrates how foreign courts can be utilized to recover a child.

After Recovery

For many searching parents the joy of recovering their children is tainted by the fear of re-abduction. Often, these parents return home with their children, only to become victims of their own fear. Knowing that the "system" failed to prevent the initial abduction, these parents live with continual insecurity.

There are many ways to implement effective safeguards against re-abduction. A parent should begin putting these safeguards in place before a child is recovered. Parents can effectively establish specific obstacles for the abductor. As mentioned earlier, the foreign national abductor can be refused entry into the United States. (See section on passports.) Warrants may be used to arrest an abductor who is able to enter the country. Should a court actually grant visitation to an abductor (it has happened), a parent can request legal safeguards be imposed by the court. (See Chapter 2.)

For more dramatic avenues, adoption may provide the protection a child needs. In some states, a child is free to be adopted if the absent parent has not paid child support nor contacted the child over a specific period of time. In these cases, it may be possible for the searching parent to have a new spouse adopt a child, depending on state law. If the adoptive parent is a male, the child takes on a new last name, and the birth records are sealed. A searching parent should contact an adoption attorney for legal requirements to this approach.

Many searching parents relocate once their children have been recovered. A parent who makes the decision to relocate may want to do some research to determine which states have the best laws and reputations in the area of parental abductions. California is a good example. Of course, relocation may not be an option for some parents. Considerations such as family support and job openings may prevent a parent from relocating.

Whether or not a parent relocates, it is important to implement safeguards. First and foremost, a previously abducted child should not be left unattended at any time. While a child should not be made to feel fearful and insecure, or like a prisoner in his or her own home, common sense should rule. A child should be transported to and from school, whether by the parent or a carpool. The child's school should be informed that only certain individuals are allowed to pick the child up. Those individuals should show identification to a school official. A child should wait in the school office until picked up. A child should also be walked to the door of his or her classroom each day. Any unauthorized person attempting to remove the child should be reported to authorities immediately.

A child should know not only his or her telephone number, but how to call collect and how to place overseas calls. Of course, a child should always be taught not to talk to strangers, but in parental abduction cases, the child usually knows the abductor. The abductor may have the assistance of a family member. The child may feel comfortable with that relative. A child must be taught not to go with anyone, even family members, unless the custodial parent has given specific permission.

A parent should have an unlisted telephone number. It is easy to trace someone through the telephone directory and get an address. Likewise, a parent should not have his or her name on the mailbox.

Changes in a custodial parent's name can hinder an abductor's chances of re-abduction. Name changes can be achieved through a variety of methods. A name change in civil court can afford a parent a new identity; however, court records, available to the public, may disclose the name change. Marriage can change the name of a female parent. While no one should even consider entering into marriage simply to get a new name, marriage does add to one's security. A parent may even be adopted. As incredible as this suggestion may sound, it is legal, it can afford a name change, and the record may be sealed.

It is not a good idea for a parent who has recovered a child to contact the abductor. This is a very sensitive issue, especially if the recovered child cries for the abductor. While a parent will want to be sensitive to a child's emotional needs, it is a parent's responsibility to protect the child from further emotional harm. Should a child insist on having contact with the abductor, safeguards should be in place before such contact comes about.

If a child is to write to the abductor, letters should be forwarded to another state or country prior to being delivered to the abductor. This will prevent the abductor from determining where the letters originated. Friends or relatives can assist in this endeavor, but make sure they are trustworthy.

A parent should always be aware of the contents of a letter that a child sends. Small, seemingly unimportant details may alert the abductor to the child's whereabouts. For example, suppose a child mentions the name of his or her pediatrician. Parents legally have access to their children's medical records. A parental abductor who knows the name of the pediatrician can request a child's records and immediately find out the child's address. Another example of a revealing detail is the name of a child's school. School information can be accessed. A parent should ask that a notice be attached to his or her child's records requesting that the parent be contacted should anyone request these records. The parent can then learn the name and address of the person requesting the information. If it is the abductor, the parent may inform authorities of the abductor's whereabouts. This is advantageous if there is a warrant for the abductor. A parent may consider asking the courts to issue restraints to prevent anyone from authorizing the release of records except by permission of the parent. If such an order is issued, it should be copied and sent to all agencies that have information on the child, with a request that it be placed in the child's file.

The habits of the parent may provide an abductor with clues on how to find the parent. For example, if the parent regularly attends bingo, bowling, or skating establishments, the abductor probably knows this. A parent's life will change once a child is recovered; many old habits may need to be broken. It is not easy. It is not simple. However, it is important to make the child feel safe and secure and not fearful.

Many factors can influence the relationship between the searching parent and the recovered child, including the age of the child when abducted, the amount of time a child was away from the searching parent, the relationship the child had with each parent, and the child's mental and emotional state. Items that were special to a child before the abduction, such as a certain toy, television show, or playmate, may trigger pleasant memories for a child. Foods, music, the smell of the searching parent's cologne or soap, or holiday traditions may also help a child remember happy times.

A recovered child may indicate a need for professional counseling. A child who is withdrawn, violent, or behaving in a way that may cause the searching parent concern should be seen by a professional. A recovered child may go through a short readjustment period, or a lengthy one. A child may wet the bed, cry for the abductor, or refuse to speak English. A searching parent must be ever sensitive to a child's needs. The trauma of an abduction is not over when a child is recovered.

5

Legal, Technical, and Diplomatic Support

MORE CHILDREN ARE RECOVERED FROM HAGUE COUNTRIES
THAN FROM NON HAGUE COUNTRIES.

Hegar, R.L., and Greif, G.L., "Parental Kidnapping Across
International Borders," *International Social Work 43* (1991,
pp. 353–363.

The purpose of this chapter is to provide a detailed picture of the agencies most likely to be of importance in a parent's search for an abducted child. The key to working effectively with any of these agencies is knowing what each one can and *cannot* do and how each one's strengths and limitations determine its usefulness in a particular search. Because knowing what agencies are most appropriate to a given situation can save time and prevent frustration, parents are urged to read the following profiles carefully.

State Department

For the searching parent of an internationally abducted child, the United States Department of State, Child Custody Division, is one of the most important resources. While the State Department will not recover a child for a searching parent, it does offer a wide range of services and information that can enable that parent to direct his or her efforts in a productive manner.

Once a parent has listed a child as missing with the local law enforcement agency and has had the child entered into the NCIC system, the parent should call the State Department. A searching parent will be assigned a case worker and be asked to provide information on the child and the abductor. The more information that is provided, the better able the worker is to evaluate a case. A parent will be required to fill out an application and provide the following:

1. As much information as possible on the abducted child: United States passport status, passport I.D. number, etc.

2. Country where abducted child has been taken or searching parent suspects the child has been taken.

3. Date child was taken, missing persons report, NCIC number.

4. United States custody order.

5. Warrants for abductor.

6. Abductor's passport status: United States passport, foreign passport, country of citizenship, possibility of dual citizenship, etc.

The parent is going to build the case, investigate, and implement the child's recovery. The information provided to the State Department will allow the department to advise and direct the parent on available courses of action as well as to provide information and assistance in initiating action, depending on the circumstances of the case.

Services provided by the State Department to a searching parent include but are not limited to;

1. Notifying the U.S. embassy in the country where a child is believed to have been taken of a possible abduction.

2. Requesting welfare and whereabouts check for the abducted child.

3. Requesting that the abductor, or family members or friends of the abductor, be contacted in an effort to locate a child or establish that child's welfare status.

4. Providing a list of attorneys who may be willing to represent a searching parent in legal action in the country where a child has been taken.

5. Making forms and application available for The Hague on behalf of the searching parent.

6. Serving as a link to the U.S. embassy abroad.

7. Providing attorney with information on parental abduction.

8. Providing searching parent with publications on parental abduction and related information.

In seeking specific assistance from the State Department, it is a good idea for the searching parent to make the request in writing, even if that parent has already made the request by phone. For example, if a searching parent wants the State Department to ask that the U.S. embassy abroad contact the abductor or the abductor's family and ask specific questions, the searching parent should list those questions in a written request. This avoids confusion and miscommunication. Each case worker at the State Department may be handling hundreds of cases. For a worker to remember the details of each and every case is probably asking too much. Since the searching parent is the coordinator of the recovery effort, it is essential that the parent make every effort to establish effective communication practices with the agencies involved. A parent should consider a written request an "order." However, this does not mean that the State Department or any other agency is bound to perform every duty or fulfill every request made by the searching parent. Searching parents should stay in contact with the State Department and keep their case workers updated on any new developments. They should request updated information from their case workers, such as any information that the U.S. embassy has been able to provide from efforts abroad.

The State Department is the central authority in the United States. Its office, located in Washington, DC, is not open for personal meetings with distraught parents. Routine communication is done by phone, fax and letters. For a parent to make a trip to Washington in hopes that his or her personal presence will elicit more attention and action from the State Department is almost certainly a waste of time. A parent may travel a lengthy distance only to be denied entrance into the building. While parents have met with State Department officials, it is unusual and not routine. While a trip to Washington may make the searching parent feel better, such a trip should be saved for more productive purposes. A visit to the appropriate foreign embassy or the passport office may prove more fruitful. Although both passports and visas may be obtained through the mail, establishing a good working relationship with the foreign embassy may be very advantageous.

The State Department can be contacted by phone, fax, or mail:

United States Central Authority
Office of Citizens' Consular Services
Division of Children's Services
Department of State
Room 4817
Washington DC 20520
Tel: (202) 647-2688
Fax: (202) 647-2835

The State Department charges no fee for services rendered on behalf of searching parents, including application to The Hague. Currently, the State Department has some 2,000 cases of abduction. Files are closed after two years if no activity is reported on a case.

The National Center for Missing and Exploited Children

Public awareness concerning missing children heightened in the early 1980s in large part because of the disappearance of a young boy named Adam Walsh. Around the time that the Adam Walsh case occurred, 29 Atlanta children were murdered. These brutal crimes led to a public outcry. Americans wanted justice, prevention and education. They wanted their children to be safe. As a result, the federal government created new laws. The Adam Walsh Foundation eventually merged with the NCMEC. Funded largely by the federal government, NCMEC is the largest and most influential missing children's organization in the United States.

The federal government also implemented grants to study the issues of missing children. It then extended funds for the study of homeless youth, runaways, child abuse and international parental abduction. The United States began prevention efforts to stop crimes against its most helpless citizens, its children.

Do not underestimate the resources and information the NCMEC has at its disposal. An example is its access to the NCIC. This is a resource to which the United States Department currently does not have access.

The NCMEC was founded by a group of concerned citizens and is a nonprofit organization. Its goal is to address the issue of missing children. The NCMEC consists of seven divisions:

1. Hotline
2. Case management
3. Publications
4. Legal
5. Photo distribution
6. Age-enhancement program
7. Outreach

The NCMEC operates a 24-hour-a-day, 7-day-a-week hotline. They are located at

NCMEC
2101 Wilson Blvd.
Arlington VA 22201

A toll-free number is provided to report missing children and to receive tips on children who are missing. Phone calls to the NCMEC are recorded so that information that may need to be passed on to authorities is accurately collected. The NCMEC is capable of handling calls in many foreign languages and provides a line for the hearing impaired. Telephone numbers are:

Hotline: 1-800-843-5678
Hearing impaired: 1-800-826-7653
Business: 1-703-235-3900

Missing children are assigned to case managers, who can provide parents with information, resources and referrals. Publications are available on the subject of parental abduction. The NCMEC also provides assistance to law enforcement and can assist a parent in filling a missing persons report.

The NCMEC will assist attorneys and congressional, state and legislative staff through their legal technical staff. Photo distribution through the NCMEC has led to the recovery of many missing children. Reports suggest that 1 in 7 children whose photos have been published have been located.

It is not unusual for a child to be missing for more than two years, especially in international parental abduction cases. For those cases, the NCMEC offers a unique service: photo age-enhancement, which allows a missing child to be "aged" photographically. This is important, as children grow quickly and can change drastically in appearance in a few years. The NCMEC offers photo age-enhancement to parents free of charge, through the Sony/QMA video imaging laboratory. In order to utilize this resource, the searching parent must have the child registered with NCMEC. A child must be gone for at least two years, and a parent should request application into the photo age-enhancement program from their case worker. If the NCMEC decides to provide this service for a particular case, the searching parent will be sent application forms and asked to provide photos of the child, the child's parents at the child's current age, and the child's siblings. For searching parents, this can be an invaluable service.

Should the NCMEC provide the searching parent with age-enhanced photos, the searching parent should distribute them to those involved in the case, e.g. law enforcement agencies, the State Department, attorneys, embassies, etc. However, *age-enhanced photos may not be used for passport photos.*

In 1990, the NCMEC received about 808 calls regarding abductions by family members (including parents and other relatives). From 1984 to 1990, the NCMEC received about 9,956 calls.

On page 90 is an example of how a child's photo was age-enhanced by

The two photos at top (each parent at age five) were combined with the photo at bottom left (child at two) to produce the age-enhanced photo of the child at five (bottom right). Photo age-enhancement by NCMEC.

the NCMEC. In the upper left-hand corner is the child's father at age five. In the upper right-hand corner is the child's mother at age five. The lower left-hand picture shows the child at age two, when she was abducted. The picture at lower right is the child at age five, through age-enhancement.

Federal Bureau of Investigation

The Federal Bureau of Investigation (FBI) investigates allegations of international parental abduction. If sufficient evidence exists to suggest that a child has been illegally taken out of the United States, a warrant will be issued for the arrest of the abductor under the 1993 International Parental Kidnapping Crime Act. (In order for a warrant to be issued, permission must first be granted by the United States Department of Justice.)

The involvement of the FBI in international parental abduction is fairly new. The Federal Kidnapping Act of 1932 (18 USC 1201) prohibited FBI involvement because parental abduction was not a crime. Only cases where children had been abducted by strangers were considered eligible for FBI involvement. When Congress passed the Parental Kidnapping Prevention Act (PKPA) in 1980 (28 USC, ss 17380a), this allowed for FBI involvement in parental abductions in which children were taken over state lines. It also allowed for Unlawful Flight to Avoid Prosecution (UFAP) warrants to be issued against abductors who fled across state lines. (Fugitive Felon Act, 18 USC 1073.)

The Missing Children Act of 1982 (Public Law 97-292; 28 USC 534a) requires the FBI to enter a missing child into the NCIC if local law enforcement agencies do not. To further FBI involvement and to lend assistance, the Juvenile and Delinquency Prevention Act of 1974 (42 USC 5778) recognizes and allows government funding of the National Center for Missing and Exploited Children. The NCMEC works with the FBI as well as other agencies in providing technical assistance and has a legal staff to consult with prosecutors in abduction cases.

With the enactment of the 1993 International Parental Kidnapping Crime Act, international parental kidnapping became a federal felony, and the FBI was empowered to investigate and handle this crime like any other federal crime, according to the guidelines established in defining this crime and establishing investigative procedure.

The FBI has 24 foreign liaison offices worldwide, covering 87 countries. These offices are dependent on the cooperation of the host country. Extradition is rarely used in international parental abduction cases at the present time. While statistics are not available on the effectiveness of the International Parental Kidnapping warrant, statistics do show that the FBI issued the following UFAP warrants for parental abductions: from 1981 through 1985, 1,054 warrants; from 1986 through 1990, 1,448 warrants; and from 1991 through 1992, 432 warrants.

Many searching parents have complained about the lack of assistance they have received from the FBI. Despite the laws just mentioned that define the role and duties of the FBI in cases of international parental abduction, a searching parent may indeed encounter obstacles. Below are described some possible problems, along with the legal information needed to counter them:

FBI refuses to investigate and obtain an International Parental Kidnapping warrant because the searching parent does not have legal custody of the abducted child.

According to the International Parental Kidnapping Crime Act of 1993, custody status of the searching parent has no basis in determining whether the accused abductor committed a crime. In fact, if the parent does not have legal custody of the child and the FBI refuses to obtain a warrant based on that fact, the FBI is in violation of the law. Any parent who is denied legal access (visitation) to their child can request a warrant.

FBI refuses to obtain a kidnapping warrant because of extradition obstacles such as cost to the department or treaty status with other country, or simply because it is a crime that is usually not prosecuted. (The maximum three-year prison sentence and fine may not justify the time and expense the FBI may have to expend to apprehend the abductor.)

If the abductor is residing in a country that does not have an extradition treaty with the United States, the FBI agent may feel it is a waste of time to obtain a warrant. Nothing could be further from the truth. While extradition problems may have a very big impact on whether a warrant will be issued, it should be noted that a warrant has often been used simply to influence a successful recovery without extradition. For example, consider two cases where warrants were issued (UFAP and International Parental Kidnapping) for abductors known to be in the Middle East. Neither country recognized the warrant nor the authority of the United States. However, when the cases entered the court system in their respective countries, the warrants were presented as evidence in the custody disputes. This helped influence a positive custody decision for both parents. (The Middle Eastern countries have extradition treaties among themselves.)

A warrant also is beneficial in restricting an abductor's rights once a child has been recovered. It may serve to influence the court, since it would make it apparent that the abductor has already committed a felony against this child. Such an influence may cause the court to deny visitation rights or require supervised visitation.

A warrant may lead to the incarceration of the abductor, thus providing some safe and secure time for the recovered child.

A warrant may influence an abductor not to return to the United States once a child has been recovered.

A warrant may influence the abductor to voluntarily return a child.

A warrant can be an insurance policy to searching parents who enter United States–friendly countries and recover their children themselves. Should a recovery be stopped in progress, the warrant may provide for an unofficial sanction of the recovery.

FBI refuses to issue a warrant based on lack of information or evidence.

It is the responsibility of the FBI to investigate and gather enough information to justify a warrant. A searching parent cannot expect a warrant to be issued just because he or she requests one. In investigating an abduction, the FBI agent will need information that the searching parent may have to provide. Failure to gather enough information to reasonably confirm a parent's complaint may result in a judge's refusal to honor the agent's request for a warrant. It may be difficult for a parent to provide certain information. If the United States attorney's office is requesting a warrant, it may be easier to obtain.

While the agent will investigate a complaint, the searching parent, again, has the burden of providing enough information to bring about a reasonable conclusion that international parental abduction has taken place. A searching parent may have to prove his or her child has been removed from the country. A note left by the abductor, a taped phone call, or information proved by family or friends may be able to establish that a child has, indeed, been abducted outside of the United States. (See "Determining Whether an Abductor Has Left the Country" in Chapter 3.)

FBI just doesn't seem to want to get involved.

Call the state attorney's office. A state attorney can order an agent to investigate a complaint if he or she feels that the complaint is valid. Influence peddling can be a great way to motivate people to do their jobs. In case a searching parent has not found out yet, recovery often has more to do with politics than with anything else. An ally in high places can be very valuable indeed.

Once the FBI has assisted a searching parent in obtaining a warrant, the agency can further provide information on the abductor. The FBI has access to immigration and customs information. The FBI provides Interpol with updated information on both the abductor and the child and may very well be the only link a parent has to Interpol services. It is important that a searching parent keep the agent updated on the case and request the agent also notify Interpol of the updates and ask Interpol to send out diffusions updating the world. An FBI agent may be one of the strongest contacts a parent has.

Each state has regional FBI offices. In order to determine who covers a specific jurisdiction, a searching parent should consult the telephone book or directory assistance operator. An agent will be assigned to the case, and a searching parent should work to support his investigation and provide all the assistance and cooperation possible.

Do not assume that a local law enforcement agency is going to issue warrants against the abductor. A local law enforcement agency may refer a case to the county or state prosecutor's office. Either is able to order an investigation.

A searching parent should be aware of different warrants and jurisdictions. A UFAP (Unlawful Flight to Avoid Prosecution) warrant can be issued when an abductor leaves the state to avoid prosecution. This is a common felony warrant issued against an abductor and was the toughest warrant until the International Parental Kidnapping warrant became available in 1993. State charges against the abductor can result in state warrants. In most states, parental abduction is a felony whether a child has been removed from the United States or not. Simply taking a child over state lines may constitute child-snatching or custodial interference. Civil charges for contempt for violation of a visitation or custody order may be lodged against the abductor in the courts. Since each state has varying laws concerning parental abduction, a searching parent may wish to contact his or her state prosecutor for more information.

If a searching parent has requested or intends to request the assistance of The Hague, it is very important that the searching parent not combine that effort with that of criminal legal action. The 1993 International Parental Kidnapping Crime Act specifically states that seeking a federal felony warrant should not automatically be a route to recovery. In many cases The Hague should be contacted first and all efforts for recovery should be tried through that avenue if possible.

If a searching parent has obtained a warrant or warrants, the FBI should request copies of those warrants. A searching parent may also want to send copies to his or her State Department case worker, missing children's case worker, and foreign legal council, as well as the U.S. embassy abroad.

During 1990, the FBI initiated investigations in 265 new cases of parental abductions. The agency assisted state and local law enforcement agencies seeking felons who had crossed state lines to avoid prosecution, arrest, or imprisonment. The FBI found 107 parentally abducted children and located or arrested 132 abductors. Although these figures do not begin to reflect the number of children who have been abducted, they do indicate a success ratio of about 1:2. These figures do not represent international abductions.

Interpol

Interpol, the International Police Association, can play an important part in the recovery of an internationally abducted child. Interpol has offices in 169 member countries. In the United States the office is known as the National Center Bureau. It is located in the United States Department of Justice in Washington, DC. The following five divisions make up the United States National Center Bureau (USNCB):

Criminal Investigation Division
Financial Fraud Division
Drugs Division
Alien/Fugitive Enforcement Division
State Liaison Division

International parental abduction cases are handled by the Alien/Fugitive Enforcement Division.

The role of Interpol is initiated once an International Parental Kidnapping warrant has been issued and the FBI transmits that information to Interpol. Interpol is able to process the warrant through member countries and alert authorities that a warrant has been issued for the abductor. Interpol will not arrest or prosecute an abductor. Its role is to forward information to the appropriate authorities when information about an abductor or missing child has been discovered. Just as NCIC has established a nationwide network in the United States to make information available to law enforcement agencies, Interpol has established a worldwide network.

Interpol uses a series of color codes to denote the priority assigned to a communication. A red flag indicates the highest priority alert.

A parent may not initiate a request for action from Interpol. This must be done through the proper federal agency. The FBI will make the determination as to whether Interpol action is warranted.

Interpol works discreetly and will not alert an abducting parent. Its goal is to provide information on an abductor or an abducted child and then to pass that information on to appropriate authorities. Interpol does not request extradition, nor will it take an abductor into custody. This is left to the appropriate law enforcement authority.

In order for Interpol to become involved in an international parental abduction case, a child must be listed as missing; a warrant must have been issued for the abductor; the abductor and child's whereabouts must be unknown; and Interpol involvement must be initiated through an appropriate agency. Interpol can be very effective in influencing foreign law enforcement agencies to act on behalf of the United States. While United States law cannot be enforced abroad, countries may view continual updated diffusions by Interpol as serious and thus be inspired to cooperate. If Interpol requests acknowledgment of a diffusion by a foreign country and the country responds, a valuable communication link has been established. Information regarding the missing child is also transmitted.

The address and phone of Interpol are below, but remember that parents should not contact Interpol to request action.

Interpol
United States Central Bureau
U.S. Department of Justice
Shoreham Bldg, Rm 800
Washington, DC 20530
(202) 616-7291 / Alien/Fugitive Division

U.S. Embassies Abroad

U.S. embassies abroad, in conjunction with the State Department, can be a vital link between a searching parent and a child. The U.S. embassy affords a diplomatic avenue in the recovery process. The U.S. embassy will not take possession of a child or provide legal advice to a searching parent. Furthermore, the embassy cannot enforce United States law in a country which does not recognize it. The U.S. embassy will not violate the law of the host country in order to facilitate the return of an abducted child. A searching parent who has the intention of securing the return of a child through illegal efforts will not be assisted by the U.S. embassy abroad; nor can the embassy assist a parent who is arrested and imprisoned in a foreign country for violating the laws. A searching parent is bound by the laws of the country that he or she enters. So what can the U.S. embassy abroad do to facilitate the return of a child? Let us continue on a more positive, and practical approach.

The U.S. embassy abroad works with the State Department in providing information and assistance to a searching parent within the laws and guidelines of that particular country. The country involved, the relationship the United States has with that country, and the particular factors in a case will determine how effective the U.S. embassy can be. For example, while the United States may enjoy a good diplomatic relationship with European countries and share common ideology in the return of abducted children as well as legal cooperation, those advantages may not exist with some Middle Eastern countries, making the recovery of a child more difficult. Still, even in the Middle East there are options available to the U.S. embassy that may facilitate the recovery of a child through cooperative and diplomatic efforts.

A parent may contact the U.S. embassy abroad directly or through the State Department. It is strongly advised that both the State Department and the embassy be aware of all communications to both agencies. (A fax machine can greatly reduce the cost of this endeavor and facilitate rapid communication.) A listing of the U.S. embassies abroad as well as their foreign counterpart in the United States are open.

The U.S. embassy abroad can attempt to do a whereabouts and welfare check on the abducted child at the parent's request. A searching parent may fear that such a check will alert the abductor to the search and cause him or her to run. For this reason, some searching parents do not want this service performed. However, if there is reason to believe that the child's life may be in danger, perhaps a parent should rethink this position. A parent who fears that the abductor will flee with the child should be aware that there are several ways a parent can prevent a child from traveling. Of course, these tactics cannot prevent the abductor from hiding the child in a more isolated manner, but they can prevent the crossing of borders.

A parent can request that the passport office not reissue a United States passport for their child. This request will be sent out to all U.S. embassies abroad. The United States issues a child's passport for five years. At the end of that time it expires. If an abducting parent tries to renew the passport and the searching parent has requested a block on reissue, the abducting parent will be refused a new passport for the child. However, it is not unusual for an abducting parent to secure a passport for the child from his country. In this case, the U.S. embassy abroad cannot prevent issuance.

If an abducted child is traveling on a foreign passport, the U.S. embassy should be made aware of the fact. Surprisingly, a searching parent may assume a child is traveling on a foreign passport, only to find out the abductor was not able to secure one. Should an abducting parent make application for a United States visa at the U.S. embassy abroad, the searching parent may be made aware of this. If a searching parent is not sure whether his or her child is traveling on a passport other than one of United States issue, the U.S. embassy abroad may be able to obtain this information, or the searching parent may be able to hire foreign counsel in order to establish the abducted child's foreign passport status.

A searching parent should address all inquiries to the counselor of the U.S. embassy abroad. The United States ambassador does not normally handle international parental abduction cases. However, there have been cases where the ambassador has gotten involved. The State Department can give the searching parent the name of the counselor at the U.S. embassy abroad.

The U.S. consulate abroad can approach the foreign minister in the country where the abducted child is believed to be and request his or her assistance in many areas. Again, cooperation with the foreign ministry is dependent on many different factors. The U.S. embassy abroad may be able to request entry and exit visa information in order to determine if the abducted child has entered the foreign country or been taking out of that country. The embassy may be able to establish time frames and may even request that a foreign minister not allow the abductor an entrance visa into another country. For example, if an abductor is working in Saudi Arabia but is a Syrian national and returns to Syria on vacation, it is possible that the U.S. embassy might ask the foreign ministry in Saudi Arabia not to permit reentry. This can be most frustrating for the abductor. Threatened with loss of livelihood, he or she may decide it is more advantageous to return the abducted child than to be unemployed.

Such action can also serve to enhance a parent's legal opportunity. If an abductor is residing in a country where it is very difficult for the searching parent to obtain legal custody or recovery of the child, but the abductor leaves that country and enters a more sympathetic one, a parent may be able to prevent the abductor from returning and thus serve legal action in the more sympathetic country.

The U.S. embassy abroad can assist a parent in utilizing the Hague Convention and working with the foreign government. Even in the most difficult of countries, the U.S. embassy will make every effort to locate a child and to determine that child's welfare. That is not to say, however, that the effort is always successful.

Changes in staff, counselor or even ambassador can greatly affect a parent's case, as well as the relationship the United States has with the host country. One can easily imagine what confusion a change in staff can have on an ongoing case. Here, a parent must use all his or her strength and resources in order to assist the U.S. embassy abroad, and to make sure everyone involved knows exactly where the case stands and what assistance is needed. Many times, new personnel are not familiar with the relationships the previous staff had with those in the foreign government, and the search may be hampered by their lack of knowledge. On the other hand, a new staff may be welcomed and may be able to facilitate a more productive dialogue. If this sounds like politics, it is. A searching parent is dealing with a diplomatic body, and everything in that body can be affected by any change, whether for better or for worse.

The U.S. embassy abroad can issue a searching parent a new passport for an abducted child if the parent has the child in his or her custody and is in the foreign country with the child. The U.S. embassy abroad will not issue a passport to a parent in the United States while the child is abroad. This is very important. If a parent has put a block on reissuing a child's passport, it would be very wise to notify the State Department and passport office that a passport request will be made for the abducted child in the foreign country once the child has been recovered. A searching parent must also be aware of exit visa requirements. A child must have a passport to leave one country and enter another. (Exceptions may exist in Mexico and Canada.) He or she may also need an exit visa. In some countries a child exiting on a new passport with no entrance visa may alarm customs and a child may not be permitted to leave. Imagine the distress of a parent who recovers a child, receives a passport from the U.S. embassy abroad, and then is detained at the airport and not permitted to leave the country with the child. A searching parent must find out what travel requirements are *before* they recover their child. The U.S. embassy abroad can provide this important information, advising a searching parent on how to facilitate exit with a recovered child. The embassy cannot issue exit visas in order for a parent to leave a foreign country. That is handled by the foreign country. However, the embassy may be able to *assist* a parent in obtaining an exit visa.

As a last note, a parent wishing to secure a passport for a child at a U.S. embassy abroad must have the required passport photos of the child, as well as the birth certificate and possibly custodial orders. The passport photos are to have been taken within the previous six months. Passport photos can be obtained in most major cities around the world.

Should a parent express an intent to illegally re-abduct a child, the U.S. embassy will in no way assist in that activity. The U.S. embassy may even report that parent's activities to the local authorities or to the abducting parent. Furthermore, should a parent succeed in recovering a child through illegal re-abduction attempts and run to the U.S. embassy for sanctuary, that parent will not be assisted. Again, the parent may be criminally liable for any illegal attempt to remove a child from the foreign country. It is imperative that a searching parent understand the legal structure of the foreign country where the child is being held. It may be that a searching parent can legally go in and simply take possession of his or her child without violating civil or criminal law.

For an excellent and inexpensive publication entitled "Key Officers in Foreign Service Posts," contact:

Superintendent of Documents
U.S. Government Printing Office
Washington DC 20402
Telephone: (202) 783-3238

It is important that the searching parent know his or her case worker in the U.S. embassy abroad as well as those in key offices. A parent coordinating efforts with the same individuals may avoid miscommunications, conflicting instructions and misunderstandings.

Foreign Embassies in the United States

A searching parent may turn to the foreign embassy located in the United States for cooperation in recovering a child. Again, much depends on the relationship the United States has with that foreign country and on the laws that prevail there. While it may be a great asset to establish a relationship with a foreign embassy, a searching parent must have some working knowledge of that country's views of child custody and other customs. It may be that a parent would harm his or her case by approaching a foreign embassy.

Although a parent may be working through the State Department and the U.S. embassy abroad as well as with a foreign attorney, he or she may still find it helpful to request the assistance of a foreign embassy in completing the necessary paperwork for visas, power of attorney, etc. A trip to Washington, DC, may help by allowing the staff of the embassy to become familiar with the case. Some parents have found that establishing a good working relationship with a foreign embassy has allowed them access to resources that they may not have known about previously, such as tourist maps, holiday schedules, and even information on foreign attorneys.

The foreign embassy can perform a variety of functions, whether a searching parent chooses to visit the embassy in person or make requests by mail.

These functions include assisting with visa application; providing information on legal aid, hotels and customs; supplying maps; filling out and witnessing forms for power of attorney; and legalizing documents. It is important that the searching parent ask the foreign embassy for specific information and not just make general requests. For example, a mother asked the Syrian embassy whether it had issued a passport for her child. Although no one investigated this question it was obvious the embassy would not provide this information, the mother did learn that the embassy purged its records every five years. This was important information because the abductor had previously registered for his military exemption through the embassy and the mother knew that he did not meet the requirement for that exemption. That registration would still be in the embassy's system. The mother divulged this information to the embassy staff in hopes that they would investigate the abductor. Although the mother cannot say for certain that they did, she is almost positive that she did generate some interest in his background. On future trips to the embassy, the mother was asked several questions about the abductor. It was obvious that the abductor's own embassy was suspicious of him and perhaps had found some indication that he had broken the law in his country. This may have prejudiced the embassy against him and ultimately served to heighten sympathy for the mother.

Many times a searching parent may be afraid to proceed with a particular action because he or she believes the abductor has "connections." In many if not most cases, these connections prove to be nonexistent. A good foreign attorney can usually determine an abductor's true position in society. Unfortunately, it must be acknowledged that if the abductor truly is extremely wealthy, politically connected, or in high social standing in his country, the foreign embassy and a foreign attorney probably will not assist a searching parent for fear of suffering possible consequences themselves. Although this does not apply in all countries, it would be well for searching parent to know the abductor's true social standing as well as the country's attitude towards bringing legal action against him or her.

A searching parent intent on recovering a child through illegal means may find that the foreign embassy will refuse to issue a visa or be of other assistance. It would be ridiculous for a searching parent to enter a foreign embassy, announce a play to re-abduct a child, then ask for assistance. A parent may find, however, that legal and diplomatic efforts to recover a child are not only encouraged but greatly assisted by the foreign embassy.

A searching parent should not enter the foreign embassy with the intention of speaking to the ambassador. The ambassador's duties do not include assisting American parents who are searching for their children. As in the U.S. embassy abroad, a parent may be referred to the counselor, or even a clerk. Since most business that pertains to the recovery of a child done at a foreign embassy will be routine paperwork, a searching parent may find that his or her most important and useful contact is an embassy employee whose job it is to issue visas, legalize documents, and witness power of attorney contracts.

If a child has been taken to a country with which the United States has no diplomatic relations, and there is not foreign embassy in the United States, it is possible that another country may intercede on behalf of the parent. The State Department can advise a searching parent on the direction to take in these cases. If this avenue does not prove fruitful, it is up to the parent to find another route and initiate the appropriate action.

6

Law

A number of United States federal laws have been enacted in an effort to address issues of parental abduction such as jurisdiction, agency responsibility, and classification of the crime. Along with federal law is the Hague Convention, which is an international treaty among signatory countries.

The United States implemented the Hague Convention through the International Child Abduction Remedies Act. This law establishes procedures in the United States to implement the Hague Convention on the Civil Aspects of International Child Abduction.

The Parental Kidnapping Prevention Act (PKPA) was enacted to settle disputes between states claiming jurisdiction and gives priority to the child's home state when one state maintains a "significant connections" position.

The National Child Search Assistance Act of 1990 states that no law enforcement agency can maintain, practice, implement, or require a "waiting period" before listing a child as missing. It also encourages law enforcement involvement.

The International Parental Kidnapping Crime Act of 1993 makes international parental kidnapping a federal felony. Of importance here is also the fact that this law does not recognize custody as an issue. Any parent denied access to his or her child by the other parent is a victim.

The Hague Convention on the Civil Aspects of International Child

Abduction is an international treaty which approaches the return of an abducted child through diplomatic processes while recognizing the legal rights granted by jurisdictional courts. The United States became a member of The Hague in 1988.

Other federal laws utilized in apprehending an abductor include laws against "unlawful flight to avoid prosecution."

Combined with state laws regarding custodial interference and child-snatching, enough federal laws exist to assist in both prevention and recovery. However, more still needs to be done.

International Child Abduction Remedies Act

(ICARA)
Public Law 100-300
100th Congress
[H.R. 3971, 29 Apr 1988]42 USC 11601 et seq

An Act

To establish procedures to implement the Convention on the Civil Aspects of International Child Abduction, done at The Hague on October 25, 1980, and for other purposes.

Be it enacted by the Senate and House of Representatives of the United States of America in Congress assembled.

Sec. 1. Short Title.

This Act may be cited as the "International Child Abduction Remedies Act."

Sec. 2. Findings and Declarations. [42 USC 11601]

(a) **Findings.** — The Congress makes the following findings:

(1) The international abduction or wrongful retention of children is harmful to their well-being.

(2) Persons should not be permitted to obtain custody of children by virtue of their wrongful removal or retention.

(3) International abductions and retention of children are increasing, and only concerned cooperation pursuant to an international agreement can effectively combat this problem.

(4) The Convention on the Civil Aspects of International Child Abduction, done at The Hague on October 25, 1980, establishes legal rights and procedures for the prompt return of children who have been wrongfully removed or retained, as well as for securing the exercise of visitation rights. Children who are wrongfully removed or retained within the meaning of the Convention are to be promptly returned unless one of the narrow exceptions set forth in the Convention applies. The Convention provides a sound treaty framework to help resolve the problem of international parental abduction and retention of children and will deter such wrongful removals and retention.

(b) **Declarations.** - The Congress makes the following declarations:

(1) It is the purpose of this Act to establish procedures for the implementation of the Convention in the United States.

(2) The provisions of the Act are in addition to and not in lieu of the provisions of the Convention.

(3) In enacting this Act the Congress recognizes —

(A) the international character of the Convention; and

(B) the need for uniform international interpretation of the Convention.

(4) The Convention and this Act empower courts in the United States to determine only rights under the Convention and not the merits of any underlying child custody claims.

Sec. 3. Definitions [42 USC 11602]

For purposes of this Act —

(1) the term "applicant" means any person who, pursuant to the Convention, files an application with the United States Central Authority or a Central Authority of any other party to the Convention for the return of a child alleged to have been wrongfully removed or retained or for arrangements for organizing or securing the effective exercise of rights of access pursuant to the Convention;

(2) the term "Convention" means the Convention on the Civil Aspects of International Child Abduction, done at The Hague on October 25, 1980;

(3) the term "Parental Locator Service" means the service established by the Secretary of Health and Human Services under section 453 of the Social Security Act (42 U.S.C. 653);

(4) the term "petitioner" means any person who, in accordance with this Act, files a petition in court seeking relief under the Convention;

(5) the term "person" includes any individual, institution, or other legal entity or other legal entity or body;

(6) the term "respondent" means any person against whose interests a petition is filed in court, in accordance with this Act, which seeks relief under the Convention;

(7) the term "rights of access" means visitation rights;

(8) the term "State" means any of the several States, the District of Columbia, and any commonwealth, territory, or possession of the United States; and

(9) the term "United States Central Authority" means the agency of the Federal Government designated by the President under section 7(a).

Sec. 4. Judicial Remedies. [42 USC 11603]

(a) **Jurisdiction of the Courts.**—The courts of the States and the United States district courts shall have concurrent original jurisdiction of actions arising under the Convention.

(b) **Petitions.**—Any person seeking to initiate judicial proceedings under the Convention for the return of a child or for arrangements for organizing or securing the effective exercise of rights of access to a child may do so by commencing a civil action by filing a petition for the relief sought in any court which has jurisdiction of such action and which is authorized to exercise its jurisdiction in the place where the child is located at the time the petition is filed.

(c) **Notice.**—Notice of an action brought under subsection (b) shall be given in accordance with the applicable law governing notice in interstate child custody proceedings.

(d) **Determination of Case.**—The court in which an action is brought under subsection (b) shall decide the case in accordance with the Convention.

(e) **Burdens of Proof.**—(1) A Petitioner in an action brought under subsection (b) shall establish by a preponderance of the evidence —

(A) in the case of an action for the return of a child, that the child has been wrongfully removed or retained within the meaning of the Convention; and

(B) in the case of an action for arrangements for organizing or securing the effective exercise of rights of access, that the petitioner has such rights.

(2) In the case of an action for the return of a child, a respondent who opposes the return of the child has the burden of establishing —

(A) by clear and convincing evidence that one of the exceptions set forth in article 13b or 20 of the Convention applies; and

(B) by a preponderance of the evidence that any other exception set forth in article 12 or 13 of the Convention applies.

(f) **Application of the Convention.**—For purposes of any action brought under this Act—

(1) the term "authorities", as used in article 15 of the Convention to refer to the authorities of the child, includes courts and appropriate government agencies;

(2) the terms "wrongful removal or retention" and "wrongfully removed or retained", as used in the Convention, include a removal or retention of a child before the entry of a custody order regarding that child; and

(3) the term "commencement of proceedings", as used in article 12 of the Convention, means, with respect to the return of a child located in the United States, the filing of a petition in accordance with subsection (b) of this section.

(g) **Full Faith and Credit.**—Full faith and credit shall be accorded by the courts of the States and the courts of the United States to the judgment of any other such court ordering or denying the return of a child, pursuant to the Convention, in an action brought under this Act.

(h) **Remedies Under the Convention Not Exclusive.**—The remedies established by the Convention and this Act shall be in addition to remedies under other laws or international agreements.

Sec. 5. Provisional Remedies. [42 USC 11604]

(a) **Authority of Courts.**—In furtherance of the objectives of article 7(b) and other provisions brought under section 4(b) of this Act may take or cause to be taken measured under Federal or State law, as appropriate, to protect the well-being of the child involved or to prevent the further removal or concealment before the final disposition of the petition.

(b) **Limitation on Authority.**—No court exercising jurisdiction of an action brought under section 4(b) may, under subsection (a) of this section, order a child removed from a person having physical control of the child unless the application requirements of State law are satisfied.

Sec. 6. Admissibility of Documents. [42 USC 11605]

With respect to any application to the United States Central Authority, or any petition to a court under section 4, which seeks relief under the Convention, or any other document or information include with such application or petition or provided after such submission which relates to the application or petition, as the case may be, no authentication of such application, petition, document, or information shall be required in order for the application, petition, document, or information to be admissible in court.

Sec. 7. United States Central Authority. [42 USC 11606]

(a) **Designation.**—The President shall designate a Federal agency to serve as the Central Authority for the United States under the Convention.
(b) **Functions.**—The United States Central Authority is authorized to issue such regulations as may be necessary to carry out its functions under the Convention and this Act.
(c) **Obtaining Information from Parent Locator Service.**—The United States Central Authority may, to the extent authorized by the Social Security Act, obtain information from the Parent Locator Service.

Sec. 8. Costs and Fees. [42 USC 11607]

(a) **Administrative Costs.**—No department, agency, or instrumentality of the Federal Government or of any State or local government may impose an application fee in relation to the administrative processing of applications being submitted under the convention.
(b) **Costs Incurred in Civil Actions.**—(1) Petitioners may be required to bear the costs of legal counsel or advisors, court costs incurred in connection with their petitions, and travel costs for the return of the child involved and any accompanying persons, except as provided in paragraph (2) and (3).

(2) Subject to paragraph (3), legal fees or court costs incurred in connection with an action brought under section 4 shall be borne by the petitioner unless they are covered by payments from Federal, State, or local legal assistance or other programs.

(3) Any court ordering the return of a child pursuant to an action brought under section 4 shall order the respondent to pay necessary expenses incurred by or on behalf of the petitioner, including court costs, legal fees, foster home or other care during the course of proceedings in the action, and transportation costs related to the return of the child, unless the respondent established that such order would be clearly inappropriate.

Sec. 9. Collection, Maintenance, and Dissemination of Information. [42 USC 11608]

(a) **In General.**—In performing its function under the Convention, the United States Central Authority may, under such conditions as the Central

Authority prescribes by regulation, but subject to subsection (c), receive from or transmit to any department, agency, or instrumentality of the Federal Government or of any State or foreign government, and receive from or transmit to any applicant, petitioner, or respondent, information necessary to locate a child or for the purpose of otherwise implementing the Convention with respect to a child, except that the United States Central Authority —

(1) may receive such information from a Federal or State department, agency, or instrumentality only pursuant to applicable Federal and State statutes; and

(2) may transmit any information received under this subsection notwithstanding any provision of law other than this Act.

(b) **Requests for Information.**—Requests for information under this section shall be submitted in such a manner and form as the United States Central Authority may prescribe by regulation and shall be accompanied or supported by such documents as the United States Central Authority may require.

(c) **Responsibility of Government Entities.**—Whenever any department, agency, or instrumentality of the United States or of any State receives a request from the United States Central Authority for information authorized to be provided to such Central Authority under subsection (a), the head of such department, agency, or instrumentality shall promptly cause a search to be made of the files and records maintained by such department, agency, or instrumentality in order to determine whether the information requested is contained in any such files or records. If such search discloses the information requested, the head of such department, agency, or instrumentality shall immediately transmit such information to the United States Central Authority, except that any information the disclosure of which —

(1) would adversely affect the national security interests of the United States or the law enforcement interests of the United States or of any State; or

(2) would be prohibited by section 9 of title 13, United States Enforcement Code shall not be transmitted to the Central Authority. The head of such department, agency, or instrumentality shall, immediately upon completion of the requested search, notify the Central Authority of the results of the search, and whether an exception set forth in paragraph (1) or (2) applies. In the event that the United States Central Authority receives information and the appropriate Federal or State department, agency, or instrumentality thereafter notifies the Central Authority that an exception set forth in paragraph (1) or (2) applies to that information, the Central Authority may not disclose that information under subsection (a).

(d) **Information Available from Parent Locator Service.**—To the extent that information which the United States Central Authority is authorized to obtain under the provisions of subsection (c) can be obtained through the Parent

Locator Service, the United States Central Authority shall first seek to obtain such information from the Parent Locator Service, before requesting such information directly under the provisions of subsection (c) of this section.

(e) **Recordkeeping.**—The United States Central Authority shall maintain appropriate records concerning its activities and the disposition of cases brought to its attention.

Sec. 10. Interagency Coordinating Group.
[42 USC 11609]

The Secretary of State, the Secretary of Health and Human Services, and the Attorney General shall designate Federal employees and may, from time to time, designate private citizens to serve on an interagency coordinating group to monitor the operation of the Convention and to provide advice on its implementation to the United States Central Authority and other Federal agencies. This group shall meet from time to time at the request of the United States Central Authority. The agency in which the United States Central Authority is located is authorized to reimburse such private citizens for travel and other expenses incurred in participating at meetings of the interagency coordinating group at rates not to exceed those authorized under subchapter 1 of chapter 57 of title 5, United States Code, for employees of agencies.

Sec. 11. Agreement for Use of Parent Locator Service
in Determining Whereabouts of Parent or Child.

Section 463 of the Social Security Act (42 USC 663) is amended —

(1) by striking "under this section" in subsection (b) and inserting "under subsection (a)";

(2) by striking "under this section" where it first appears in subsection (c) and inserting "under subsection (a), (b), or (e)"; and

(3) by adding at the end the following new subsection:

> "(e) The Secretary shall enter into an agreement with the Central Authority designated by the President in accordance with section 7 of the International Child Abduction Remedies Act, under which services of the Parent Locator Service established under section 453 shall be made available to such Central Authority upon its request for the purpose of locating any parent or child on behalf of an applicant to such Central Authority within the meaning of section 3 (1) of that Act. The Parent Locator Service shall charge no fees for services requested pursuant to this subsection."

Sec. 12. Authorization of Appropriations.
[42 USC 11610]

There are authorized to be appropriated for each fiscal year such sums as may be necessary to carry out the purposes of the Convention and this Act.

Parental Kidnapping Prevention Act of 1980

Public Law 96-611
96th Congress
[28 Dec 1980]
94 Stat 3566

An Act

To Amend title XVIII of the Social Security Act to provide for Medicare coverage of pneumococcal vaccine and its administration.

Sec. 2. The amendments made by this Act shall take effect on, and apply to services furnished on or after, July 1, 1981.

Short Title

Sec. 6. Section 6 to 10 of this Act may be cited as the "Parental Kidnapping Prevention Act of 1980".

Findings and Purposes

Sec. 7. (a) The Congress finds that —

(1) there is a large and growing number of cases annually involving disputes between persons claiming rights of custody and visitation of children under the laws, and in the courts, of different States, the District of Columbia, the Commonwealth of Puerto Rico, and the territories and possessions of the United States;

(2) the laws and practices by which the courts of those jurisdictions determine their jurisdiction to decide such disputes, and the effect to be given the decisions of such disputes by the courts of other jurisdictions, are often inconsistent and conflicting;

(3) those characteristics of the law and practices of such cases, along with the limits imposed by a Federal system on the authority of each such jurisdiction to conduct investigations and take other actions outside its own boundaries, contribute to a tendency of parties involved in such disputes

to frequently resort to seizure, restraint, concealment, and interstate transportation of children, the disregard of court orders, excessive re-litigation of cases, obtaining of conflicting orders by the courts of various jurisdictions, and interstate travel and communication that is so expensive and time consuming as to disrupt their occupation and commercial activities; and

(4) among the results of those conditions and activities are the failure of the courts of such jurisdictions to give full faith and credit to the judicial proceedings of the other jurisdictions, the deprivation of rights of liberty and property without due process of law, burdens on commerce among such jurisdictions and with foreign nations, and harm to the welfare of children and their parents and other custodians.

(b) For those reasons it is necessary to establish a national system for locating parents and children who travel from one such jurisdiction to another and are concealed in connection with such disputes, and to establish national standards under which the courts of such jurisdictions will determine their jurisdiction to decide such decisions by the courts of other such jurisdictions.

(c) The general purposes of sections 6 to 10 of the Act are to —

(1) promote cooperation between State courts to the end that a determination of custody and visitation is rendered in the State which can best decide the case in the interest of the child;

(2) promote and expand the exchange of information and other forms of mutual assistance between States which are concerned with the same child;

(3) facilitate the enforcement of custody and visitation decrees of sister States;

(4) discourage continuing interstate controversies over child custody in the interest of greater stability of same environment and of secure family relationships for the child;

(5) avoid jurisdictional competition and conflict between State courts in matters of child custody and visitation which have in the past resulted in the shifting of children from State to State with harmful effects on their well being; and

(6) deter interstate abductions and other unilateral removals of children undertaken to obtain custody and visitation awards.

Full Faith and Credit Given to Child Custody Determinations

Sec. 8. (a) Chapter 115 of title 28, United States Code, is amended by adding immediately after section 1838 the following new section:

"1738A. Full faith and credit given to child custody determinations.

(a) The appropriate authorities of every state shall enforce according to its terms, and shall not modify except as provided in subsection (f) of this section, any child custody determination made consistently with the provisions of this section by a court of another State.

(b) As used in this section, the term —

(1) 'child' means a person under the age of eighteen;

(2) 'contestant' means a person, including a parent, who claims a right to custody or visitation of a child;

(3) 'custody determination' means a judgment, decree, or other order of a court providing for the custody or visitation of a child, and includes permanent and temporary orders, and initial orders and modifications;

(4) 'home State' means the State in which, immediately preceding the time involved, the child lived with his parents, a parent, or a person acting as a parent, for at least six consecutive months, and in the case of a child less than six weeks old, the State in which the child lived from birth with any such persons. Periods of temporary absence of any of such persons are counted as part of the six-month or other period;

(5) 'modification' and 'modify' refer to a custody determination which modifies, replaces, supersedes or otherwise is made subsequent to, a prior custody determination concerning the same child, whether made by the same court or not;

(6) 'person acting as a parent' means a person, other than a parent, who has physical custody of a child and who had either been awarded custody by a court or claims a right to custody;

(7) 'physical custody' means actual possession and control of a child; and

(8) 'State' means a State of the United States, the District of Columbia, the Commonwealth of Puerto Rico, or a territory or possession of the United States.

(c) A child custody determination made by a court of a State is consistent with the provisions of this section only if—

(1) such court has jurisdiction under the law of such State; and

(2) one of the following conditions is met:

(A) such State (i) is the home State of the child on the date of the commencement of the proceeding, or (ii) had been the child's home State within six months before the date of the commencement of the proceeding and the child is absent from such State because of his removal or retention by a contestant or for other reasons, and a contestant continues to live in such State;

(B) (i) it appears that no other State would have jurisdiction under subparagraph (A), and (ii) it is in the best interest of the child that a court of such State assume jurisdiction because (I) the child and his parents, or the child and at least one contestant, have a significant connection with such State other than mere physical presence in such State, and (II) there is available in such State substantial evidence concerning the child's present or future care, protection, training, and personal relationships;

(C) the child is physically present in such State and (i) the child has been abandoned, or (ii) it is necessary in an emergency to protect the child because he had been subjected to or threatened with mistreatment or abuse;

(D) (i) it appears that no other State would have jurisdiction under subparagraph (A), (B), (C), or (E), or another State has declined to exercise jurisdiction on the ground that the State whose jurisdiction is in issue is the more appropriate forum to determine the custody of the child, and (ii) it is in the best interest of the child that such court assume jurisdiction; or

(E) the court has continuing jurisdiction pursuant to subsection (d) of this section.

(d) The jurisdiction of a court of a State which has made a child custody determination consistently with the provisions of this section continues as long as the requirement of subsection (c) (1) of the section continues to be met and such State remains the residence of the child or of any Contestant.

(e) Before a child custody determination is made, reasonable notice and opportunity to be heard shall be given to the contestants, any parent whose parental rights have not been previously terminated and any person who has physical custody of a child.

(f) A court of a State may notify a determination of the custody of the same child made by a court of another State, if—

(1) it has jurisdiction to make such a child custody determination: and

(2) the court of the other State no longer has jurisdiction, or it has declined to exercise such jurisdiction to modify such determination.

(g) A court of a State shall not exercise jurisdiction in any proceeding for a custody determination commenced during the pendency of a proceeding in a court of another State where such court of the other State is exercising jurisdiction consistently with the provisions of this section to make a custody determination."

(b) The table of sections at the beginning of chapter 115 of title 28, United States Code, is amended by inserting after the item relating to section 1738 the following new item:

"1738A. Full Faith and Credit Given to Child Custody Determinations.

(C) In furtherance of the purposes of section 1738A of title 28, United States Code, as added by subsection (a) of this section, State courts are encouraged to —

(1) afford priority to proceedings for custody determinations; and

(2) award to the person entitled to custody or visitation pursuant to a custody determination which is consistent with the provisions of such section 1738A, necessary travel expenses, attorneys' fees, costs of private investigations, witness fees or expenses, and other expenses incurred in connection with such custody determination in any case in which —

(A) a contestant has, without the consent of the person entitled to custody or visitation pursuant to a custody determination which is consistent with the provisions of such section 1738A, (i) wrongfully removed the child from the physical custody of such person, or (ii) wrongfully retained the child after a visit or other temporary relinquishment of physical custody; or

(B) the court determines it is appropriate."

Use of the Federal Parent Locator Service in Connection with the Enforcement or Determination of Child Custody and in Cases of Parental Kidnapping of a Child

Sec. 9. (a) Section 454 of the Social Security Act is amended —

(1) by striking out "and" at the end of paragraph (15);

(2) by striking out the period at the end of paragraph (16) and inserting in lieu thereof "; and"; and

(3) by inserting after paragraph (16) the following new paragraph:

"(17) in the case of a State which has in effect an agreement with the Secretary entered into pursuant to section 463 for the use of the Parent Locator Service established under section 453, to accept and transmit to the Secretary requests for information authorized under the provisions of the agreement to be furnished by such service to authorized persons, and to impose and collect (in accordance with regulations of the Secretary) a fee sufficient to cover the costs to the State and to the Secretary incurred by reason of such requests, to transmit to the Secretary from time to time (in accordance with such regulations) so much of the fees collected as are attributable to such costs to the Secretary so incurred, and during the period that such agreement is in effect, otherwise to comply with such agreement and regulations of the Secretary with respect thereto."

(b) Part D of title IV of the Social Security Act is amended by adding at the end thereof the following new section:

"Use of Federal Parent Locator Service in Connection with the Enforcement or Determination of Child Custody and in Cases of Parental Kidnapping of a Child

"**Sec. 463.** (a) The Secretary shall enter into an agreement with any State which is able and willing to do so, under which the services of the Parent Locator Service established under section 453 shall be made available to such State for the purpose of determining the whereabouts of any absent parent or child when such information is to be used to locate such parent or child for the purpose of—

(1) enforcing any State or Federal law with respect to the unlawful taking or restraining of a child; or

(2) making or enforcing a child custody determination.

(b) An agreement entered into under this section shall provide that the State agency described in section 454 will, under procedures prescribed by the Secretary in regulations, receive and transmit to the Secretary requests from authorized persons for information as to (or useful in determining) the whereabouts of any absent parent or child when such information is to be used to locate such parent or child for the purpose of—

(1) enforcing any State or Federal law with respect to the unlawful taking or restraint of a child; or

(2) making or enforcing a child custody determination.

(c) Information authorized to be provided by the Secretary under this section shall be subject to the same conditions with respect to disclosure as information authorized to be provided under section 453, and a request for information by the Secretary under this section shall be considered to be a request for information under section 453 which is authorized to be provided under such section. Only information as to the most recent address and place of employment of any absent parent or child shall be provided under this section.

(d) For purposes of this section —

(1) the term 'custody determination' means a judgment, decree, or other order of a court providing for the custody or visitation of a child, and includes permanent and temporary orders, and initial orders and modification;

(2) the term 'authorized person' means —

(A) any agent or attorney of any State having an agreement under this section, who had the duty or authority under the law of such State to enforce a child custody determination;

(B) any court having jurisdiction to make or enforce such a child custody determination, or any agent of such court; and

(C) any agent or attorney of the United States, or of a State having an agreement under this section, who has the duty or authority to investigate, enforce, or bring prosecution with respect to the lawful taking or restraint of a child."

(c) Section 455(a) of such Act is amended by adding after paragraph (3) the following: "except that no amount shall be paid to any State on accounts of amounts expended to carry out an agreement which it has entered into pursuant to section 463."

(d) No agreement entered into under section 463 of the Social Security Act shall become effective before the date on which section 1738A of title 28, United States Code (as added by this title) becomes effective.

Parental Kidnapping

Sec. 10. (a) In view of the findings of the Congress and the purposes of sections 6 to 10 of the Act set forth in section 302, the Congress hereby expressly declares its intent that section 1073 of title 18, United States Code, apply to cases involving parental kidnapping and interstate or international flight to avoid prosecution under applicable State felony statutes.

(b) The Attorney General of the United States, not later than 120 days after the enactment of this section (and once every 6 months during the 3-year period), shall submit a report to the Congress with respect to steps taken to comply with the intent of the Congress set forth in subsection (a). Each such report shall include —

(1) data relating to the number of applications for complaints under section 1073 of title 18, United States Code, in cases involving parental kidnapping;

(2) data relating to the number of complaints issued in such cases; and

(3) such other information as may assist in describing the activities of the Department of Justice in conformance with such intent.

National Child Search Assistance Act of 1990

Public Law 101-647
[29 Nov 1990]
42 USC ss 5780

ss 5780. State Requirements.
Each State reporting under the provisions of this title shall [42 USCS ss 5779 et seq.-] —

(1) ensure that no law enforcement agency within the State establishes or maintains any policy that requires the observance of any waiting period before accepting a missing child or unidentified person report;

(2) provide that each such report and all necessary and available information, which, with respect to each missing child report, shall include —

(A) the name, date of birth, sex, race, height, weight, and eye and hair color of the child;

(B) the date and location of the last known contact with the child; and

(C) the category under which the child is reported missing; is entered immediately into the State law enforcement system and the National Crime Information Center computer networks and made available to the Missing Children Information Clearinghouse within the State or other agency designated within the State to receive such reports; and

(3) provide that after receiving reports as provided in paragraph (2), the law enforcement agency that entered the report into the National Crime Information Center shall —

(A) no later than 60 days after the original entry of the record into the State law enforcement system and National Crime Information Center computer networks, verify and update such record with any additional information, including, where available, medical and dental records.

(B) institute or assist with appropriate search and investigative procedures; and

(C) maintain close liaison with the National Center for Missing and Exploited Children for the exchange of information and technical assistance in the missing children cases.

International Parental Kidnapping Crime Act of 1993

Public Law 13-173
103d Congress
[2 Dec 1993]
107 Stat 1998

An Act

To amend title 18, United States Code, with respect (H.R. 3378) to parental kidnapping and for other purposes.

Be it enacted by the Senate and House of Representatives of the United States of America in Congress assembled,

Sec. 1. Short Title.

This Act may be cited as the "International Parental Kidnapping Crime Act of 1993."

Sec. 2. Title 18 Amendment.

(a) **In General.**—Chapter 55 (relating to kidnapping) of title 18, United States Code, is amended by adding at the end the following:

"1204. International Parental Kidnapping.

(a) Whoever removes a child from the United States or retains a child (who has been in the United States) outside of the United States with the intent to obstruct the lawful exercise of parental rights shall be fined under this title or imprisoned not more than 3 years, or both.

(b) **As used in this section —**

   (1) the term 'child' means a person who has not attained the age of 16 years; and

   (2) the term 'parental rights' with respect to a child, means the right to physical custody of the child —

      (A) whether joint or sole (and includes visitation rights), and

      (B) whether arising by operation of law, court order, or legally binding agreement of the parties.

(c) It shall be an affirmative defense under this section that —

   (1) the defendant acted within the provisions of a valid court order granting the defendant legal custody or visitation rights and that order was obtained pursuant to the Uniform Child Custody Jurisdiction Act and was in effect at the time of the offense;

   (2) the defendant was fleeing an incidence or pattern of domestic violence;

   (3) the defendant had physical custody of the child pursuant to a court order granting legal custody or visitation rights and failed to return the child as a result of circumstances beyond the defendant's control, and the defendant notified or made reasonable attempts to notify the other parent or lawful custodian of the child of such circumstances within 24 hours after the visitation period had expired and returned the child as soon as possible.

(d) This section does not detract from the Hague Convention on the Civil Aspects of International Parental Child Abduction, done at The Hague on October 25, 1980."

(b) **Sense of the Congress.** — It is the sense of the Congress that, inasmuch as use of the procedures under the Hague Convention on the Civil Aspects of International Parental Child Abduction has resulted in the return of many children, those procedures, in circumstances in which they are applicable, should be the option of first choice for a parent who seeks the return of a child who has been removed from the parent.

(c) **Clerical Amendment.** — The table of sections at the beginning of chapter 55 of title 18, United States Code, is amended by adding at the end of the following:

"1204. International Parental Kidnapping.

Sec. 3. State Court Programs Regarding Interstate and International Parental Child Abduction.

   (Appropriation authorization)

There is authorized to be appropriated $250,000 to carry out under the State Justice Institute Act of 1984 (42 U.S.C. 10701–10713) national, regional, and in-State training and educational programs dealing with criminal and civil aspects of interstate and international parental child abduction."

Hague Convention on the Civil Aspects of International Child Abduction

The States signatory to the present Convention, firmly convinced that the interests of children are of paramount importance in matters relating to their custody, [and] desiring to protect children internationally from the harmful effects of their wrongful removal or retention and to establish procedures to ensure their prompt return to the State of their habitual residence, as well as to secure protection for rights of access, have resolved to conclude a Convention to this effect, and have agreed upon the following provisions —

Chapter I — Scope of the Convention

Article 1
The objects of the present Convention are —
(a) to secure the prompt return of children wrongfully removed to or retained in any contracting State: and
(b) to ensure that rights of custody and of access under the law of one Contracting State are effectively respected in the other States.

Article 2
Contracting States shall take all appropriate measures to secure within their territories the implementation of the objects of the Convention. For this purpose they shall use the most expeditious procedures available.

Article 3
The removal of the retention of a child is to be considered wrongful where —
(a) it is in breach of rights of custody attributed to a person, an institution, or any other body, either jointly or alone, under the law of the State in which the child was habitually resident immediately before the removal or retention; and
(b) at the time of removal or retention those rights were actually exercised, either jointly or alone, or would have been so exercised but for the removal or retention.

The rights of custody mentioned in sub-paragraph (a) above, may arise in particular by operation of law or by reason of a judicial or administrative decision, or by reason of an agreement having legal effect under the law of that State.

Article 4

The Convention shall apply to any child who was habitually resident in a Contracting State immediately before may breach of custody or access rights. The Convention shall cease to apply when the child attains the age of 16 years.

Article 5

For the purpose of this Convention —

(a) "rights of custody" shall include rights relating to the care of the person of the child and, in particular, the right to determine the child's place of residence;

(b) "rights of access" shall include the right to take a child for a limited period of time to a place other than the child's habitual residence.

Chapter II — Central Authority

Article 6

A Contracting State shall designate a Central Authority to discharge the duties which are imposed by the convention upon such authorities.

Federal States, States with more than one system of law, or States having autonomous territorial organizations shall be free to appoint more than one Central Authority and to specify the territorial extent of their powers. Where a State has appointed more than one Central Authority, it shall designate the Central Authority to which applications may be addressed for transmission to the appropriate Central Authority within that State.

Article 7

Central Authorities shall cooperate with each other and promote cooperation amongst the competent authorities in their respective States to secure the prompt return of children and to achieve the other objects of this Convention.

In particular, either directly or through any intermediary, they shall take all appropriate measures —

(a) to discover the whereabouts of a child who has been wrongfully removed or retained;

(b) to prevent further harm to the child or prejudice to interested parties by taking or causing to be taken provisional measures;

(c) to secure the voluntary return of the child or to bring about an amicable resolution of the issues;

(d) to exchange, where desirable, information relating to the social background of the child;

(e) to provide information of a general character as to the law of their State in connection with the application of the Convention;

(f) to initiate or facilitate the institution of judicial or administrative proceedings with a view to obtaining the return of the child and, in a proper case, to make arrangements for organizing or securing the effective exercise of rights of access;

(g) where the circumstances so require, to provide or facilitate the provision of legal aid and advice, including the participation of legal counsel and advisers;

(h) to provide such administrative arrangements as may be necessary and appropriate to secure the safe return of the child;

(i) to keep each other informed with respect to the operation of this Convention and, as far as possible, to eliminate any obstacles to its application.

Chapter III — Return of Children

Article 8

Any person, institution, or other body claiming that a child has been removed or retained in breach of custody rights may apply either to the Central Authority of the child's habitual residence or to the Central Authority of any other Contracting State for assistance in securing the return of the child.

The application shall contain —

(a) information concerning the identity of the applicant, of the child, and of the person alleged to have removed or retained the child;

(b) where available, the date of birth of the child;

(c) the grounds on which the applicant's claim for return of the child is based;

(d) all available information relating to the whereabouts of the child and the identity of the persons with whom the child is presumed to be.

The application may be accompanied or supplemented by —

(e) an authenticated copy of any relevant decision or agreement;

(f) a certificate or an affidavit emanating from a Central Authority, or other competent authority of the State of the child's habitual residence, or from a qualified person, concerning the relevant law of state;

(g) any other relevant document.

Article 9

If the Central Authority which serves an applicant referred to in Article 8 has reason to believe that the child is in another Contracting State, it shall directly and without delay transmit the application to the Central Authority of that Contracting State and inform the requesting Central Authority, or the applicant, as the case may be.

Article 10

The Central Authority of the State where the child is shall take or cause to be taken all appropriate measures in order to obtain the voluntary return of the child.

Article 11

The judicial or administrative authorities or Contracting States shall act expeditiously in proceedings for the return of children. If the judicial or administrative authority concerned has not reached a decision within six weeks from the date of commencement of the proceedings, the applicant or the Central Authority of the requested State, on its own initiative or if asked by the Central Authority of the requesting State, shall have the right to request a statement of the reasons for the delay. If a reply is received by the Central Authority of the requested States, that Authority shall transmit the reply to the Central Authority of the requesting State, or to the applicant, as the case may be.

Article 12

Where a child has been wrongfully removed or retained in terms of Article 3 and, at the date of the commencement of the proceedings before the judicial or administrative authority of the Contracting State where the child is, a period of less than one year has elapsed from the date of the wrongful removal or retention, the authority concerned shall order the return of the child forthwith. The judicial or administrative authority, even where the proceedings have been commenced after the expiration of the period of one year referred to in the preceding paragraph, shall also order the return of the child, unless it is demonstrated that the child is now settled in its new environment. Where the judicial or administrative authority in the requested State has reason to believe that the child has been taken to another State, it may stay the proceedings or dismiss the application for the return of the child.

Article 13

Notwithstanding the provisions of the preceding Article, the judicial or administrative authority of the requested State is not bound to order the return of the child if the person, institution, or other body which opposes its return establishes that —

(a) the person, institution, or other body having the care of the person of the child was not actually exercising the custody rights at the time of removal or retention, or had consented to or subsequently acquiesced in the removal or retention; or

(b) there is grave risk that his or her return would expose the child to physical or psychological harm, or otherwise place the child in an intolerable situation. The judicial or administrative authority may also refuse to order the return of the child if it finds that the child objects to being returned and has attained an age and degree of maturity at which it is appropriate to take account of its views.

In considering the circumstances referred to in this Article, the judicial and administrative authorities shall take into account the information relating to the social background of the child provided by the Central Authority or other competent authority of the child's habitual residence.

Article 14
In ascertaining whether there has been a wrongful removal or retention within the meaning of Article 3, the judicial or administrative authorities of the requested State may take notice directly of the law, and of judicial or administrative decisions, formally recognized or not in the State of the habitual residence of the child, without recourse to the specific procedures for the proof of that law or for the recognition of foreign decisions which would otherwise be applicable.

Article 15
The judicial or administrative authorities of a Contracting State may, prior to the making of an order for the return of the child, request that the applicant obtain from the authorities of the State of habitual residence of the child a decision or other determination that the removal or retention was wrongful within the meaning of Article 3 of the Convention, where such a decision or determination may be obtained in that State. The Central Authorities of the Contracting States shall so far as practicable assist applicants to obtain such a decision or determination.

Article 16
After receiving notice of wrongful removal or retention of a child in the sense of Article 3, the judicial or administrative authorities of the Contracting State to which the child has been removed or in which it has been retained

shall not decide on the merits of rights of custody until it has been determined that the child is not to be returned under this Convention or unless an application under this Convention is not lodged within a reasonable time following receipt of notice.

Article 17
The sole fact that a decision relating to custody has been given in or is entitled to recognition in the requested State shall not be a ground for refusing to return a child under this Convention, but the judicial or administrative authorities of the requested State may take account of the reasons for that decision in applying this Convention.

Article 18
The provisions of this Chapter do not limit the power of a judicial or administrative authority to order the return of the child at any time.

Article 19
A decision under this Convention concerning the return of the child shall not be taken to be a determination on the rights of any custody issue.

Article 20
The return of the child under the provisions of Article 12 may be refused if this would not be permitted by the fundamental principles of the requested State relating to the protection of human rights and fundamental freedoms.

Chapter IV — Rights of Access

Article 21
An application to make arrangements for organizing or securing the effective exercise of rights of access may be presented to the Central Authorities of the Contracting States in the same way as an application for the return of a child. The Central Authorities are bound by the obligations of cooperation which [are] set forth in Article 7 to promote the peaceful enjoyment of access rights and the fulfillment of any conditions to which the exercise of those rights may be subject. The Central Authorities shall take steps to remove, as far as possible, all obstacles to the exercise of such rights. The Central Authorities, either directly or through intermediaries, may initiate or assist in the institution of proceedings with a view to organizing or protecting these rights and securing respect for the conditions to which the exercise of these rights may be subject.

Chapter V— General Provisions

Article 22

No security, bond, or deposit, however described, shall be required to guarantee the payment of costs and expenses in the judicial or administrative proceedings falling within the scope of this Convention.

Article 23

No legalization or similar formality may be required in the context of this Convention.

Article 24

Any application, communication, or other document sent to the Central Authority of the requested State shall be in the original language, and shall be accompanied by a translation into the official language or one of the official languages of the requested State, or where that is not reasonable, a translation into French or English. However, a Contracting State may, by making a reservation in accordance with Article 42, object to the use of either French or English, but not both, in any application, communication, or other document sent to its Central Authority.

Article 25

Nationals of the Contracting States and persons who are habitually resident within the States shall be entitled in matters concerned with the application of this Convention to legal aid and advice in any other Contracting State on the same conditions as if they themselves were nationals of and habitually resident in that State.

Article 26

Each Central Authority shall bear its own costs in applying this Convention. Central Authorities and other public services of a Contracting State shall not impose any charges in relation to applications submitted under this Convention. In particular, they may not require any payment from the applicant towards the costs and expenses of the proceedings or, where applicable, those arising from the participation of legal counsel or advisors. However, they may require the payment of the expenses incurred or to be incurred in implementing the return of the child. However, a Contracting State may, by making a reservation in accordance with Article 42, declare that it shall not be bound to assume any costs referred to in the preceding paragraph resulting from the participation of legal counsel or advisers or from court proceedings, except insofar as those costs may be covered by its system of legal aid and advice.

Upon ordering the return of a child or issuing an order concerning rights of access under this Convention, the judicial or administrative authorities may, where appropriate, direct the person who removed or retained the child, or who prevented the exercise of rights of access, to pay necessary expenses incurred by or on behalf of the applicant, including travel expenses, any costs incurred or payments made for locating the child, the costs of legal representation of the applicant, and those of returning the child.

Article 27
When it is manifest that the requirements of the Convention are not fulfilled or that the application is otherwise not well founded, a Central Authority is not bound to accept the application. In that case, the Central Authority shall forthwith inform the applicant or the Central Authority through which the application was submitted, as the case may be, of its reasons.

Article 28
A Central Authority may require that the application be accompanied by a written authorization empowering it to act on behalf of the applicant, or to designate a representative so to act.

Article 29
This Convention shall not preclude any person, institution, or body who claims that there has been a breach of custody or access rights within the meaning of Article 3 or 21 from applying directly to the judicial or administrative authorities of a Contracting State, whether or not under the provisions of this Convention.

Article 30
Any application submitted to the Central Authorities or directly to the judicial or administrative authorities of a Contracting State in accordance with the terms of this Convention, together with documents and any other information appended thereto or provided by a Central Authority, shall be admissible in the courts or administrative authorities of the Contracting States.

Article 31
In relation to a State which in matters of custody of children has two or more systems of law applicable in different territorial units —
(a) any reference to habitual residence in that State shall be construed as referring to habitual residence in a territorial unit of that State;
(b) any reference to the law of the State of habitual residence shall be construed as referring to the law of the territorial unit in that State where the child habitually resides.

Article 32
In relation to a State which in matters of custody of children has two or more systems of law applicable to different categories of persons, any reference to the law of that State shall be construed as referring to the legal system specified by the law of that State.

Article 33
A State within which different territorial units have their own rules of law in respect of custody of children shall not be bound to apply this Convention where a State with a unified system of law would not be bound to do so.

Article 34
This Convention shall take priority in matters within its scope over the **Convention of 5 October 1961 Concerning the Powers of Authorities and the Law Applicable in Respect of the Protection of Minors**, as between Parties to both Conventions. Otherwise the present Convention shall not restrict the application of an international instrument in force between the State of origin and the State addressed or other law of the State address for the purposes of obtaining the return of a child who has been wrongfully removed or retained or of organizing access rights.

Article 35
This Convention shall apply as between Contracting States only to wrongful removals or retentions occurring after its entry into force in those States. Where a declaration has been made under Article 39 or 40, the reference in the preceding paragraph to a Contracting State shall be taken to refer to the territorial unit or units in relation to which this Convention applies.

Article 36
Nothing in this Convention shall prevent two or more Contracting States, in order to limit restrictions to which the return of the child may be subject, from agreeing among themselves to derogate from any provisions of this Convention which may imply such a restriction.

Article 37
The Convention shall be open for signature by the States which were members of the Hague Conference on Private International Law at the time of its Fourteenth Session. It shall be ratified, accepted, or approved and the instruments of ratification, acceptance, or approval shall be deposited with the Ministry of Foreign Affairs of the Kingdom of The Netherlands.

Article 38
Any other State may accede to the Convention. The instrument of accession shall be deposited with the Ministry of Foreign Affairs of the Kingdom of The Netherlands. The Convention shall enter into force for State acceding to it on the first day of the third calendar month after the deposit of its instrument of accession. The accession will have effect only as regards the relations between the acceding State and such Contracting States as will have declared their acceptance of the accession. Such a declaration will also have to be made by any member State ratifying, accepting or approving the Convention after an accession. Such declarations shall be deposited at the Ministry of Foreign Affairs of the Kingdom of The Netherlands; this ministry shall forward, through diplomatic channels, a certified copy to each of the Contracting States. The Convention will enter into force as between the acceding State and the State that has declared its acceptance of the accession on the first day of the third calendar month after the deposit of the declaration of acceptance.

Article 39
Any State may, at the time of signature, ratification, acceptance, approval, or accession, declare that the Convention shall extend to all the territories for the international relations of which it is responsible, or to one or more of them. Such a declaration, as well as any subsequent extention, shall be notified to the Ministry of Foreign Affairs of the Kingdom of The Netherlands.

Article 40
If a Contracting State has two or more territorial units in which systems of law are applicable in relation to matters dealt with in this Convention, it may at the time of signature, ratification, acceptance, approval, or accession, declare that this Convention shall extend to all its territorial units or only two or more of them and may modify this declaration by submitting another declaration at any time. Any such declaration shall be notified to the Ministry of Foreign Affairs of the Kingdom of The Netherlands and shall state expressly the territorial units to which the Convention applies.

Article 41
Where a Contracting State has a system of government under which executive, judicial, and legislative powers are distributed between central and other authorities within that State, its signature, or ratification, acceptance or approval of, or accession, to this Convention, or its making of any declaration in terms of Article 40 shall carry no implication as to the internal distribution of powers within that State.

Article 42

Any State may, not later than the time of ratification, acceptance, approval, or accession, or at the time of making a declaration in terms of Article 39 or 40, make one or both of the reservations provided for in Article 24 and Article 26, third paragraph. No other reservation shall be permitted.

Any State may at any time withdraw a reservation it has made. The withdrawal shall be notified to the Ministry of Foreign Affairs of the Kingdom of The Netherlands. The reservation shall cease to have effect on the first day of the third calendar month after the notification referred to in the preceding paragraph.

Article 43

The Convention shall enter into force on the first day of the third calendar month after the deposit of the third instrument of ratification, acceptance, approval, or accession referred to in Articles 37 and 38. Thereafter the Convention shall enter into force —

(1) for each State ratifying, accepting, approving, or acceding to it subsequently, on the first day of the third calendar month after the deposit of its instrument of ratification, acceptance, approval, or accession;

(2) for any territory or territorial unit to which the Convention had been extended in conformity with Article 39 or 40, on the first day of the third calendar month after the notification referred to in that Article.

Article 44

The Convention shall remain in force for five years from the date of its entry into force in accordance with the first paragraph of Article 443 even for States which subsequently have ratified, accepted, approved it, or acceded to it. If there has been no denunciation, it shall be renewed tacitly every five years. Any denunciation shall be notified to the Ministry of Foreign Affairs of the Kingdom of The Netherlands at least six months before the expiry of the five year period. It may be limited to certain of the territories or territorial units to which the Convention applies. The denunciation shall have effect only as regards the State which has notified it. The Convention shall remain in force for the other Contracting States.

Article 45

The Ministry of Foreign Affairs of the Kingdom of The Netherlands shall notify the States Members of the Conference, and the States which have acceded in accordance with Article 38, of the following —

(1) the signatures and ratifications, acceptances, and approvals referred to in Article 37;

(2) the accessions referred to in Article 38;

(3) the date on which the Convention enters into force in accordance with Article 43;

(4) the extensions referred to in Article 39;

(5) the declarations referred to in Articles 38 and 40;

(6) the reservations referred to in Article 24 and Article 26, third paragraph, and the withdrawals referred to in Article 42;

(7) the denunciations referred to in Article 44.

In witness whereof the undersigned, being duly authorized thereto, have signed this Convention.

Done at The Hague, on the 25th day of October, 1980, in the English and French languages, both texts being equally authentic, in a single copy which shall be deposited in the archives of the Government of the Kingdom of The Netherlands, and of which a certified copy shall be sent, through diplomatic channels, to each of the States Members of the Hague Conference of Private International Law at the date of its Fourteenth Session.

Recommendations of the American Bar Association

In a report prepared by the American Bar Association supported by the Office of Juvenile Justice and Delinquency Prevention, Office of Justice Programs, United States Department of Justice, Dr. Linda K. Girdner and Patricia M. Hoff, Esq., address the problem of obstacles to recovery that are actually created by the United States justice system. That report, entitled *Obstacles to the Recovery and Return of Parentally Abducted Children*, was published in March 1994 and included the following recommendations:

> Continuing education and training in laws applicable to parental abduction cases should be provided to judges and attorneys. Collaborative efforts with the American Bar Association Family Law Section, The National Council of Family and Conciliation Courts, and similar organizations should be encouraged and supported through funding from the Office of Juvenile Justice and Delinquency Prevention.
>
> Diverse methods of disseminating information should be used, including satellite teleconferencing, interactive computer learning modules, articles in scholarly and practical publications, bench books for judges, and

manuals giving practice tips for attorneys.... [Experienced persons] should serve as mentors for those with less experience. In addition, a parental abduction curriculum should be developed for circulation to law schools. Appellate judges should also have the opportunity for continuing education relating to the PKPA [Parental Kidnapping Prevention Act] and UCCJA [Uniform Child Custody Jurisdiction Act]. If appellate judges were more informed, the decisions of lower court judges would not be overturned....

Continuing legal education is needed for attorneys so they can better understand their ethical responsibility and liability in these cases. Disciplinary actions should be taken against attorneys when appropriate.

Congress should amend the PKPA to include an express Federal cause of action (the right to take the case to Federal court) when conflicting custody decrees exist as a result of the actions of courts of two or more States with respect to the same child.

Congress should enact legislation establishing a national computerized child custody registry so that all child custody determinations and information about filings related to child custody will be readily accessible to courts throughout the country. The registry could be combined with a national child support registry.

Congress should amend the PKPA to provide a time limitation on continuing modification jurisdiction after the custodial parent and the child have left the State. The provision would apply only if the State had not set a specific time limit of its own.

Congress should amend the PKPA to clarify what constitutes the proper exercise of emergency jurisdiction, including:
• Specifying that it can only be temporary.
• Clarifying that it can be used to modify custody, but only temporarily, even when another State has continuing jurisdiction.
• Exempting emergency proceedings from the prohibition against simultaneous proceedings.
• Providing for a short-term exemption from the notice requirement in limited emergency circumstance.

Congress should amend the PKPA to clarify ambiguous and confusing language, including:
• Specifying, to the greatest extent possible, the various types of custody determinations to which the PKPA should be applied.
• Defining what constitutes declination of jurisdiction.
• Expanding the definition of State to include native American tribes.

The National Conference of Commissioners on Uniform State Laws should review State enactments of the UCCJA and promulgate amendments to the uniform law.

State legislatures should amend current State enactments to achieve greater uniformity and specificity. These include:

• Adding provisions allowing temporary foster care placement of abducted children pending return to the lawful custodian.

• Deleting provisions that weaken the continuing modification jurisdiction mandate.

• Adding "subject matter" to the UCCJA jurisdiction section to clarify that the requirements are not personal jurisdiction requirements and cannot be stipulated or waived.

State legislatures should review laws relating to parental abduction, spouse abuse, and child abuse to determine if battered spouses and abused children are further victimized by existing laws and procedures in the event of a parental abduction. Consideration should be given to the need to protect victims, comply with the intent of parental abduction laws, and provide due process safeguards. Changes should include:

• Mandating that disclosure to the other contestant of the present address of an abused contestant be waived in relation to the affidavit requirement.

• Extending the emergency jurisdiction provision of the UCCJA to include abuse of a parent or sibling of an abducted child.

• Adding child abuse and domestic violence as defenses against criminal charges of parental kidnapping.

State legislatures should pass record-flagging statutes and statutes to prevent abductions. State court rules to permit out-of-State attorney appearances should also be adopted.

State legislatures should fund State missing children clearinghouses and departments of law enforcement at a level that allows them to carry out their functions of locating, recovering, and returning parentally abducted children.

State legislatures should make parental abduction a felony when the child either is being concealed, has been removed from the State, or is otherwise at risk of harm. These circumstances should apply to any case in which the abduction is in derogation of the custody rights of another parent or family member, whether or not a custody order has been issued by a court.

No child should remain missing or be withheld from the left-behind parent because of the parent's lack of funds. National, State, and local bar associations should encourage attorneys to take parental abduction cases pro bono or on a sliding scale. Legal aid and legal service programs should give high priority to parental abduction cases so that more low income parents could have their children returned to them.

State laws and regulations should also be clarified so that left-behind parents are clearly eligible for financial aid under victims' assistance and criminal restitution programs.

Educational efforts that bring existing research to the attention of judges, attorneys, law enforcement, and the public should be developed to dispel current myths regarding parental abduction and to change the actions taken in these cases. Professional groups and the public should learn of the deleterious effects of parental abductions on children so as to heighten their awareness of the seriousness of this problem.

Other significant findings of this report include:

Almost 40 percent ... reported that law enforcement procedures in their States required the existence of a violation of a State criminal statute before the police would take a missing child report ... contrary to federal law.

Many clearinghouse respondents were unaware of law enforcement policies and procedures in their States regarding parental abduction cases, despite their function to provide information and assist in these cases.

To obtain a complete copy of *Obstacles to the Recovery and Return of Parentally Abducted Children*, contact:

Juvenile Justice Clearinghouse
Department F
P.O. Box 6000
Rockville MD 20850
Telephone: 1-800-638-8736
Ask for report number NCJ 144535.

(Note: There is a fee for this report. Inquire of the operator.)

Directory

Passport Offices

Boston Passport Agency
Thomas P. O'Neill Federal Bldg.
Room 247
10 Cause Way Street
Boston MA 02222
Telephone (617) 565-6698
(617) 565-6990

Chicago Passport Agency
Suite 380, Kluczynski Fed. Bldg.
230 S. Dearborn Street
Chicago IL 60604-1564
Telephone (312) 353-5426
(312) 353-7155/7163

Honolulu Passport Agency
Room C-106 New Federal Building
300 Ala Moana Boulevard
Honolulu HI 96850
Telephone (808) 541-1918

Los Angeles Passport Agency
Room 13100, 11000 Wilshire Blvd.
Los Angeles CA 90024-3615
Telephone (213) 209-7070
(213) 209-7075

San Francisco Passport Agency
Suite 200, 525 Market Street
San Francisco CA 94105-2773
Telephone (415) 974-7972
(415) 974-9941

Stamford Passport Agency
One Landmark Square
Broad & Atlantic Street
Stamford CT 06901-2767
Telephone (203) 325-4401
(203) 325-3538/3530

Miami Passport Agency
3rd Fl., Federal Office Bldg.
51 Southwest 1st Avenue
Miami FL 33130-1680
Telephone (305) 536-5395 English
(305) 536-4681
(305) 536-4448 Spanish

New Orleans Passport Agency
Postal Services Building
701 Loyola Ave. Room T-12005
New Orleans LA 70113-1931
Telephone (504) 589-6728
(504) 589-6161

New York Passport Agency
Room 270 Rockefeller Center
630 Fifth Avenue
New York NY 10111-0031
Telephone (212) 541-7700
(212) 541-7710

Philadelphia Passport Agency
Room 4426, Federal Building
600 Arch Street
Philadelphia PA 19106-1684
Telephone (215) 597-7482
(215) 597-7480

Seattle Passport Office
Room 992, Federal Office Bldg.
915 Second Avenue
Seattle WA 98174-1091
Telephone (206) 553-7941
(206) 553-7945

Washington Passport Agency
1425 K Street NW
Washington DC 20524-0002
Telephone (202) 647-0518

Embassies

This list of Embassies represents U.S. embassies abroad and their foreign counterparts. Embassies with no counterparts are not listed. In requesting services of a U.S. embassy abroad, regarding International Parental Abduction, correspondence should be directed to the Consular Office of the Embassy. * denotes Hague country.

Foreign Embassies in the U.S.	*U.S. Embassies Abroad*
ALBANIA, Embassy of The Republic of 1511 K Street NW #1010 Washington, D.C. 20005 Phone (202) 223-4942 Fax (202) 628-7342	American Embassy Tirana Rruga E. Elbansanit 103; PSC 59, Box 100 (A), APO AE 09624 Telephone [355]-42-32875 Fax [355]-42-32222
ALGERIA, Embassy of Democratic & Popular Republic of 2118 Kalorama Road NW Washington, D.C. 20008 Telephone (202) 265-2800	American Embassy 4 Chemin Cheikh Bachir El Ibrahimi, B.P. Box 549 (Alger-Gare) 16000; Algiers Telephone [213] (2) 601-425\255\186 Fax [213] (2) 603979

Foreign Embassies in the U.S.	*U.S. Embassies Abroad*

ANTIGUA & BARBUDA,
Embassy of
3400 International Drive NW #4M
Washington, D.C. 20008
Telephone (292) 362-5211
Fax (202) 362-5225

American Embassy
FPO AA 34054-0001
St. Johns, Antigua & Barbuda
Telephone [809] 462-3505\06
Fax [809] 462-3516

*ARGENTINA, Embassy of
Argentine Republic
1600 New Hampshire Avenue NW
Washington, D.C. 20009
Telephone (202) 939-6400
Fax (202) 332-3171

American Embassy
3400 Columbia 1425; Unit
4334, APO AA 34034
Buenos Aires, Argentina
Telephone Box 54 (1) 777-4533\34
Fax [54] (1) 777-3547

ARMENIA, Embassy of
The Republic of
1660 L Street NW #210
Washington, D.C. 20036
Telephone (202) 628-5766

American Embassy
#18 Gen Bagramian, Yerevan
Telephone Box 7 (8852) 151-144
Box 7 (8852) 524-661
Fax [7] (8852) 151-138

*AUSTRALIA, Embassy of
1601 Massachusetts Avenue, NW
Washington, D.C. 20036
Telephone (202) 797-3000
Fax (202) 797-3168

American Embassy
Moonah Pl., Canberra, A.C.T.
2600, Canberra. APO AP 96549
Box 61 (6) 270-5000
Fax [61] (6) 270-5970

*AUSTRIA, Embassy of
3524 International Ct. N.W.
Washington, D.C. 20008-3035
Telephone (202) 895-6700
Fax (202) 895-6750

American Embassy
Boltzmanngasse 16, A-1091
Unit 27937, Vienna, Austria
Telephone [43] (1) 31-339
Fax [243] (1) 310-0682

*BAHAMAS, Embassy of the
Commonwealth of
2220 Massachusetts Avenue N.W.
Washington, D.C. 20008
Telephone (202) 319-2660
Fax (202) 319-2668

American Embassy
Queen St., P.O. Box N-8197
Nassau, Bahamas
Telephone (809) 322-1181
and (809) 328-2206
Fax (809) 328-7838

Foreign Embassies in the U.S.	*U.S. Embassies Abroad*
BAHRAIN, Embassy of the State of 3502 International Dr. N.W. Washington, D.C. 20008 Telephone (202) 342-0741	American Embassy P.O. Box 26431 or FPO AE 09834-5100 Manama Telephone [973] 273-300 Fax [973] 272-594
BANGLADESH, Embassy of The People's Republic of 2201 Wisconsin Ave. N.W. Washington, D.C. 20007 Telephone (202) 342-8372	American Embassy Diplomatic Enclava Madani Avenue, Baridhara or G.P.O. Box 323, Dhaka 1212 Telephone [880] (2) 884700\22 Fax [880] (2) 883744
BARBADOS, Embassy of 2144 Wyoming Ave. N.W. Washington, D.C. 20008 Telephone (202) 939-9200 Fax (202) 332-7467	American Embassy P.O. Box 302, Bridgetown or FPO AA 34055 Telephone (809) 436-4950 Fax (809) 329-5246
BELARUS, Embassy of The Republic of 1619 New Hampshire Ave. N.W. Washington, D.C. 20005 Telephone (202) 986-1604 Fax (202) 986-1805	American Embassy Starovilenskaya #46, Minsk Telephone (7) [0172] 34-65-37
BELGIUM, Embassy of 3330 Garfield St. N.W. Washington, D.C. 20008 Telephone (202) 333-6900 Fax (202) 333-3079	American Embassy 27 Boulevard du Regent, B-1000 Brussels, or APO AE 09724, Brussels Fax [32] (2) 511-2725
BELIZE, Embassy of 2535 Massachusetts Ave. N.W. Washington, D.C. 20008 Telephone (202) 332-9636 Fax (202) 332-6888	American Embassy Gabourel Ln. & Hutson St. Belize City or P.O. Box 286; APO: Belize, Unit 7401, APO AA 34025 Telephone [501] (2) 771611 Fax [501] (2) 30802

Foreign Embassies in the U.S.	*U.S. Embassies Abroad*

BENIN, Embassy of the
Republic of (DEHOMEX)
2737 Cathedral Ave. N.W.
Washington, D.C. 20008
Telephone (202) 232-6656
Fax (202) 332-6888

American Embassy
RVE Caporal Bernard Anani,
B.P. 3012, Cotonov, Benin
Telephone [229] 30-06-50
Fax [229] 30-14-39
30-19-74

BOLIVIA, Embassy of
3014 Massachusetts Ave. N.W.
Washington, D.C. 20008
Telephone (202) 483-4410
Fax (202) 328-3712

American Embassy
Banco Popular Del Peru Bldg.
Corner of Calles Mercado &
Coloni or P.O. Box 425
La Paz, Bolivia or APO AA 34032
Telephone [591] (2) 350251
                               350120
Fax [591] (2) 359875

BOTSWANA, Embassy of the
Republic of
3400 International Dr. N.W. #7M
Washington, D.C. 20008
Telephone (202) 244-4990
Fax (202) 244-4164

American Embassy
P.O. Box 90, Gaborone, Botswana
Telephone [267] 353-982
Fax [267] 356-947

BRAZIL, Embassy of
3006 Massachusetts Ave. N.W.
Washington, D.C. 20008
Telephone (202) 244-4990
Fax (202) 244-4164

American Embassy
Avenidadas Nacoes, Lote3;
Brasilia, Brazil or
Unit 3500, APO AA 34030
Telephone [55] (61) 321-7272
Fax [55] (61) 225-9136

BRUNEI, Embassy of the
State of Brunei Darussalam
2600 Virginia Ave. N.W. #300
Washington, D.C. 20037
Telephone (202) 342-0159
Fax (202) 342-0158

American Embassy
3rd FL-teck Guan Plaza
Jalan Sultan, BanDar Seri
Begawan, Brunei or Amemb Box B,
APO AP 96440, BanDar Seri
Telephone [673] (2) 229670
Fax [673] (2) 225293

Foreign Embassies in the U.S.	*U.S. Embassies Abroad*

BULGARIA, Embassy of the
Republic of
1621 22nd St. N.W.
Washington, D.C. 20008
Telephone (202) 387-7969
Fax (202) 234-7973

American Embassy
1 Saborna St., Sofia, Bulgaria
Unit 25402, APO AE 09213-5740
Telephone [359] (2) 88-48-01\
02\03\04\05
Fax [359] (2) 80-9-77

*__BURKINA FASO__, Embassy of
2340 Massachusetts Ave. N.W.
Washington, D.C. 20008
Telephone (202) 332-5577

American Embassy
01 B.P. 35, Ouagadougou, Burkina
Telephone [226] 30-67-23\24\25
Fax [226] 31-23-68
Fax [226] 31-23-68

BURMA, Embassy of the Union
of Myan Mar
2300 S St. N.W.
Washington, D.C. 20008
Telephone (202) 332-9044
Fax (202) 332-9046

American Embassy
581 Merchant St. (GP0521):
RAN GOON, Burma or
AMEMB Box B, APO AP 96546
Telephone [95] (1) 82055 or 82182
Fax [95] (1) 8049

BURUNDI, Embassy of the
Republic of
2233 Wisconsin Ave. N.W. #212
Washington, D.C. 20007
Telephone (202) 342-2574

American Embassy
B.P. 34, Avenu des Etats-Unis,
BUJUMBURA, Burundi
Telephone [257] 223-454
Fax [257] 222-926

CAMEROON, Embassy of
the Republic of
2349 Massachusetts Ave. N.W.
Washington, D.C. 20008
Telephone (202) 265-8790

American Embassy
Rve Nachtigal, B.P. 817
YAOUNDE, Cameroon
Telephone [237] 234014
Fax [237] 230753

*__CANADA__, Embassy of
501 Pennsylvania Ave. N.W.
Washington, D.C. 20001
Telephone (202) 682-1740
Fax (202) 682-7726

American Embassy
100 Wellington St., KIP 5TI
Ottawa, Ontario, Canada or
P.O. Box 5000
Ogdensburg, N.Y. 13669-0430
Telephone (613) 238-5335
Fax (613) 238-5720

Foreign Embassies in the U.S.   U.S. Embassies Abroad

CAPE VERDE, Embassy of
  the Republic of
3415 Massachusetts Ave. N.W.
Washington, D.C. 20007
Telephone (202) 965-6820
Fax (202) 965-1207

American Embassy
Rua Abilio Macedo 81; C.P. 201
Praia, Cape Verde
Telephone [238] 61-56-16
Fax [238] 61-13-55

CENTRAL AFRICAN
  REPUBLIC, Embassy of
1618 22nd St. N.W.
Washington, D.C. 20008
Telephone (202) 483-7800
Fax (202) 332-9893

American Embassy
Avenue David Dacko, B.P. 924
Bangui, Central African Republic
Telephone [236] 61-02-00
                61-02-10
                61-25-78
Fax [236] 61-44-94

CHAD, Embassy of the Republic
2002 R St. N.W.
Washington, D.C. 20009
Telephone (202) 462-4009
Fax (202) 265-1937

American Embassy
Ave. Felix Eboue, B.P. 413
'DJAMENA, Chad
Telephone [235] (51) 62-18
                40-09
                61-11
Fax [235] (51) 33-72

*****CHILE**, Embassy of
1732 Massachusetts Ave. N.W.
Washington, D.C. 20036
Telephone (202) 785-1746
Fax (202) 887-5579

American Embassy
Codina Bldg., 134 Agustina
Santiago, Chile
Unit 4127, APO AA 34033
Telephone [56] (2) 671-0133
Fax [56] (2) 699-1141

CHINA, Embassy of the People's
  Republic of
2300 Connecticut Ave. N.W.
Washington, D.C. 20008
Telephone (202) 328-2500

American Embassy
Xiu Shui Bei Jie 3
100600 Beijing, China or
PSC 461, Box 50
FPO AP 96521-0002
Beijing
Telephone [86] (1) 532-3831
Fax [86] (1) 532-3178

Foreign Embassies in the U.S.	*U.S. Embassies Abroad*

COLOMBIA, Embassy of
2118 Lerox Pl. N.W.
Washington, D.C. 20008
Telephone (202) 387-8338
Fax (202) 232-8643

American Embassy
Calle 38, No. 8-61, BOGOTA
or P.O. Box AA3831, BOGOTA
Columbia or APO AA 34038,
    BOGATA
Telephone [57] (1) 285-1300
Fax [57] (1) 288-5687

CONGO, Embassy of the
    Republic of
4891 Colorado Ave. N.W.
Washington, D.C. 20011
Telephone (202) 726-0825
Fax (202) 726-1860

American Embassy
Avenue Amilcar Cabral
Brazzaville, Congo
Mail: B.P. 1015
Brazzaville, Congo
Telephone [242] 83-20-70
Fax [242] 83-63-38

COSTA RICA, Embassy of
2114 S St. N.W.
Washington, D.C. 20008
Telephone (202) 234-2945
Fax (202) 265-4795

American Embassy
Pavas, San Jose,
Costa Rica
Mail: APO AA 34020
Telephone [506] 20-39-39

COTE DIVOIRE, Embassy of the
    Republic of
2424 Massachusetts Ave. N.W.
Washington, D.C. 20008
Telephone (202) 797-0300

American Embassy
5 Rue Jesse Owens, 01
B.P. 1712 Abidjan
Cote Divoire (Ivory Coast)
Telephone [225] 21-09-79
                21-46-72
Fax [225] 22-32-59

*CROATIA, Embassy of the
    Republic of
236 Massachusetts Ave. N.W.
Washington, D.C. 2002
Telephone (202) 543-5580

American Embassy
Andrije Hebrangaz
Zagreb, Croatia
Mail: Unit 25402, APO AE 09213
Telephone [38] (41) 444-8000
Fax [38] (41) 440-235

Foreign Embassies in the U.S.	*U.S. Embassies Abroad*
*CYPRUS, Embassy of the Republic of 2211 R St. N.W. Washington, D.C. 20008 Telephone (202) 462-5772	American Embassy Metochiov & Ploutarchou St. Nicosia, Cyprus Mail: APO AE 09836 Telephone [357] (2) 476100 Fax [357] (2) 465944

CYPRUS, Embassy of the
Republic of
2211 R St. N.W.
Washington, D.C. 20008
Telephone (202) 462-5772

American Embassy
Metochiov & Ploutarchou St.
Nicosia, Cyprus
Mail: APO AE 09836
Telephone [357] (2) 476100
Fax [357] (2) 465944

CZECH REPUBLIC,
Embassy of the
3900 Spring of Freedom St. N.W.
Washington, D.C. 20002
Telephone (202) 363-6315
Fax (202) 966-8540

American Embassy
Trziste 15, 11801 Prague, Czech
Mail: Unit 25402,
APO AE 09213-5630
Telephone [42] (2) 536-641 or 646
Fax [42] (2) 532-457

DENMARK, Royal Danish
Embassy
3200 Whitehaven St. N.W.
Washington, D.C. 20008
Telephone (202) 234-4300
Fax (202) 328-1470

American Embassy
Dag Hammarskjolds
Alle 24, 2100 Copenhagen O
Denmark
Mail: APO AE 09716
Telephone [45] (31) 42-31-44
Fax [45] (35) 43-02-23

DJIBOUTI, Embassy of
Republic of
1156 15th St. N.W. #515
Washington, D.C. 20005
Telephone (202) 331-0270
Fax (202) 331-0302

American Embassy
Plateau du Serpent Blvd.
Marechal Joffre, Djibouti or
B.P. 185 Djibouti
Telephone [253] 35-39-95
Fax [253] 35-39-40

DOMINICAN REPUBLIC,
Embassy of the
1715 22nd St. N.W.
Washington, D.C. 20008
Telephone (202) 332-6280
Fax (202) 265-8057

American Embassy
Corner of Calle Cesar Nicolas
Penson & Calle Leopoldo
Navarro Santo Domingo,
Dominican Republic
Mail: Unit 5500
APO AA 34041-0008
Telephone [809] 541-2571
Fax [809] 686-7437

Foreign Embassies in the U.S.	*U.S. Embassies Abroad*
*ECUADOR, Embassy of 2535 15th St. N.W. Washington, D.C. 20009 Telephone (202) 234-7200	American Embassy Avenida 12 de Octubre y Avenida Patria, Quito, Ecuador Mail: P.O. Box 538 Quito, Ecuador or APO AA 34039-3420 Telephone [593] (2) 562-890 Fax [593] (2) 505-052
EGYPT, Embassy of the Arab Republic of 3522 International Ct. N.W. Washington, D.C. 20008 Telephone (202) 895-5400 Fax (202) 895-5497	American Embassy North Gatel 8, Kamel El-Din Salah St. Garden City, Cairo, Egypt Mail: APO AE 09 839-4900 Telephone [20] (2) 355-7371 Fax [20] (2) 357-3200
EL SAVADOR, Embassy of 2308 California St. N.W. Washington, D.C. 20008 Telephone (202) 265-9671	American Embassy Final Blvd. & Station Antiguo Cuscatlan, San Salvador El Salvador Mail: Unit 3116, APO AA 34023 Telephone [503] 78-4444 Fax [503] 78-6011
EQUATORIAL GUINEA, Embassy of 57 Magnolia Ave. Mount Vernon, N.Y. 10553 Telephone (914) 738-9584 Fax (914) 667-6838	American Embassy Calle de los Ministros, Malabo Equatorial Guinea Mail: P.O. Box 597 Malabo, Equatorial Guinea Telephone [240] (9) 2185 or 2406 Fax [240] (9) 2164
ERITREA, Embassy of the State of 910 17th St. N.W. #400 Washington, D.C. 20006 Telephone (202) 429-1991 Fax (202) 429-9004	American Embassy 34 Zera Yacob St. Asmara, Eritrea Mail: P.O. Box 211, Asmara, Eritrea Telephone [291] (1) 123-720 Fax [291] (1) 127-584

Foreign Embassies in the U.S.   *U.S. Embassies Abroad*

ESTONIA, Embassy of
1030 15th St. N.W. #1000
Washington, D.C. 20005
Telephone (202) 789-0320
Fax (202) 789-0471

American Embassy
Kentmanni, 20, EE 0001
Tallinn, Estonia
Telephone [372] (6) 312-021
Fax [372] (6) 312-025

ETHIOPIA, Embassy of
2134 Kalorama Rd. N.W.
Washington, D.C. 20008
Telephone (202) 234-2281
Fax (202) 328-7950

American Embassy
Entoto St. P.O. Box 1014
Addis Ababa, Ethiopia
Telephone [251] (1) 550-666
Fax [251] (1) 552-191

FIJI, Embassy of the Republic of
2233 Wisconsin Ave. N.W. #240
Washington, D.C. 20007
Telephone (202) 337-8320
Fax (202) 337-1996

American Embassy
31 Loftus St., Suva, Fiji
Mail: P.O. Box 218 Suva, Fiji
Telephone [679] 314-466
Fax [679] 300-081

*****FINLAND**, Embassy of
3216 New Mexico Ave. N.W.
Washington, D.C. 20016
Telephone (202) 363-2430
Fax (202) 363-8233

American Embassy
Itainen Puistotie 14A
SF-00140 Helsinki, Finland
Mail: APO AE 09723
Telephone [358] (0) 171931
Fax [358] (0) 174681

*****FRANCE**, Embassy of
4101 Reservoir Rd. N.W.
Washington, D.C. 20007
Telephone (202) 944-6000
Fax (202) 944-6166

American Embassy
2 Avenue Gabriel
75 382 Paris Cedex 08
Paris, France
Mail: Unit 21551 APO AE 09777
Telephone [33] (1) 4296-12-02
                           4261-80-75
Fax [33] (1) 4266-9783

GAMBIA, Embassy of the
1155 15th St. N.W. #1000
Washington, D.C. 20005
Telephone (202) 785-1399
Fax (202) 785-1430

American Embassy
Fajara, Kairaba Ave.
P.M.B. No. 19
Banjul, Gambia
Telephone [220] 392856
Fax [220] 392475

Foreign Embassies in the U.S.	*U.S. Embassies Abroad*

GEORGIA, Embassy of
the Republic of
1511 K St. N.W. #424
Washington, D.C. 20008
Telephone (202) 393-6060

American Embassy
#25 Antonely St.
380026 Tbilsi, Georgia
Telephone [7] 8832-98-99-68
Fax [7] 8832-93-37-59

*****GERMANY**, Embassy of the
Federal Republic of
4645 Reservoir Rd. N.W.
Washington, D.C. 20007
Telephone (202) 298-4000
Fax (202) 298-4249

American Embassy
Deichmanns Ave. 29
53170 Bonn, Germany
Mail: Unit 21701 APO AE 09080
Telephone [49] (228) 3391
Fax [49] (228) 339-2663

GHANA, Embassy of
3512 International Dr. N.W.
Washington, D.C. 20008
Telephone (202) 686-4520
Fax (202) 686-4527

American Embassy
Ring Rd. East Accra
Ghana
Mail: P.O. Box 194
Accra, Ghana
Telephone [233] (21) 775347
Fax [233] (21) 776008

*****GREECE**, Embassy of
2221 Massachusetts Ave. N.W.
Washington, D.C. 20008
Telephone (202) 939-5800
Fax (202) 939-5824

American Embassy
91 Vasilissis Sophias Blvd.
10160 Athens, Greece
Mail: PSC 108 APO AE 09842
Telephone [30] (1) 721-2951
                    721-8401
Fax [30] (1) 646-6282

GRENADA, Embassy of
1701 New Hampshire, Ave. N.W.
Washington, D.C. 20009
Telephone (202) 265-2561

American Embassy
P.O. Box 54
St. George's, Grenada
Telephone (809) 444-1173
                    (809) 444-1178
Fax (809) 444-4820

Foreign Embassies in the U.S.	*U.S. Embassies Abroad*

GUATEMALA, Embassy of
2220 R St. N.W.
Washington, D.C. 20008
Telephone (202) 745-4952
Fax (202) 745-1908

American Embassy
7-01 Avenida de la Reforma
Zone 10 Guatemala City,
Guatemala
Mail: APO AA 34024
Telephone [502] (2) 31-15-41
Fax [502] (2) 318885

GUINEA, Embassy of
the Republic of
2112 Leroy Pl. N.W.
Washington, D.C. 20008
Telephone (202) 483-9420
Fax (202) 483-8688

American Embassy
2d Blvd. And 9th Ave.
Conakry, Guinea or
B.P. 603 Conakry, Guinea
Telephone [224] 44-15-20 thru 23
Fax [224] 44-15-22

GUINEA-BISSAU, Embassy of
the Republic of
918 16th St. N.W.
Mezzanine Suite
Washington, D.C. 20006
Telephone (202) 872-4222
Fax (202) 872-4226

American Embassy
Avenida Domingos Ramos
Bissau, Guinea-Bissau or
1067 Bissau Codex, Bissau
Guinea-Bissau
Telephone [245] 20-1139 or 1145
Fax [245] 20-1159

GUYANA, Embassy of
2490 Tracy PL. N.W.
Washington, D.C. 20008
Telephone (202) 265-6900

American Embassy
99-100 Young & Duke St.
Kingston, Georgetown, Guyana
Mail: P.O. Box 10507
Georgetown, Guyana
Telephone [592] (2) 549000-9
Fax [592] (2) 58497

HAITI, Embassy of
the Republic of
2311 Massachusetts Ave. N.W.
Washington, D.C. 20008
Telephone (202) 332-4090
Fax (202) 745-7215

American Embassy
Harry Truman Blvd.
Port-au-Prince, Haiti
Mail: P.O. Box 1761
Port-au-Prince, Haiti
Telephone [509] 22-0354,
    22-0368 or 22-0200
Fax [509] 23-1541

Foreign Embassies in the U.S.	*U.S. Embassies Abroad*

*HONDURAS, Embassy of
3007 Tilden St. N.W.
Washington, D.C. 20008
Telephone (202) 966-7702
Fax (202) 966-9751

American Embassy
Avenido La Paz
Tegucigalpa, Honduras or
AP No. 3453 Amemb, Honduras
Mail: APO AA 34022
Telephone [504] 36-9320
                     38-5114
Fax [504] 36-9037

*HUNGARY, Embassy of
the Republic of
3910 Shoemaker St. N.W.
Washington, D.C. 20008
Telephone (202) 362-6730
Fax (202) 966-8135

American Embassy
V. Szabadsag Ter 12
Budapest, Hungary
Mail: Unit 25402
APO AE 09213-5270
Telephone [36] (1) 112-6450
Fax [36] (1) 132-8934

ICELAND, Embassy of
2022 Connecticut Ave. N.W.
Washington, D.C. 20008
Telephone (202) 265-6653
Fax (202) 265-6656

American Embassy
Laufasvegur 21 Box 40
Reykjavik, Iceland
Mail: Usemb PSC 1003, Box 40
FPO AE 09728-6340
Telephone [354] (1) 629100
Fax [354] (1) 629139

INDIA, Embassy of
2107 Massachusetts Ave. N.W.
Washington, D.C. 20008
Telephone (202) 939-7000
Fax (202) 939-7027

American Embassy
Shanti Path, Chanaky apuri 110021
New Delhi, India
Telephone [91] (11) 600651
Fax [91] (11) 6872028

INDONESIA, Embassy of the
Republic of
2020 Massachusetts Ave. N.W.
Washington, D.C. 20036
Telephone (202) 775-5200
Fax (202) 775-5365

American Embassy
Medan Merdeka Selatan 5
Jakarta, Indonesia
Mail: Box 1 APO AP 96520
Telephone [62] (21) 360-360
Fax [62] (21) 386-2259

Foreign Embassies in the U.S.	*U.S. Embassies Abroad*
*IRELAND, Embassy of 2234 Massachusetts Ave. N.W. Washington, D.C. 20008 Telephone (202) 462-3939	American Embassy 42 Elgin Rd. Ballsbridge Dublin, Ireland Telephone [353] (1) 6687122 Fax [353] (1) 6689946
*ISRAEL, Embassy of 3514 International Dr. N.W. Washington, D.C. 20008 Telephone (202) 364-5500 Fax (202) 364-5610	American Embassy 71 Hayarkon St. Tel Aviv, Israel Mail: PSC 98, Box 100 APO AE 09830 Telephone [972] (3) 517-4338 Fax [972] (3) 663449
*ITALY, Embassy of 1601 Fuller St. N.W. Washington, D.C. 20009 Telephone (202) 328-5500	American Embassy Via Veneto 119/A 00187-Rome, Italy Mail: PSC 59, Box 100 APO AE 09624 Telephone [39] (6) 46741 Fax [39] (6) 488-2672
JAMAICA, Embassy of 1850 K St. N.W. #355 Washington, D.C. 20006 Telephone (202) 452-0660 Fax (202) 452-0081	American Embassy Jamaica Mutual Life Center 2 Oxford Rd. 3rd FL Kingston, Jamaica Telephone [809] 929-4850 Fax [809] 926-6743
JAPAN, Embassy of 2520 Massachusetts Ave. N.W. Washington, D.C. 20008 Telephone (202) 939-6700 Fax (202) 328-2187	American Embassy 10-5 Akasaka 1-Chome Minato-KU (107) Tokyo, Japan Mail: Unit 45004, Box 258 APO AP 96337-0001 Telephone [81] (3) 3224-5000 Fax [81] (3) 3505-1862

Foreign Embassies in the U.S.	*U.S. Embassies Abroad*

JORDAN, Embassy of the
Hashemite Kingdom
3504 International Dr. N.W.
Washington, D.C. 20008
Telephone (202) 966-2664
Fax (202) 966-3110

American Embassy
P.O. Box 354
Amman, Jordan
Mail: APO AE 09892-0200
Telephone [962] (6) 820-101
Fax [962] (6) 820-121

KAZAKHSTAN, Embassy of
the Republic of
3421 Massachusetts Ave. N.W.
Washington, D.C. 20008
Telephone (202) 333-4504
Fax (202) 333-4509

American Embassy
99/97 Furmanova St. 480012
Almaty, Kazakhstan
Telephone [7] (3272) 63-34-05
                                53-17-70
Fax [7] (3272) 63-38-83

KENYA, Embassy of
the Republic of
2249 R St. N.W.
Washington, D.C. 20008
Telephone (202) 387-6101

American Embassy
Moi\Haile Selassie Ave.
Nairobi, Kenya or
P.O. Box 30137,
Nairobi, Kenya
Mail: Unit 64100, APO AE 09831
Telephone [254] (2) 334141
Fax [254] (2) 340838

KOREA, Embassy of
2450 Massachusetts Ave. N.W.
Washington, D.C. 20008
Telephone (202) 939-5600

American Embassy
82 Sejong-Ro Chongro-Ku
Seoul, Korea
Mail: Amemb Unit 15550
APO AP 96205-0001
Telephone [82] (2) 397-4114
Fax [82] (2) 738-8845

KUWAIT, Embassy of the
State of
2940 Tilden St. N.W.
Washington, D.C. 20008
Telephone (202) 966-0702
Fax (202) 966-0517

American Embassy
P.O. Box 77
Safat, Kuwait
Mail: Unit 69000
APO AE 09880
Telephone [965] 242-4151 thru 59
Fax [965] 244-2855

Foreign Embassies in the U.S.	*U.S. Embassies Abroad*

KYRGYZSTAN, Embassy of the
Kyrgyz Republic
1511 K St. N.W. #705
Washington, D.C. 20005
Telephone (202) 347-3732
Fax (202) 347-3718

American Embassy
Erkindik Prospekt #66
720002 Bishkek, Kyrgyzstan
Telephone [7] (3312) 22-29-20
22-26-31
Fax [7] (3312) 22-35-51

LAOS, Embassy of
the Lao People's
Democratic Republic
2222 S St. N.W.
Washington, D.C. 20008
Telephone (202) 332-6416
Fax (202) 332-4923

American Embassy
Rue Bartholonie
B.P. 114 Vientiane, Laos
Mail: Amemb Box V
APO AP 96546
Telephone [856] 2220
2357
3570
Fax [856] 4675

LATVIA, Embassy of
4325 17th St. N.W.
Washington, D.C. 20011
Telephone (202) 726-8213

American Embassy
Raina Blvd. 7 226050
Riga, Latvia
Telephone [46] (9) 882-0046
Fax [46] (9) 882-0047

LEBANON, Embassy of
2560 28th St. N.W.
Washington, D.C. 20008
Telephone (202) 939-6300
Fax (202) 939-6324

American Embassy
Antelias P.O. Box 70-840
Beirut, Lebanon or
PSC 815 Box 2
FPO AE 09836-0002
Telephone [961] (1) 402-200
403-300
Fax [961] (1) 407-112

LESOTHO, Embassy of
the Kingdom of
2511 Massachusetts Ave. N.W.
Washington, D.C. 20008
Telephone (202) 797-5534
Fax (202) 234-6815

American Embassy
P.O. Box 33 Maseru 100
Maseru, Lesotho
Telephone [266] 312666
Fax [266] 310-116

Foreign Embassies in the U.S.	*U.S. Embassies Abroad*
LIBERIA, Embassy of the Republic of 5201 16th St. N.W. Washington, D.C. 20011 Telephone (202) 291-0761	American Embassy 111 United Nations Dr. Monrovia, Liberia or P.O. Box 10-0098 Mamba Point Monrovia, Liberia Telephone [231] 222991 to 222994 Fax [231] 223-710
*LUXEMBOURG**, Embassy of 2200 Massachusetts Ave. N.W. Washington, D.C. 20008 Telephone (202) 265-4171 Fax (202) 328-8270	American Embassy 22 Blvd. Emmanuel-Servais 2535 Luxembourg, or PSC 11 APO AE 09132 5380 Telephone [352] 460123 Fax [352] 461401
LITHUANIA, Embassy of the Republic of 2622 16th St. N.W. Washington, D.C. 20009 Telephone (202) 234-5860 Fax (202) 328-0466	American Embassy Akmenu 6 232600 Vilnius Lithuania or APO AE 09723 Telephone [370] (2) 223-031 Fax [370] (2) 222-779
MADAGASCAR, Embassy of Democratic Republic of 2374 Massachusetts Ave. N.W. Washington, D.C. 20008 Telephone (202) 265-5525	American Embassy 14-16 RVE Rainitoro Antsahavola Antananarivo, Madagascar or B.P. 620 Antananarivo, Madagascar Telephone [261] (2) 212-57 200-89 207-18 Fax [261] 234-539
MALAWI, Embassy of 2408 Massachusetts Ave. N.W. Washington, D.C. 20008 Telephone (202) 797-1007	American Embassy P.O. Box 30016 Lilongwe, Malawi Telephone [265] 783-166 Fax [265] 780-471

Foreign Embassies in the U.S.   U.S. Embassies Abroad

MALAYSIA, Embassy of
2401 Massachusetts Ave. N.W.
Washington, D.C. 20008
Telephone (202) 328-2700
Fax (202) 483-7661

American Embassy
376 Jalan Tun Razak
50400 Kuala Lumpur Malaysia
or P.O. Box 10035
50700 Kuala Lumpur Malaysia
or APO AE 96535-8152
Telephone [60] (3) 248-9011
Fax [60] (3) 242-2207

MALI, Embassy of the Republic
2130 R St. N.W.
Washington, D.C. 20008
Telephone (202) 332-2249
Fax (202) 939-8950

American Embassy
Rue Rochester NY and Rue
Mohamed V Bamako, Mali
Telephone [223] 225470
Fax [223] 223712

MALTA, Embassy of
2017 Connecticut Ave. N.W.
Washington, D.C. 20008
Telephone (202) 462-3611
Fax (202) 387-5470

American Embassy
2d Fl. Development House
St. Anne St. Floriana, Malta
Mail: P.O. Box 535
Valletta, Malta
Telephone [356] 235960
Fax [356] 243229

MARSHALL ISLANDS, Embassy
of the Republic of the
2433 Massachusetts Ave. N.W.
Washington, D.C. 20008
Telephone (202) 234-5414
Fax (202) 232-3236

American Embassy
P.O. Box 1379 Majuro,
Republic of the Marshall
Islands 96960-1379
Telephone [692] 247-4011
Fax [692] 247-4021

MAURITANIA, Embassy of
The Islamic Republic of
2129 LeRoy Pl N.W.
Washington, D.C. 20008
Telephone (202) 232-5700

American Embassy
B.P. 222 Novakchott,
Mauritania
Telephone [222] (2) 52660
                          52663
Fax [222] (2) 51592

Foreign Embassies in the U.S.	*U.S. Embassies Abroad*
*MAURITIUS, Embassy of 4301 Connecticut Ave. N.W. #441 Washington, D.C. 20008 Telephone (202) 244-1491 Fax (202) 966-0983	American Embassy Roger House (4th Fl.) John Kennedy St. Port Louis, Mauritus Telephone [230] 2089763 Fax [230] 2089534
*MEXICO, Embassy of 1911 Pennsylvania Ave. N.W. Washington, D.C. 20006 Telephone (202) 728-1600 Fax (202) 728-1698	American Embassy Paseo de La Reforma 305 Colonia Cuauhtemoc 06500 Mexico DF Mail: P.O. Box 3087 Laredo, TX 78044-3087 Telephone [52] (5) 211-0042 Fax [52] (5) 511-9980
MICRONESIA, Embassy of The Federated States of 1725 N St. N.W. Washington, D.C. 20036 Telephone (202) 223-4383 Fax (202) 223-4391	American Embassy P.O. Box 1286 Pohnpei Federated States of Micronesia 96941 Telephone [691] 320-2187 Fax [691] 320-2186
MONGOLIA, Embassy of 2833 M St. N.W. Washington, D.C. 20007 Telephone (202) 333-7117 Fax (202) 298-9227	American Embassy PSC 461, Box 300 FPO AP 96521-0002 Ulaanbaatar, Mongolia Telephone [976] (1) 329095 329096 Fax [976] (1) 320-776
MOROCCO, Embassy of The Kingdom of 1601 21st St. N.W. Washington, D.C. 20009 Telephone (202) 462-7979 Fax (202) 265-0161	American Embassy 2 Ave. De Marrakech Rabat, Morocco or PSC 74, Box 003 APO AE 09718 Telephone [212] (7) 7622-65 Fax [212] (7) 7656-61

Foreign Embassies in the U.S.	*U.S. Embassies Abroad*
MOZAMBIQUE, Embassy of The Republic of 1990 M. St. N.W. #570 Washington, D.C. 20036 Telephone (202) 293-7146 Fax (202) 835-0245	American Embassy Avenida Kaunda 193 Maputo, Mozambique or P.O. Box 783 Maputo, Mozambique Telephone [258] (1) 49-27-97 Fax [258] (1) 49-01-14
NAMIBIA, Embassy of The Republic of 1605 New Hampshire Ave. N.W. Washington, D.C. 20009 Telephone (202) 986-0540 Fax (202) 986-0443	American Embassy Ausplan Bldg. 15 Lossen St. Windhoek, Namibia or Private Bag 12029 Åusspannplatz Windhoek, Namibia Telephone [264] (61) 221-601 Fax [264] (61) 229-792
NEPAL, Royal Nepalese Embassy 2131 Le Roy Pl N.W. Washington, D.C. 20008 Telephone (202) 667-4550 Fax (202) 667-5534	American Embassy Pani Pokhari Kathmandu, Nepal Telephone [977] (1) 411179 Fax [977] (1) 419963
*****NETHERLANDS**, Embassy of The 4200 Linnean Ave. N.W. Washington, D.C. 20008 Telephone (202) 244-5300 Fax (202) 362-3430	American Embassy Lange Voorhout 102 The Hague, Netherlands or PSC 72, Box 1000, APO AE 09715 Telephone [31] (70) 310-9209 Fax [31] (70) 361-4688
*****NEW ZEALAND**, Embassy of 37 Observatory Cir. N.W. Washington, D.C. 20008 Telephone (202) 328-4800	American Embassy 29 Fitzherbert Ter. Thorndon Wellington New Zealand or P.O. Box 1190 Wellington, New Zealand or PSC 467, Box 1 FPO AP 96 531-1001 Telephone [64] (4) 472-2068 Fax [64] (4) 472-3537

Foreign Embassies in the U.S.	*U.S. Embassies Abroad*

NICARAGUA, Embassy of
1627 New Hampshire Ave. N.W.
Washington, D.C. 20009
Telephone (202) 939-6570
Fax (202) 939-6574

American Embassy
Km. 4½ Carretera Sur.
Managua, Nicaragua or
APO AA 34021
Telephone [505] (2) 666010
                       666013
                       666015
Fax [505] (2) 666046

NIGER, Embassy of
  The Republic of
2204 R St., N.W.
Washington, D.C. 20008
Telephone (202) 483-4224
Fax (202) 483-3169

American Embassy
Rue Des Ambassades
Niamey, Niger or
B.P. 11201 Niamey, Niger
Telephone [227] 72-26-61
   through 64
Fax [227] 73-31-67

NIGERIA, Embassy of
  The Federal Republic of
1333 16th St. N.W.
Washington, D.C. 20036
Telephone (202) 986-8400

American Embassy
2 Eleke Crescent
Lagos, Nigeria or
P.O. Box 554,
Lagos, Nigeria
Telephone [234] (1) 261-0097
Fax [234] 10 261-0257

***NORWAY**, Royal Norwegian
  Embassy
2720 34th St. N.W.
Washington, D.C. 20008
Telephone (202) 333-6000
Fax (202) 337-0870

American Embassy
Drammen Sveien 18
0244 Oslo 2 Norway or
PSC69, Box 1000
APO AE 09707
Telephone [47] 22-44-85-50
Fax [47] 22-43-07-77

OMAN, Embassy of The Sultanate
2535 Belmont Rd. N.W.
Washington, D.C. 20008
Telephone (202) 387-1980
Fax (202) 745-4933

American Embassy
P.O. Box 202 Code No. 115
Mudcat, Oman
Telephone [968] 698-989
Fax [968] 695-157

Foreign Embassies in the U.S.	U.S. Embassies Abroad

PAKISTAN, Embassy of
2315 Massachusetts Ave. N.W.
Washington, D.C. 20008
Telephone (202) 939-6200
Fax (202) 387-0484

American Embassy
Diplomatic Enclave Ramna 5
Islamabad, Pakistan or
P.O. Box 1048
Islamabad, Pakistan or
PSC 1212 Box 2000 Unit 6220
APO AF. 09812-2000
Telephone [92] (51) 826161 through 3
Fax [92] (51) 214222

*PANAMA**, Embassy of
The Republic of
2862 McGill Terrace N.W.
Washington, D.C. 20008
Telephone (202) 483-1407
Fax (202) 483-8413

American Embassy
Apartado 6959 Panama 5
Rep. De Panama or
Unit 0945 APO AA 34002
Telephone [507] 27-1777
Fax [507] 27-1964

PAPUA NEW GUINEA,
Embassy of
1615 Hew Hampshire Ave. N.W.
3rd Fl.
Washington, D.C. 20009
Telephone (202) 745-3680
Fax (202) 745-3679

American Embassy
Armit St. Port Moresby,
Papua New Guinea
Mail: P.O. Box 1492
Port Moresby, Papua New Guinea
or APO AE 96553
Telephone [675] 213-423

PARAGUAY, Embassy of
2400 Massachusetts Ave. N.W.
Washington, D.C. 20008
Telephone (202) 483-6960
Fax (202) 234-4508

American Embassy
1776 Mariscal Lopex Ave.
Asuncion, Paraguay
Mail: Casilla Postal 402
Asuncion, Paraguay or
Unit 4711 APO AA 34036-0001
Telephone (595) (21) 213-715
Fax [595] (21) 213-728

PERU, Embassy of
1700 Massachusetts Ave. N.W.
Washington, D.C. 20036
Telephone (202) 467-9300
Fax (202) 328-7614

American Embassy
P.O. Box 1995 Lima, Peru or
APO AA 34031
Telephone [51] (14) 338-000
Fax [51] (14) 316682

Foreign Embassies in the U.S.	*U.S. Embassies Abroad*
PHILIPPINES, Embassy of the 1600 Massachusetts Ave. N.W. Washington, D.C. 20036 Telephone (202) 467-9300 Fax (202) 328-7614	American Embassy 1201 Roxas Blvd. Manila, Philippines or APO AP 96440 Telephone [63] (2) 521-7116 Fax [63] (2) 522-461
*****POLAND**, Embassy of The Republic of 2640 16th St. N.W. Washington, D.C. 20009 Telephone (202) 234-3800 Fax (202) 328-6271	American Embassy Aleje Ujazdowskle 29131 Warsaw, Poland, Mail: AmEmbassy Warsaw, Box 5010 APO AE 09213-5010 Telephone [48] (2) 628-3041 Fax [48] (2) 628-8298
*****PORTUGAL**, Embassy of 2125 Kalorama Rd. N.W. Washington, D.C. 20008 Telephone (202) 328-8610 Fax (202) 462-3726	American Embassy Avenidadas Forcas Armadas 1600 Lisbon Portugal Mail: 38 APO AE 09726 Telephone [351] (1) 726-6600 726-6659 726-8670 Fax [351] (1) 726-9109
QATAR, Embassy of The State of 600 New Hampshire Ave. N.W. #1180 Washington, D.C. 20037	American Embassy P.O. Box 2399 Doha, Qutar Telephone [974] 864701 through 3 Fax [974] 861669
*****ROMANIA**, Embassy of 1607 23rd St. N.W. Washington, D.C. 20008 Telephone (202) 332-4846 Fax (202) 232-4748	American Embassy Strada Tudor Arghezi 7–9 or AmCon Gen (Buch) Bucharest, Romania Mail: Unit 25402 APO AE 09213-5260 Telephone [40] (1) 312-0149 Fax [40] (1) 312-5567

Foreign Embassies in the U.S.   U.S. Embassies Abroad

RUSSIAN FEDERATION,
  Embassy of
1125 16th St. N.W.
Washington, D.C. 20036
Telephone (202) 628-7551
Fax (202) 628-8548

American Embassy
Novinskiy Bul'var 19123
Moscow, Russia
Mail: APO AE 09721
Telephone [7] (095) 252-2451
Fax [7] (095) 255-9965

RWANDA, Embassy of
  The Republic of
1714 New Hampshire Ave. N.W.
Washington, D.C. 20009
Telephone (202) 232-2882
Fax (202) 232-4544

American Embassy
Blvd. de la Revolution
B.P. 28 Kigal, Rwanda
Telephone [250] 75601 through 3
Fax [250] 72128

SAUDI ARABIA, Embassy of
601 New Hampshire Ave. N.W.
Washington, D.C. 20037
Telephone (202) 342-3800

American Embassy
Amemb, Unit 61307
APO AE 09803-1307 or
P.O. Box 94309
Riyadh, Saudi Arabia 11693
Telephone [966] (1) 488-3800
  Ext. 1115, 1116, 1117
Fax [966] (1) 488-7275 or 3278

SENEGAL, Embassy of
  The Republic of
2112 Wyoming Ave. N.W.
Washington, D.C. 20008
Telephone (202) 234-0540

American Embassy
B.P. 49 Ave. Jean XXIII
Dakar, Senegal
Telephone [221] 23-42-96
    23-34-24
USIS Telephone [221] 23-59-28
    23-11-82
Fax [221] 22-29-91

SEYCHELLES, Embassy of
  the Republic of
820 Second Ave. #900 F
New York, N.Y. 10017
Telephone (212) 687-9766
Fax (212) 922-9177

American Embassy
Box 148, Unit 62501
APO AE 09815-2501 or
Victoria House Box 251
Victoria Mahe, Seychelles
Telephone (248) 225256
Fax (248) 225189

Foreign Embassies in the U.S.	*U.S. Embassies Abroad*

SIERRA LEONE, Embassy of
1701 19th St. N.W.
Washington, D.C. 20009
Telephone (202) 939-9261

American Embassy
Corner Walpole & Siaka, Stevens St.
Freetown, Sierra Leone
Telephone [232] (22) 226-481
Fax [232] (22) 225-471

SINGAPORE, Embassy of
The Republic of
3501 International Pl. N.W.
Washington, D.C. 20008
Telephone (202) 537-3100
Fax (202) 537-0876

American Embassy
30 Hill St. Singapore 0617
Mail: FPO AP 96534
Telephone [65] 338-0251
Fax [65] 338-4550

SLOVAK REPUBLIC,
Embassy of The
2201 Wisconsin Ave. N.W. #380
Washington, D.C. 20007
Telephone (202) 965-5161
Fax (202) 965-5166

American Embassy
Hviezdoslavovo Namestie 4
81102 Bratislava, Slovakia
Telephone [42] (7) 330861
Fax [42] (7) 335-439

***SLOVENIA**, Embassy of
The Republic of
1300 19th St. N.W. #410
Washington, D.C. 20036
Telephone (202) 828-1650

American Embassy
P.O. Box 254 Prazakova 4
61000 Ljubljana, Slovenia
Telephone [386] (61) 301-427
301-472
Fax [386] (61) 301-402

SOUTH AFRICA, Embassy of
3051 Massachusetts Ave. N.W.
Washington, D.C. 20008
Telephone (202) 232-4400
Fax (202) 265-1607

American Embassy
877 Pretorius St., Pretoria,
South Africa or P.O. Box 99536
Pretoria, South Africa
Telephone [27] (12) 342-1048
Fax [27] (12) 342-2244

***SPAIN**, Embassy of
2700 15th St. N.W.
Washington, D.C. 20009
Telephone (202) 265-0190
Fax (202) 332-5451

American Embassy
Serrano 75 28006 Madrid Spain
Mail: APO AE 09642
Telephone [34] (1) 577-4000
Fax [34] (1) 577-5735

Foreign Embassies in the U.S.	*U.S. Embassies Abroad*

SRI LANKA, Embassy of The
Democratic Socialist Republic of
2148 Wyoming Ave. N.W.
Washington, D.C. 20008
Telephone (202) 483-4025
Fax (202) 232-7181

American Embassy
210 Galle Rd.
Colombo 3, Sri Lanka or
P.O. Box 106
Colombo, Sri Lanka
Telephone [94] (1) 44-80-07
Fax [94] (1) 43-73-45

SUDAN, Embassy of
The Republic of
2210 Massachusetts Ave. N.W.
Washington, D.C. 20008
Telephone (202) 338-8565
Fax (202) 667-2406

American Embassy
P.O. Box 699 Khartoum, Sudan
or APO AE 09829
Telephone [249] 74700
74611

SURINAME, Embassy of
The Republic of
4301 Connecticut Ave. N.W. #10
Washington, D.C. 20008
Telephone (202) 244-7488
Fax (202) 244-5878

American Embassy
Dr. Sophie Redmondstraat 129
Paramaribo, Suriname or
P.O. Box 1821
Telephone [597] 472900
477881
Fax [597] 410025

SWAZILAND, Embassy of
The Kingdom of
3400 International Dr. N.W. #3M
Washington, D.C. 20008
Telephone (202) 362-6683
Fax (202) 244-8059

American Embassy
Central Bank Bldg., Warner St.
Mbabane, Swaziland or
P.O. Box 199
Mbabane, Swaziland
Telephone [268] 46441, 46445
Fax [268] 45959

*SWEDEN, Embassy of
600 New Hampshire Ave. N.W.
#1200
Washington, D.C. 20037
Telephone (202) 944-5600
Fax (202) 342-1319

American Embassy
Strandvagen 101
S-115 89 Stockholm Sweden
Telephone [46] (8) 783-5300
Fax [46] (8) 661-1964

Foreign Embassies in the U.S.	*U.S. Embassies Abroad*
*SWITZERLAND, Embassy of 2900 Cathedral Ave. N.W. Washington, D.C. 20008 Fax (202) 387-2564	American Embassy Jubilaeumstrasse 93 3005 Bern Switzerland Telephone [41] (31) 357-7011 Fax [41] (31) 357-7344
SYRIAN ARAB REPUBLIC, Embassy of the 2215 Wyoming Ave. N.W. Washington, D.C. 20008 Telephone (202) 232-6313 Fax (202) 265-4585	American Embassy P.O. Box 29 Damascus, Syria Telephone [963] (11) 332-814 714-108 Fax [963] (11) 224-7938
TANZANIA, Embassy of The United Republic of 2139 R St. N.W. Washington, D.C. 20008 Telephone (202) 939-6125 Fax (202) 797-8408	American Embassy P.O. Box 9123 Dar Es Salaam, Tanzania Telephone [255] (51) 66010 66013 Fax [255] (51) 66701
THAILAND, Embassy of 2300 Kalorama Rd. N.W. Washington, D.C. 20008 Telephone (202) 483-7200 Fax (202) 234-4498	American Embassy 95 Wireless Rd. Bangkok, Thailand or APO AP 96546 Telephone [66] (2) 252-5040 Fax [66] (2) 254-2990
TOGO, Embassy of The Republic of 2208 Massachusetts Ave. N.W. Washington, D.C. 20008 Telephone (202) 234-4212 Fax (202) 232-3190	American Embassy Rue Pelletier Carentou & Rue Vauban, Lome, Togo or B.P. 852 Lome, Togo Telephone [228] 21-77-17 21-29-91 Fax [228] 21-79-52

Foreign Embassies in the U.S.	*U.S. Embassies Abroad*

TRINIDAD & TOBAGO,
Embassy of
1708 Massachusetts Ave. N.W.
Washington, D.C. 20036
Telephone (202) 467-6490
Fax (202) 785-3130

American Embassy
P.O. Box 752
Port-of-Spain,
Trinidad & Tobago
Telephone [809] 622-6372
                     622-6176
Fax [809] 628-5462

TUNISIA, Embassy of
1515 Massachusetts Ave. N.W.
Washington, D.C. 20005
Telephone (202) 862-1850
Fax (202) 862-1858

American Embassy
144 Ave. de La Liberte
1002 Tunis-Belvedere
Tunisia
Telephone [216] (1) 782-566
Fax [216] (1) 789-719

TURKEY, Embassy of
The Republic of
1714 Massachusetts Ave. N.W.
Washington, D.C. 20036
Telephone (202) 659-8200

American Embassy
110 Ataturk Blvd.
Ankara, Turkey or
PSC 93, Box 5000
APO AE 09823
Telephone [90] (312) 468-9110
Fax [90] (312) 467-0019

UGANDA, Embassy of
The Republic of
5909 16th St N.W.
Washington, D.C. 20011
Telephone (202) 726-7100
Fax (202) 726-1727

American Embassy
P.O. Box 7007
Kampala, Uganda
Telephone [256] (41) 259792
                     259793

UKRAINE, Embassy of
3350 M St. N.W.
Washington, D.C. 20036
Telephone (202) 333-0606
Fax (202) 333-0817

American Embassy
10 Yuria Kotsyuninskovo
252053 Kiev 53
Ukraine
Telephone [7] (044) 244-7349
                     244-7344
Fax [7] (044) 244-7350

Foreign Embassies in the U.S.	*U.S. Embassies Abroad*
UNITED ARAB EMIRATES, Embassy of The 3000 K St. N.W. #600 Washington, D.C. 20007 Telephone (202) 338-6500 Fax (202) 337-7029	American Embassy Al-Sudan St. Abu Dhabi United Arab Emirates or P.O. Box 4009 Abu Dhabi United Arab Emirates Telephone [971] (2) 4366-691 Fax [971] (2) 434-771
***UNITED KINGDOM OF GREAT BRITAIN & NORTHERN IRELAND**, Embassy of the 3100 Massachusetts Ave. N.W. Washington, D.C. 20008 Telephone (202) 462-1430 Fax (202) 898-4255	American Embassy 24\31 Grosvenor Sq. W. 1A 1AE London, England or PSC 801 Box 40 FPO AE 09498-4040 Telephone [44] (71) 499-9000 Fax [44] (71) 409-1637
URUGUAY, Embassy of 1918 F St. N.W. Washington, D.C. 20006 Telephone (202) 331-1313 Fax (202) 331-8141	American Embassy Lauro Muller 1776 Montevideo, Uruguay or APO AA 34035 Telephone [598] (2) 23-60-61 48-77-77 Fax [598] (2) 48-86-11
UZBEKISTAN, Embassy of The Republic of 1511 K St. N.W. #619 & 623 Washington, D.C. 20005 Telephone (202) 638-4266 Fax (202) 638-4268	American Embassy 82 Chelanzanskaya Telephone [7] (3712) 77-14-07 Fax [7] (3712) 77-69-53

Foreign Embassies in the U.S.   U.S. Embassies Abroad

VENEZUELA, Embassy of The Republic of 1099 30th St. N.W. Washington, D.C. 20007 Telephone (202) 342-2214 Fax (202) 387-2489	American Embassy Avenida Francisco de Miranda & Avenida Principal de la Floresta Caracas, Venezuela or P.O. Box 62291 Caracas, Venezuela or APO AA 34037 Telephone [58] (2) 285-2222 Fax [58] (2) 285-0336
WESTERN SAMOA, Embassy of 820 Second Ave. #800 New York, N.Y. 10017 Telephone (212) 599-6196 Fax (212) 599-0797	American Embassy P.O. Box 3430 Apia, Western Samoa Telephone (685) 21631 Fax (685) 22030
ZAIRE, Embassy of The Republic of 1800 New Hampshire Ave. N.W. Washington, D.C. 20009 Telephone (202) 234-7690	American Embassy 310 Avenue des Aviateurs Kinshasa, Zaire or APO AE 09828 Telephone [243] (12) 21532 Fax [243] (12) 21232
ZAMBIA, Embassy of The Republic of 2419 Massachusetts Ave. N.W. Washington, D.C. 20008 Telephone (202) 265-9717 Fax (202) 332-0826	American Embassy Corner of Independence & United Nations Ave. Lusaka, Zambia Mail: P.O. Box 31617 Lusaka, Zambia Telephone [2601] 228-595 228-601 Fax [2601] 261-538
***ZIMBABWE**, Embassy of The Republic of 1608 New Hampshire Ave. N.W. Washington, D.C. 20009 Telephone (202) 332-7100 Fax (202) 483-9326	American Embassy 172 Herbert Chitapo Ave. Harare, Zimbabwe Mail: P.O. Box 3340 Telephone [263] (4) 794-521 728-957 Fax [263] (4) 796-488

State Clearinghouses
for Missing Children

ALABAMA
Alabama Department of Public
 Safety
Missing Childrens Bureau
P.O. Box 1511
Montgomery, AL 36102-1511
Telephone (205) 242-4207
 (800) 228-7688 (in state)
Contact: Lt. Roscoe Howell

ARIZONA
Arizona Department of Public
 Safety
Intelligence Division
P.O. Box 6638
Phoenix, AZ 85005-6638
Telephone (602) 223-2158
Contact: Annette Barnard

ARKANSAS
Arkansas Office of the Attorney
 General
Missing Children Services Program
Tower Building, Suite 200
323 Center Street
Little Rock, AR 72201
Telephone (501) 682-1323
 (800) 448-3014 (in state)
 (800) 843-5678 (national)
Contact: Carol Robinson

CALIFORNIA
California State Department of
 Justice
Missing/Unidentified Persons

P.O. Box 903387
Sacramento, CA 94203-3870
Telephone (916) 227-3290
 (800) 222-3463 (in state)
Contact: Jeannine Willie

COLORADO
Colorado Bureau of Investigation
Crime Information Center
690 Kipling, Suite 3000
Denver, CO 80215
Telephone (303) 239-4251
Contact: Carol Clark

CONNECTICUT
Connecticut State Police
Missing Persons Unit
P.O. Box 2794
1111 Country Club Road
Middletown, CT 06457
Telephone (203) 685-8420
Contact: Susan Lomotta

DELAWARE
Delaware State Police
State Bureau of Identification
P.O. Box 430
Dover, DE 19903
Telephone (302) 739-5883
Contact: Rodney B. Hegman

DISTRICT OF COLUMBIA
Metropolitan Police Department
D.C. Missing Persons/Youth Divi-
 sion

1700 Rhode Island Avenue N.E.
Washington, D.C. 20018
Telephone (202) 576-6771
Contact: Lt. Maupin

FLORIDA
Florida Department of Law
  Enforcement
Missing Children Information
  Clearinghouse
P.O. Box 1489
Tallahassee, FL 32302
Telephone (904) 488-5224
  (800) 342-0821 (in state)
Contact: Donna Uzzell

GEORGIA
Georgia Bureau of Investigation
Intelligence Unit
P.O. Box 370808
Decatur, GA 30037-0808
Telephone (404) 244-2554
  (800) 282-6564 (in state)
Contact: Terry Craven

ILLINOIS
Illinois State Police, I SEARCH
500 Iles Park Place
Springfield, IL 62718-1002
Telephone (217) 524-6596
  (800) 843-5763 (in state)

INDIANA
Indiana State Police
309 State Office Building
100 North Senate Avenue
Indianapolis, IN 46204-2259
Telephone (317) 232-8310
  (800) 831-8953 (in state)
Contact: Andre Clark

IOWA
Iowa Division of Criminal Investi-
  gation
Wallace State Office Building
Des Moines, IA 50319
Telephone (515) 281-7958
  (800) 346-5507 (in state)
Contact: Steven Conlon

KANSAS
Kansas Bureau of Investigation
Special Services Division
1620 S.W. Tyler Street
Topeka, KS 66612
Telephone (913) 296-8200
  (800) 572-7463
Contact: Special Agent Charles
  Sexson

KENTUCKY
Kentucky State Police
Missing Child Information Center
1240 Airport Road
Frankfort, KY 40601
Telephone (502) 227-8799
Contact: Lt. Kelly McCloud

LOUISIANA
Louisiana Clearinghouse for
  Missing and Exploited Children
Department of Health and Human
  Resources
P.O. Box 3318
Baton Rouge, LA 70821
Telephone (504) 342-4011
Contact: Jennifer Hembree

MAINE
Maine State Police
Criminal Investigation Division

36 Hospital Street
Augusta, ME 04333
Telephone (800) 452-4664 (in state)
Contact: Lt. Gerard Therrien

MARYLAND
Maryland Center for Missing Children
Maryland State Police
1201 Reisterstown Road
Pikesville, MD 21208-3899
Telephone (410) 290-0780
    800 637-5437
Contact: Thomas Wills

MASSACHUSETTS
Massachusetts State Police
Missing Persons Unit
West Grove Street
Middleboro, MA 02346
Telephone 800 447-5269 (nationwide)
    (800) 622-5999 (in state)
Contact: Sgt. John Murphy

MICHIGAN
Michigan State Police
Special Operation Divisions
Prevention Services Section
714 South Harrison Road
East Lansing, MI 48823
Telephone (517) 336-6680
Contact: Sgt. Sandra K. Thompson

MINNESOTA
Minnesota State Clearinghouse
Bureau of Criminal Apprehension
1246 University Avenue
St. Paul, MN 55104

Telephone (612) 642-0610
Contact: David E. Kanefelkamp

MISSISSIPPI
Mississippi State Highway Patrol
P.O. Box 958
Jackson, MS 39205
Telephone (601) 987-1599
Contact: Judy M. Tucker

MISSOURI
Division of Drug and Crime Control
Missing Persons
Missouri State Highway Patrol
P.O. Box 568
Jefferson City, MO 65102
Telephone (314) 751-3313 ext. 178
Contact: Kirt Muller

MONTANA
Missing/Unidentified Persons
    Clearinghouse
Montana Department of Justice
303 North Roberts Street
Helena, MT 59620
Telephone (406) 444-3817
    (800) 332-6617 (in state)
Contact: Bill Erwin

NEBRASKA
Nebraska State Patrol
Criminal Identification
Box 94907
Lincoln, NE 68509-4907
Telephone (402) 471-4545
Contact: David Kohrell

NEVADA
Nevada Office of the Attorney
    General

Crime Prevention Coordinator
555 E. Washington
Suite 3900
Las Vegas, NV 89101
Telephone (702) 486-3420
Contact: Robert Dunson

NEW HAMPSHIRE
New Hampshire State Police
Troop E
P.O. Box 235
West Ossipee, NH 03890
Telephone (603) 271-1166
   (800) 852-3411 (in state)
Contact: Detective Kim Bossey

NEW JERSEY
New Jersey State Police
Missing Persons Unit
P.O. Box 7068
West Trenton, NJ 08628
Telephone (609) 882-2000 ext.
   2895
   (800) 709-7090 (in state)
Contact: William Fox

NEW MEXICO
New Mexico Department of Public
   Safety
Communications Bureau/NCIC
   Section
P.O. 1628
Santa Fe, NM 87504-1628
Telephone (505) 827-9187
Contact: Art Trujillo

NEW YORK
New York Division of Criminal
   Justice Services

Missing and Exploited Children
   Clearinghouse
Executive Park Tower, Stuyvesant
   Plaza
Albany, NY 12203
Telephone (518) 457-6326
   (800) 346-3543 (nationwide)
Contact: James Stanco

NORTH CAROLINA
North Carolina Department of
   Crime Control and Public
   Safety Center for Missing Per-
   sons
116 West Jones Street
Raleigh, NC 27603-1335
Telephone (919) 733-3718
   (800) 522-5437
Contact: John Goad

NORTH DAKOTA
North Dakota Clearinghouse for
   Missing Children
North Dakota Radio Communica-
   tions
P.O. Box 5511
Bismarck, ND 58502-5511
Telephone (701) 224-2121
   (800) 472-2121 (in state)
Contact: Rick Hessinger

OHIO
Ohio Department of Education
Missing Child Education Program
65 South Front Street
Room 719
Columbus, OH 43266-0308
Telephone (614) 466-6830
   (800) 325-5604 (in state)
Contact: Dr. Jerry Klenke

OKLAHOMA
Oklahoma State Bureau of Investigation
Criminal Information Unit
P.O. Box 11497
Oklahoma City, OK 73136
Telephone (405) 848-6724
Contact: Mary Jane Cook

OREGON
Oregon State Police
Missing Children Clearinghouse
Public Service Building
Salem, OR 97310
Telephone (503) 378-3720 ext. 4412
Contact: Judy Hayes

PENNSYLVANIA
Pennsylvania State Police
Missing Persons Unit
Bureau of Criminal Investigation
1800 Elmerton Avenue
Harrisburg, PA 17110
Telephone (717) 783-5524
Contact: Capt. Roger Peacock

RHODE ISLAND
Rhode Island State Police
Missing and Exploited Childrens Unit
311 Danielson Pike
North Scituate, RI 02857
Telephone (401) 444-1000
    (401) 444-1125 (direct line)
    (800) 544-1144 (in state)
    (800) 286-8626
Fax (401) 444-1133
Contact: Lt. Armand H. Bilodeau, Jr., or Isaballe R. Verducci

SOUTH CAROLINA
South Carolina Law Enforcement Division
Missing Persons Information Center
P.O. Box 21398
Columbia, SC 29221-1398
Telephone (803) 737-9000
    (800) 322-4453 (in state)
Contact: Dottie Cronise

SOUTH DAKOTA
Division of Criminal Investigation
Attorney General's Office
500 East Capitol
Pierre, SD 57501
Telephone (605) 773-3331
Contact: Doug Lake

TENNESSEE
Tennessee Bureau of Investigation
Special Investigation Unit
1148 Foster Ave.
Nashville, TN 37210
Telephone (615) 741-0430
Contact: Elic-Cheryl Autson

TEXAS
Texas Department of Public Safety
Criminal Intelligence Services
P.O. Box 4087
Austin, TX 78773-0001
Telephone (512) 465-2814
    (800) 346-3243 (in state)
Contact: Deanna Tidwell

VERMONT
Vermont Department of Public Safety
Vermont State Police

103 South Main Street
Waterbury, VT 05676
Telephone (802) 244-8727

VIRGINIA
Virginia State Police Department
Missing Children's Clearinghouse
P.O. Box 27472
Richmond, VA 23261-7472
Telephone (804) 674-2026
  (800) 822-4453 (in state)
Fax (804) 674-2105
Contact: Lt. George Crowder

WASHINGTON
Missing Children Clearinghouse
Washington State Patrol

P.O. Box 2347
Olympia, WA 98507-2347
Telephone (360) 753-3960
  (800) 543-5678
Fax (360) 586-8231
Contact: Vonda Barber

WYOMING
Wyoming Office of the Attorney
  General
Division of Criminal Investigation
316 West 22nd Street
Cheyenne, WY 82002
Telephone (307) 777-7537
Fax (307) 777-7545
Contact: Rich Wilson

Appendix A: State Department Publication on International Parental Child Abduction

The following information is reprinted verbatim from International Parental Abduction, *Department of State Publication 10052, and is presented as advice and information for searching parents.*

PART I

HOW TO GUARD AGAINST INTERNATIONAL CHILD ABDUCTION

How vulnerable is your child?

In International Parental Child Abduction, an ounce of prevention is worth a pound of cure. You and your child are most vulnerable when your relationship with the other parent is broken or troubled, the other parent has close ties to another country, and the other country has traditions or laws that may be prejudicial to a parent of your gender or to aliens in general.

Cross-Cultural Marriages:
Should you or your child
visit the country of the other parent?

Many cases of international parental child abduction are actually cases in which the child traveled to a foreign country with the approval of both parents but was later prevented from returning to the United States. Sometimes the marriage is neither broken nor troubled, but the foreign parent, upon returning to his or her country of origin, decides not to return to the

U.S. or to allow the child to do so. A person who has assimilated a second culture may find a return to his or her roots traumatic and may feel a pull to shift loyalties back to the original culture. A person's personality may change when he or she returns to the place where they grew up.

In some traditional societies, children must have their father's permission and a woman may have to have her husband's permission to travel. If you are a woman, to prevent your own child's detention abroad, find out about the laws and traditions of the country you plan to visit or to allow your child to visit, and consider carefully the effect that a return to his roots might have on your husband.

Precautions That Any Vulnerable Parent Should Take

Even if your marriage is legally intact, you may feel that your child is vulnerable to abduction by your spouse. Be alert to the possibility and be prepared — keep a list of the addresses and telephone numbers of the other parent's relatives, friends, and business associates both here and abroad. Keep a record of other important information on the other parent, including these numbers: passport, social security, bank account, driver's license, and auto license. In addition, keep a written description of your child, including hair color and eye color, height, weight, and any special physical characteristics. Take color photographs of your child every six months. If your child should be abducted, this information could be vital in locating your child.

The National Center for Missing and Exploited Children has other suggestions that a parent can take if he or she fears the other parent will abduct their child. Teach your child to use the telephone; practice making collect calls; instruct him or her to call home immediately if anything unusual happens, such as anyone telling the child that you have died or that you don't love the child anymore. If you feel your child is vulnerable to abduction, get professional counseling from a social worker or a lawyer. Do not merely tell a friend about your fears.

The Importance of a Custody Decree

Under the laws of many American states and many foreign countries, if there is no decree of custody, both parents are considered to have legal custody of their child and a parent-snatched child is generally not considered legally abducted. If you are contemplating divorce or separation, or are divorced or separated, or even if you were never legally married to the other parent, obtain a decree of sole custody for your child as soon as possible. If you have or would prefer to have a joint custody decree, make certain that it prohibits your child from traveling abroad without your permission.

How to Draft or Modify a Custody Decree

A well-written custody decree is an important line of defense against international parental child abduction. The American Bar Association (ABA) and the National Center for Missing and Exploited Children (NCMEC) have developed recommendations for writing custody decrees to help prevent the abduction of your child if your spouse is an alien or a U.S. citizen with ties to a foreign country. For instance, court-ordered supervised visitation and/or impounding the other parent's passport may be advisable. If the country to which your child might be taken is a member of the Hague Convention on International Child Abduction (see page 196) the custody decree should state that the parties agree that the terms of the Hague Convention apply should an abduction occur. The ABA also suggests having the court require the alien parent or the parent with ties to a foreign country to post a bond. This may be useful both as a deterrent to abduction and, if forfeited because of an abduction, a source of revenue for you in your efforts to locate and recover your child.

For further information, you may contact the National Center for Missing and Exploited Children. The address of the NCMEC is on page 88.

Prevention: How a Custody Decree Can Help

Obtain several certified copies of your custody degree from the court that issued it. Give a copy to your child's school. A school that is aware of a custody decree has a basis for refusing a child to a non-custodial parent and for notifying both the custodial parent and the police if a problem should arise.

U.S. Passports

If you have a U.S. court order that either grants you sole custody of your child or prohibits your child from traveling without your permission, you can prevent the issuance of a U.S. passport for your child. Call the Office of Citizenship Appeals and Legal Assistance, Office of Passport Services in the Department of State on 202-326-6168. You will need to follow your call with a written request and enclose a certified copy of your custody decree. The address is: 1425 K Street N.W., Room 300, Washington, D.C. 20522-1708.

Your child's name will be entered in a computerized passport name check list and the Passport Office can refuse to issue the child a passport anywhere in the United States or at any U.S. embassy or consulate abroad. A passport already issued to your child cannot be revoked, however.

Foreign Passports — The Problem of Dual Nationality

Most U.S. Citizen Children Who Fall Victim to International Parental Abduction Possess Dual Nationality. While the Department of State will make every effort to avoid issuing a U.S. passport if the custodial parent has provided a custody decree, the Department cannot prevent embassies and consulates of other countries in the United States from issuing their passports to children who are also their nationals. You can, however, request the foreign embassy and consulates not to issue a passport to your child. Send them a written request, along with certified copies of any custody decrees, court orders, or warrants you have. In your letter, inform then that you are sending a copy of this request to the Department of State. If your child is only a U.S. citizen, you can request that no visa for that country be issued in his or her U.S. passport. No international law requires compliance with such requests, but some countries will comply voluntarily.

PART II

HOW TO SEARCH FOR A CHILD ABDUCTED ABROAD

Note: If your child has been abducted to a country that is a party to the Hague Convention on International Child Abduction, see page 179 before you read further. At present, besides the United States, **Argentina, Australia, Austria, Belize, Burkina Faso, Canada, Denmark, Ecuador, France, Germany, Greece, Hungary, Ireland, Israel, Luxembourg, Mexico, Monaco, Netherlands, New Zealand, Norway, Poland, Portugal, Romania, Spain, Sweden, Switzerland, United Kingdom**, and the former **Yugoslavia** are parties to the Convention.

Where to Report Your Missing Child

1. If your child has been abducted and you do not know where he or she is, file a missing person report with your local police department and request that your child's name and description be entered into the "missing persons" section of the National Crime Information Center (NCIC) computer. This is provided for under the Missing Children's Act of 1982 (see

page 29. The abductor does not have to be charged with a crime when you file a missing person report. In addition, through Interpol, the international criminal police organization, your local police can request that a search for your child be conducted by the police in the country where you believe your child may have been taken. You may be able to achieve all of the above even if you do not have a custody decree.

2. Report the abduction to the National Center for Missing and Exploited Children (NCMEC) at 1-800-843-5678. With the searching parent's permission, the child's photograph and description may be circulated to the media in the country to which you believe the child may have been taken.

At the same time that you report your child missing, you should contact a lawyer to obtain a decree of sole custody if you do not already have one. In many states, a married parent can obtain a temporary decree of sole custody if the other parent has taken their child.

3. Have your child's name entered into the U.S. passport name check system (see page 58). Even if your child is already abroad, his or her name should be in the system so that a U.S. passport application for your child can be denied anywhere — abroad or in the United States.

4. The Department of State, when requested to do so, conducts welfare and whereabouts searches for American citizens abroad. In an emergency, the Office of Citizens Consular Services (CCS) will cable such a request for you to the U.S. embassy or consulate responsible for the area to which you believe your child has been abducted. Call us on 1-202-736-7000 and have ready as much as you can of the following information on the child:
— full name
— date and place of birth
— passport, number, date, and place of issuance

and on the abductor
— full name (and any aliases),
— date and place of birth,
— passport number, date, and place of issuance,
— occupation
— probable date of departure
—flight information
— details of ties to a foreign country, such as the names, addresses, and telephone numbers of friends, relatives, place of employment, or business connections there.

A consular officer overseas, working with this information, will try to find your child. The consular officer may also request information from local officials on your child's entry or residence in the country. Unfortunately, not every country maintains such records in a retrievable form, and some countries may not release such information.

We may also ask you for photographs of both your child and the abducting parent because these are often helpful to foreign authorities trying to find a missing child.

The Search and Recovery — a Basic Guide

It is possible that none of the institutions listed above (the police, the NCMEC, or the Department of State) will succeed in locating your child right away and you will need to carry out the search on your own. As you search, you should, however, keep these institutions informed of your actions and progress.

This booklet attempts to cover the international aspects of your search and recovery effort, but for other information, you should have a more basic guide. The National Center for Missing and Exploited Children publishes *Parental Kidnapping: How to Prevent an Abduction and What to Do If Your Child Is Abducted.* For a copy, call 703-235-3900, or write the NCMEC at: 2101 Wilson Boulevard, Suite 550; Arlington, VA, 22201. This publication guides you through the legal system, helps you organize your search, and supplies a list of local support groups.

We have relied heavily on the NCMEC guide for the following list of suggestions:

Further Steps to Take in Your Search

• One of the best ways to find your child overseas is through establishing friendly contact with relatives and friends of the other parent, either here or abroad. You may have more influence with such persons than you suspect, and their interest in your child's welfare may lead them to cooperate with you.

• Under the U.S. Department of Health and Human Services, the Office of Child Support Enforcement maintains the Federal Parent Locator Service (FPLS). The primary purpose of this service is to locate parents who are delinquent in child support payments, but the service will also search for parental abductors *when requested to do so by a judge or law enforcement agent.*

• Using the abductor's social security number, the FPLS searches the records maintained by such federal agencies as the Internal Revenue Service, Veterans Administration, Social Security Administration, Department of Defense, and the National Personnel Records Center. An abductor who has had a connection with any of the above might, even from abroad, renew a connection with one of them. To learn how to access the services of the FPLS, contact your local or State Child Support Enforcement Office. These offices are listed under government listings in your telephone directory.

• To obtain information on requests that may have been made by the abductor to your child's school for the transfer of your child's records, you can contact the principal of the school. Your will need to give the school a certified copy of your custody decree.

• You can find out from the National Center for Missing and Exploited Children how to prepare a poster on your child. A poster may assist foreign authorities in attempting to locate your child.

• You can ask your local prosecutor to contact the U.S. Postal Inspection Service to see if a "mail cover" can be put on any address that you know of in the United States to which the abductor might write.

• You can ask local law enforcement authorities to obtain, by subpoena or search warrant, credit card records that may show where the abductor is making purchases. In the same manner, you can try to obtain copies of telephone company bills of the abductor's friends or relatives who may have received collect calls from the abductor.

PART III

ONE POSSIBLE SOLUTION:
THE HAGUE CONVENTION

The most difficult and frustrating element for most parents whose child has been abducted abroad is that U.S. laws and court orders are not directly enforceable abroad. Each sovereign country has jurisdiction within its own territory and over persons present within its border, and no country can force another to decide cases or enforce laws within its confines in a particular way. Issues that have to be resolved between sovereign nations can only be handled by persuasion or by international agreement.

The increase in international marriages since World War II increased international child custody cases to the point where 23 nations, meeting at the Hague Conference on Private International Law in 1976, agreed to seek a treaty to deter international child abduction. Between 1976 and 1980, the United States was a major force in preparing and negotiating the Hague Convention on the Civil Aspects of International Child Abduction. The Convention came into force for the United States on July 1, 1988, and applies to abductions or wrongful retentions that occurred on or after that date. In the United States, federal legislation, the International Child Abduction Remedies Act (P.L. 100-300), was enacted to implement the Convention in this country.

The United States actively encourages other countries to become party to the Convention. As of April 1993, the Convention is also in effect with *Argentina, Australia, Austria, Belize, Burkina Faso, Canada, Denmark, Ecuador, France, Germany, Hungary, Ireland, Israel, Luxembourg, Mexico, Netherlands, New Zealand, Norway, Poland, Portugal, Spain, Sweden, Switzerland, United Kingdom,* and the former *Yugoslavia*. It will be in effect with *Greece, Monaco, and Romania* as of June 1, 1993. Other countries are working toward ratification. Contact the Office of Citizens Consular Services (CCS) to learn if additional countries have joined.

If your child has been abducted to a country that is not a party to the Convention, see Part IV in, "Legal Solutions in Countries Not Party to the Hague Convention."

What Is Covered by the Convention

The countries that are parties to the Convention have agreed with each other that, subject to certain limited exceptions, a child wrongfully removed to or retained in a party country shall promptly be returned to the party country where the child habitually resided before the wrongful removal or retention. The Convention also provides a means for helping parents to exercise visitation rights abroad.

There is a treaty obligation to return an abducted child below the age of 16 if application is made within one year from the date of the wrongful removal or retention. After one year, the court is still obligated to order the child returned unless the person resisting return demonstrates that the child is settled in the new environment. A court may refuse to order a child returned if there is a grave risk that the child would be exposed to physical or psychological harm or otherwise placed in an intolerable situation. A court may also decline to return the child if the child objects to being returned and has reached an age and degree of maturity at which the court can take account of the child's views. Finally, the return of the child may be refused if the freedoms would violate the fundamental principles of human rights and freedoms of the country where the child is being held. These exceptions have been interpreted narrowly by courts in the United States and the other countries party to the Convention.

How to Invoke the Hague Convention

You do not need to have a custody decree to invoke the Convention. However, to apply for the return of your child, you must have been actually exercising a "custodial right" at the time of the abduction and you must not have consented to the removal or retention of the child. If there was no court order in effect at the date of the abduction, custodial rights are provided in the statutes of most states.

You may apply for the return of your child or the ability to exercise your visitation rights. You can also ask for assistance in locating your child and for information on your child's welfare.

Each country that is a party to the Convention has designated a Central Authority to carry out specialized duties under the Convention. You may submit an application either to the U.S. Central Authority or directly to the Central Authority of the country where the child is believed to be held. The Central Authority for the United States is the Department of State's Office of Citizens Consular Services (CCS)....

The Role of the U.S. Central Authority (CCS)

CCS will review your application to ensure that it complies with the Convention. If it does, we will forward it to the foreign Central Authority and work with that authority until your case is resolved. If the abducting parent does not voluntarily agree to the return of your child, you may be required to retain an attorney abroad, see "How to Proceed" on page 65.

The Department of State is prohibited from acting as an agent or attorney in your case. We can, however, help in many other ways. We can give you information on the operating procedures of the Central Authority in the country where your child is believed to be located. We can help you obtain information on the laws of the state in which your child resided prior to the abduction and can transmit statements concerning the wrongfulness of the abduction under the laws of that state. Six weeks after court action commences, we can request a status report.

The Central Authority in the country where your child is located, however, has the primary responsibility of responding to your application. In the words of the Convention, those countries "agree to ensure that rights of custody and access under the law of one Contracting State are effectively respected in the other Contracting State."

PART IV

LEGAL SOLUTIONS IN COUNTRIES NOT PARTY TO THE HAGUE CONVENTION

If your child has been abducted to a country that is not a party to the Hague Convention, you can seek legal remedies against the abductor, in the United State and abroad, from both the civil and criminal justice systems. The family court system where you get your custody decree is part of the civil justice system. At the same time you are using that system, you can also use the criminal justice system consisting of the police, prosecutors, and the FBI. We will discuss each system in turn.

Using the Civil Justice System

How to Proceed

After you obtain a custody decree in the United States, your next step is to use the civil justice system in the country to which your child has been abducted.

The Office of Citizens Consular Services (CCS) can provide information on the customs and the legal practices in the country where your child is. We can also give you general information on how to serve process abroad or obtain evidence from abroad, and on how to have documents authenticated for use in a foreign country. You may write or telephone CCS for two information sheets: *Retaining a Foreign Attorney*, and *Authentication* [Legalization] *of Documents in the United States for Use Abroad*.

To obtain authoritative advice on the laws of a foreign country or to take legal action in that country, you should retain an attorney there. U.S. consular and diplomatic officers are prohibited by law from performing legal services (see 22 C.F.R. 92.81). We can, however, provide you with a list of attorneys in a foreign country who speak English, who may be experienced in parental child abduction or family law, and who have expressed a willingness to represent Americans abroad. U.S. embassies and consulates abroad prepare these lists. A note of caution: *Attorney fees can vary widely from country to country.* The fee agreement that you make with your local attorney should be put into writing as soon as possible to avoid potentially serious misunderstanding later.

Although officers at U.S. embassies and consulates cannot take legal action on behalf of U.S. citizens, consular officers can assist in clarifying communication problems with a foreign attorney. Consular officers may at least at times be able to inquire about the status of proceedings in the foreign court, and they will coordinate with your attorney to ensure that your rights as provided for by the laws of that foreign country are respected.

Once you retain a foreign attorney, send him or her a certified copy of your custody decree and of any court orders and/or state and federal warrants. Also send copies of your State's laws on custody and parental kidnapping and the Federal Parental Kidnapping Prevention Act and copies of reported cases of your State's enforcement of foreign custody decrees under Section 23 of the Uniform Child Custody Jurisdiction Act. The National Center for Missing and Exploited Children can help you gather these materials (address on page 88).

What Are Your Chances of Enforcing Your U.S. Custody Abroad?

A custody decree issued by a court in the United States has no binding legal force abroad, although it may have persuasive force in some countries. Foreign courts decide child custody cases on the basis of their own domestic relations law. This may give a "home court" advantage to a person who has abducted a child to the country of his or her origin. You could also be disadvantaged if the country has a cultural bias in favor of a mother or a father. A U.S. custody decree may, however, be considered by foreign courts and authorities as evidence and, in some cases, may be recognized and enforced by them on the basis of comity (the voluntary recognition by courts of one jurisdiction of the laws and judicial decisions of another.) Your chances of having your U.S. court order enforced depend, to a large degree, upon the tradition of comity that the legal system of the country in question has with the U.S. legal system. CCS can give you some information on these traditions.

Using the Criminal Justice System: What Are the Risks?

Law enforcement authorities in the United States and abroad may be valuable sources of information. In some cases, however, formal resort to the criminal justice system (filing of charges, issuance of an arrest warrant, transmission of an extradition request to a foreign government under an applicable treaty, and criminal prosecution) may be counterproductive and should be considered a last resort. This is especially true if the other country concerned is a party to the Hague Convention.

CCS can obtain information on the criminal justice system of a particular country and on whether or not it is likely to cooperate in some form in parental abduction cases. Your decision on whether or not to try to utilize the criminal justice system depends upon the circumstances of your case, but you should understand that you are likely to lose control of your case to a large extent when formal charges have been filed and an arrest warrant has been issued. You should also realize that extradition of the abductor to the United States is unlikely, and that neither extradition nor prosecution of the abductor guarantees the return of your child and may in some cases complicate, delay, or ultimately jeopardize return.

Presumably, your overriding interest is to obtain the return of your child. That is not the primary responsibility of the prosecutors. When the criminal justice system becomes involved in a case, there are several interests at stake, some of which are in conflict: the interests of the child, the interests of each party/guardian and other immediate family members, the interests of the civil justice system in a stable and workable custody arrangement, and the interests of the criminal justice system in apprehending, prosecuting, and punishing those who have violated criminal laws of their jurisdiction in connection with a parental child abduction.

Another factor to consider is the possible reaction of the abductor to the filing of criminal charges and the threat of ultimate prosecution and punishment. Although some individuals might be intimidated enough to return the child (with or without agreement by the prosecutors to the condition that the charges be dropped), others might go deeper into hiding, particularly if they are in a country where they have family or community support. If an abductor is ultimately brought to trial, how far are you willing to go in pursuing criminal prosecution? Unless you are prepared to testify in court against the abductor, you should not pursue criminal prosecution. A final factor to consider is the effect on the child of seeing the abducting parent prosecuted and perhaps incarcerated, with you playing an active role in that process.

The Steps to Take in Case
You Decide to Use the Criminal Justice System

Once you have a custody decree and have decided to pursue criminal remedies, you or your attorney may contact your local prosecutor or law enforcement authorities to request that the abducting parent be criminally prosecuted and that an arrest warrant be issued, if provided for by your state law. In some states, parental child abduction or custodial interference is a misdemeanor; however, in most states it is a felony. If you are able to obtain a warrant, the local prosecutor can contact the FBI or your state's U.S. Attorney to request the issuance of a Federal Unlawful Flight to Avoid Prosecution (UFAP) warrant for the arrest of the abductor. The Federal Parental Kidnapping Prevention Act of !980 provides for the issuance of this warrant.

Once a warrant has been issued for the abductor's arrest, ask local law enforcement authorities or the FBI to enter the abductor's name in the "wanted persons" section of the National Crime Information Center (NCIC) computer.

Prosecution of Agents or Accomplices of the Abductor

Find out if your state has laws that allow legal action to be taken against agents or accomplices to an abduction. Consider whether such actions would be useful in learning your child's whereabouts or compelling the return of your child.

Implications of an Arrest Warrant for a U.S. Citizen

If the abducting parent is a U.S. citizen and the subject of a federal arrest warrant, the FBI or U.S. Attorney's office can ask the Department of State, Passport Services, to revoke the person's U.S. passport. This may or may not be a burden to an abducting parent who, as a dual national, may carry a foreign passport. However, an abducting parent who is only a U.S. citizen becomes an undocumented alien in a foreign country if his or her U.S. passport is revoked. Some countries may deport undocumented aliens or at least make it difficult for them to remain in the country.

To arrange for a U.S. passport to be revoked, the FBI or U.S. Attorney must send a copy of the UFAP warrant to the Department of State's Office of Citizenship Appeals and Legal Assistance (Telephone 202-326-6168). The regulatory basis for revocation of passports is found in the Code of Federal Regulations: 22C.F.R. 51.70, et seq.

In certain circumstances you may decide that revoking the abducting parent's passport will not achieve the desired result. For example, if you know the location of the other parent, there is always the possibility of negotiation and a settlement or, at least, there is the possibility of communication with your child. However, if the abducting parent is threatened with passport revocation, he or she might choose to flee with your child again. In child abduction cases, Passport Services does not revoke an abductor's passport automatically. Instead they will work with the Office of Citizens Consular Services to make a decision, taking into consideration your wishes, the location of your child, and other specific details of your case.

Implications of a Warrant for a Non–U.S. Citizens

Even if the abductor is not a U.S. citizen, the existence of a UFAP warrant is important. Such a warrant may encourage the abducting parent to return the child voluntarily, especially if he or she has business or other reasons to travel to the United States. The warrant also serves to inform the foreign government that the abduction of the child is a violation of U.S. law and that the abductor is a federal fugitive. An arrest warrant is also necessary if your wish to have authorities seek extradition of the abductor.

The Possibility of Extradition

Through Interpol and other international links, national law enforcement authorities in many countries regularly cooperate in the location and apprehension of international fugitives. Extradition, the surrender of a fugitive or prisoner by one jurisdiction for criminal prosecution or service of a sentence in another jurisdiction, is rarely a viable approach in international child abduction cases. Extradition is utilized only for criminal justice purposes in cases that local prosecutors believe can be successfully prosecuted due to the sufficiency of the evidence, which would presumably include your testimony. Moreover, it must be remembered that extradition does not apply to the abducted or wrongfully retained child, but only to the abductor. There is no guarantee that the child will be returned by foreign authorities in connection with extradition of the alleged wrongdoer. Threatened with impending extradition, abducting parents in other countries have hidden the child or children with a friend or relative in the foreign country.

Another reason that extradition is seldom useful is that the offenses of parental child abduction or custodial interference are covered by only a few of the extradition treaties now in force between the United States and more than 100 foreign countries. Most of these treaties contain a list of covered offenses and were negotiated before international parental child abduction became a widely recognized phenomenon. With respect to these older treaties, there was thus no intent on the part of the negotiators to cover such conduct, and it cannot therefore be validly argued that parental child abduction is a covered extraditable offense, even if the language used in the list of offenses covered by a given treaty appears somewhat broad (e.g., "abduction" or "kidnapping" or "abduction/kidnapping of minors").

In negotiating more modern extradition treaties, the United States has tried to substitute a "dual" criminality" approach for a rigid list of extraditable offenses, or at least has tried to combine the two. Under an extradition treaty with a duel criminality provision, an offense is covered if it is a felony in both countries. Accordingly, if the underlying conduct involved in parental child abduction or custodial interference is a felony in both the U.S. and foreign jurisdictions involved, then that conduct is an extraditable offense under an extradition treaty based on duel criminality.

Despite the fact that parental child abduction may be covered by certain extradition treaties, you should be aware of potential difficulties in utilizing them, apart from the possible counterproductive effects already discussed. Specifically, nearly all civil law countries (in contrast with common law countries like the United States, United Kingdom, Canada, Australia) will not extradite their own nationals. Nearly all the nations of Latin America and Europe are civil law countries. Whatever the terms of any applicable extradition treaty, experience has also shown that foreign governments are generally reluctant at best (and often simply unwilling) to extradite anyone (their own citizens, U.S. citizens, or third country nationals) for parental child abductions.

For extradition to be possible, therefore:

• your local prosecutor must decide to file charges and pursue the case, and you probably must be prepared to testify in any criminal trial;

• there must be an extradition treaty in force between the United States and the country in question;

• the treaty must cover the conduct entailed in parental child abduction or custodial interference;

• if the person sought is a national of the country in question, that country must be willing to extradite its own nationals;

and,

• the country in question must be otherwise willing to extradite persons for parental child abduction/custodial interference (i.e., not refuse to do so for "humanitarian" or other policy reasons).

The Possibility of Prosecution
of an Abductor in a Foreign Country

A final possibility in the area of criminal justice is prosecution of the abductor by the authorities of the foreign country where he or she is found. In many countries (not the United States), nationals of the country can be prosecuted for acts committed abroad under the "nationality" basis for criminal jurisdiction, if the same conduct would constitute a criminal offense under local law. U.S. law enforcement authorities can request such a prosecution and forward the evidence that would have been used in a U.S. prosecution. U.S. witnesses may, of course, have to appear and testify in the foreign proceeding. Like the courses of action discussed above, this approach may be counterproductive and will not necessarily result in the return of the child.

PART V

OTHER SOLUTIONS:
SETTLING OUT OF COURT;
PROMOTING COMMUNICATION
BETWEEN PARENTS AND CHILDREN

Legal procedures can be long and expensive. You may have greater success working in an area even more difficult than the legal system — the area of negotiation with the abducting parent. In some cases, friends or relatives of the abductor may be able to help you establish amicable relations with the abductor and may be willing to help mediate a compromise. A decrease in tension might bring about the return of your child, but, even if it does not, it can increase your chances of being able to visit the child and participate in some way in the child's upbringing. Sometimes compromise and some kind of reconciliation are the only solution.

Obtaining Information on Your Child's Welfare

If your child has been found, but cannot be recovered, you can request that a U.S. consular officer visit the child. If the consul succeeds in seeing your child, he or she will send you a report on your child's health, living conditions, schooling, and other information. Sometimes consular officers are also able to send you letters or photos from the child. If the abducting parent will not permit the consular officer to see your child, the U.S. embassy or consulate will request the assistance of local authorities, either to arrange for such a visit or to have a local social worker make a visit and provide a report on your child's health and welfare. Contact the Office of Consular Services (CCS) to request such a visit.

Working with Foreign Authorities

In child abduction cases, consular officers routinely maintain contact with local child welfare and law enforcement officers. If there is evidence of abuse or neglect of the child, the U.S. embassy or consulate will request that local authorities become involved to ensure the child is protected. This may mean removal of your child from the home for placement in local foster care.

The Question of Desperate Measures

Consular officers cannot take possession of a child abducted by a parent or aid parents attempting to act in violation of the laws of a foreign country. Consular officers must act in accordance with the laws of the country to which they are accredited.

Before considering desperate measures, you should read the information available from the National Center for Missing and Exploited Children about the emotional trauma inflicted on a child who is a victim of abduction and re-abduction. The NCCMEC discourages re-abduction not only because it is illegal, but also because of possible psychological harm to the child.

Attempts to use self-help measures to bring an abducted child to the United States from a foreign country may endanger your child and others, prejudice any further judicial efforts you might wish to make in that country to stabilize the situation, and result in your arrest and imprisonment in that country. In imposing a sentence, the foreign court will not necessarily give weight to the fact that the would-be-abductor was the custodial parent in the United States or otherwise had a valid grievance under a U.S. court order (e.g., failure of the foreign parent to honor the terms of a joint custody order).

If you do succeed in leaving the foreign country with your child, you and anyone who assisted you may be the target of arrest warrants and extradition requests in the United States or any other country where you are found. Even if you are not ultimately extradited and prosecuted, an arrest followed by extradition proceedings can be very disruptive and disturbing for both you and your child.

Finally, there is no guarantee that the chain of abductions would end with the one committed by you. A parent who has re-abducted a child may have to go to extraordinary lengths to conceal his or her whereabouts, living in permanent fear that the child may be re-abducted again.

Appendix B:
Resource Guides

Below each of the following addresses is a list of helpful publications available from that source.

Juvenile Justice Clearinghouse
Department F
P.O. Box 6000
Rockville MD 20850
Telephone: 1-800-638-8736
Email: askncjrs@aspensys.com

Law Enforcement Policies and Practices Regarding Missing Children and Homeless Youth. 1993. #NCJ114218. $13.00.
Obstacles to the Recovery and Return of Parentally Abducted Children. 1994. 877 page report. #NCJ144535. $22.80.
OJJDP Annual Report on Missing Children. 1990. #NCJ130582.
Parental Abductors: Four Interviews. 1993. #NCJ147866 (43 min.) $12.50

Superintendent of Documents
U.S. Government Printing Office
Washington DC 20402
Telephone: (202) 783-3238

A Safe Trip Abroad. #9493. $1.00.
Background Notes. Pamphlets on each of 170 countries. $2.00 each.
Diplomatic List. #7894. Call for price.
Foreign Consular Offices in U.S. $6.50.
Key Officers of Foreign Service Posts. $1.75.

Passport Information. #9915. Free.
Tips for Travelers to Central & South America. #9682. $1.00.
Tips for Travelers to Cuba. #9232. $1.00.
Tips for Travelers to Eastern Europe. #9329. $1.00.
Tips for Travelers to Mexico. #9309. $1.00.
Tips for Travelers to Russia. #9971. $1.00.
Tips for Travelers to South Asia. #9601. $1.00.
Tips for Travelers to the Caribbean. #9906. $1.00.
Tips for Travelers to the Middle East & North Africa. #9972. $1.00.
Tips for Travelers to the People's Republic of China. #9189. $1.00.
Tips for Travelers to Sub-Saharan Africa. #9628. $1.00.
U.S. Consul Help for Americans Abroad. #9782. Free.
Your Trip Abroad. #9926. $1.00.

American Bar Association
Center on Children & the Law
1800 M. St.
Washington, DC 20036
Tel (202) 662-1720
Fax (202) 662-1755

A Judge's Guide to Risk Factors for Family Abduction and Child Recovery. 1995.
    L. Girdner, Ph.D. & J. Johnston, Ph.D.
Parental Kidnapping: Prevention & Remedies. 1995.

Office of Citizens Consular Services
Bureau of Consular Affairs
Department of State
Room 4817
Washington DC 20520
Telephone: (202) 647-2688

International Parental Child Abduction. Free. Also inquire about publications on dual citizenship or nationality; Islamic family law; and custody disputes involving Iran, Japan, Jordan, Pakistan, Philippines, Saudi Arabia, and Thailand.

Appendix C:
Supporting Agencies

The following agencies are presented to the reader for information purposes. Their appearance here should not necessarily be viewed as a personal endorsement by the author.

International Center for the Search and
Recovery of Missing Children
5449 South Highway 436, Suite 216
Orlando, Florida 32822
Telephone: (407) 382-7762
Fax: (407) 382-8673
http://jimmyasap.org

Interpreters for: Chinese, French, German, Japanese, Spanish, Vietnamese.

Our Goals:

- Assist parents in the search for their missing children at no cost to the parent!
- Work to provide as much media exposure to the missing child's case as is possible, because such exposure has helped find missing children when other methods have failed.
- Assist law enforcement by referring all leads obtained to the proper authorities.
- I.C.S.R.M.C. operates a 24 hour, seven day a week international missing child hotline to receive leads on missing children cases.
- Assist in ground search activities when called upon to do so.
- Provide computer searches (as needed).
- Ground and aerial surveillance to assist in the missing child case.
- Maintain a multi-lingual staff with several languages available upon request.
- Maintain a capability to do on site case work.

Vanished Children's Alliance
National Headquarters
2095 Park Avenue
San Jose, California 95126
Telephone: 1-800-VANISHED
(408) 296-1113
Fax: (408) 296-1117

The Vanished Children's Alliance (VCA), headquartered in San Jose, California, is a national non-profit organization dedicated to the prevention and recovery of missing and abducted children. Since its inception in 1980, VCA has assisted the families of over 18,000 missing and abducted children; of these, the majority have been found. VCA has provided hundreds of training and prevention education classes and workshops to professionals and the public both nationally and locally. VCA is recognized by the United States Department of Justice, the National Center for Missing and Exploited Children, the State of California Office of Criminal Justice Planning, and by many law enforcement agencies and victim parents across the country as experts in the field of missing and exploited children. *VCA is the oldest and most experienced organization of its kind in California and one of the three oldest in the United States.*

Agency services include:
• providing educational training and materials;
• acting as liaison between searching parents/guardians of missing children and the law enforcement agencies both locally and nationally.
• providing technical assistance for searching parents/guardians;
• registering missing children and active case management;
• distributing missing children photos, descriptive information, posters, flyers and brochures;
• utilizing our computerized database on all reported missing children;
• networking with other credible victim serving non-profit organizations, law enforcement and social services agencies;
• maintaining an updated national referral list of professionals who can provide assistance to families of missing children;
• counseling and on-going emotional support to victim families and victim children;
• acting as expert witnesses for court cases, if needed;
• fingerprinting of children;
• multi-lingual translation services;
• speaker's bureau; and
• in-house legal assistance.
All services to victim families and their children are provided free of charge.

Child Find of America Inc.
7 Innis Avenue
P.O. Box 277
New Paltz, New York 12561-9277
Telephone: (914) 255-1848
Fax: (914) 255-5706

Child Quest International
1625 The Alameda, Suite 400
San Jose, CA 95126
Tel: (408) 287-HOPE
Fax: (408) 287-4676
http://www.childquest.org

Committee for Missing Children
934 Stone Mill Run
Lawrenceville, GA 30245
Tel: (800) 525-8204
Fax: (770) 962-5766

Children's Rights Council of
   Japan
P.O. Box 583
Max Meadows, VA 24360
Tel: (540) 637-3799
E-mail: emari@earthlink.net

Islamic Family Law
Kristine Uhlman
http://www.halcyon.com/harenet/
   umhani
E-mail: umhani@aol.com

Reunite
P.O. Box 4
London WC1X 3DX
England
Tel: 0171-404-8356
Fax: 0171-242-1512
Website: www.dircon.co.uk/users/
   reunite
E-mail: reunite@dircon.co.uk

IAF
Bundesgeschaftsstelle
Landesgeschaftsstelle Hessen
Kasseler Straße 1a
60486 Frankfurt/Main
Germany
Tel: (0-69) 7-07-50-87
          7-07-50-88
Fax (0-69) 7-07-50-92

Appendix D:
Hague Country Profiles

*The following country profiles are presented as a basic guide and infor-
mation. While all attempts have been made to present up-to-date fac-
tual information, it is up to the reader to contact foreign embassies or
the United States Department of State for current travel advisories, passport and visa regulations, changes in country status, etc.*

*The phrase "Member of The Hague" as used in this Appendix
signifies that the country is a signatory to the Hague Convention on the
Civil Aspects of International Child Abduction.*

AUSTRALIA

Member of The Hague since June 1, 1988. Travel requirements to Australia include a valid U.S. passport, visa, and onward/return transportation.
Children have been successfully recovered from Australia.

The Commonwealth of Australia is located in the southwestern Pacific
Ocean. The capital is Canberra. Other major cities include Sydney, Mel-
bourne, and Brisbane.

Embassy of Australia
1601 Massachusetts Ave. NW
Washington DC 20036
Telephone: (202) 797-3000
Fax: (202) 797-3168

Central Authority
International Civil and Privacy Branch
Attorney General's Department
Robert Garran Offices
Barton, Alt 2600

Consulate Phone Numbers:

CA (213) 469-4300
   (415) 362-6160
HI (808) 524-5050

IL (312) 645-9440
NY (212) 245-4000
TX (713) 629-9131

AUSTRIA

Member of The Hague since October 1, 1988. The Republic of Austria is located in Central Europe. A passport is required for entry into Austria; however, a visa is not required for stays up to three months.

The capital of Austria is Vienna. Other major cities include Graz, Linz, Salzburg, and Innsbruck.

Embassy of Austria
3524 International Ct. NW
Washington DC 20008-3035
Telephone: (202) 895-6700
Fax: (202) 895-6750

Central Authority
Bundesministerium für justiz
Abteilung 1 10
Postfach 63
A-1016 Vienna

Consulate Phone Numbers:

CA (310) 444-9310
IL (312) 222-1515

NY (212) 737-6400

ARGENTINA

Member of The Hague since June 1, 1991. A passport is required for travel into the country. Visas are not required for stays up to three months.

The Argentine Republic is located in southern South America. Its capital is Buenos Aires. Other major cities include Cordoba, San Justo, and Rosario.

Embassy of Argentine Republic
1600 New Hampshire Ave. NW
Washington DC 20009
Telephone: (202) 939-6400
Fax: (202) 332-3171

Central Authority
Ministerio de Relaciones Exteriores y
    Culto
Direccion de Asuntos Juridicos
Reconquista 1088 — 3rd Floor
Buenos Aires (c.p. 1003)

Consulate Phone Numbers:

CA (305) 373-1889
IL (312) 263-7435
LA (504) 523-2823

PR (809) 754-6500
TX (713) 871-8935
NY (212) 603-0415

BAHAMAS

Member of The Hague since January 1, 1994. Travel requirements include proof of United States citizenship, photo I.D. and onward/return ticket for entrance into the country. Those planning on arriving in the Bahamas in their own plane or boat should contact the consulate or tourist office for entry requirements. One may be required to show proof of ownership (title), insurance coverage, and/or a temporary import permit.

The Bahamas are a group of islands located in the Caribbean. The capital city is Nassau.

Embassy of the Commonwealth of Bahamas
2220 Massachusetts Ave. NW
Washington DC 20008
Telephone: (202) 319-2660
Fax: (202) 319-2668

Central Authority
The Honorable Minister of Foreign Affairs of the Commonwealth of the Bahamas

Consulate Phone Numbers:

FL (305) 373-6295

NY (212) 421-6420

BELIZE

Member of The Hague since September 1, 1989. A passport is required for entry into the country. A visa is not required for stays up to one month; however, a return/onward ticket is required. A minor child traveling alone with only one parent, or with someone other than his parent may need written authorization allowing the child to travel from the absent parent, or possibly a custody decree. Consult the Belize embassy or consulate for further information. Immunizations may be required for travel.

Belize is located in Central America. Its capital is Belmopan.

Embassy of Belize
2535 Massachusetts Ave. NW
Washington DC 20008
Telephone: (202) 332-9636
Fax: (202) 332-6888

Central Authority
Ministry of Social Services and Community Development
Belmopan

Consulate Phone Number:

NY (212) 599-0233

BOSNIA-HERZEGOVINA

A member of The Hague since December 1, 1991. A United States passport is required to enter the country. Those planning on traveling to the area are urged to contact the embassy of State Department for travel advisories and entry requirements. Children have been successfully recovered from Bosnia through legal channels. Because of civil war in the area, the country is extremely unstable.

The capital city is Sarajevo.

Central Authority
No known address

BURKINA FASO

Member of The Hague since November 1, 1992. Passport and visa are required for entry into the country. Immunizations may be required. Travelers may be required to stop at occasional police roadblocks. Travelers who have entry and/or exit visas or stamps on their passports may be refused admittance into the country. The United States passport agency can provide information and assistance in these cases.

Burkina Faso is located in Sub-Saharan Africa. The capital city is Ouagadougou.

Embassy of Burkina Faso
2340 Massachusetts Ave. NW
Washington DC 20008
Telephone: (202) 332-5577

Central Authority
Le Ministère de l'Action
    Sociale et de la Famille
01 BP 515
Ouagadougou 01

Consulate Phone Numbers:

GA (404) 378-7278
CA (213) 824-5100

LA (504) 945-3152

CANADA

Member of The Hague since July 1, 1988. To enter Canada, a United States citizen must have proof of citizenship.
Legal aid is available in Canada.

Embassy of Canada
501 Pennsylvania Ave. NW
Washington DC 20001
Telephone: (202) 682-1740
Fax: (202) 682-7726

Consulate Phone Numbers:

CA (213) 687-7432	MN (612) 333-4641
(415) 495-6021	NY (212) 768-2400
GA (404) 157-6810	(716) 852-1247
IL (312) 427-1031	OH (216) 771-0150
MA (617) 262-3760	TX (214) 922-9806
MI (313) 567-2340	WA (206) 443-1777

Canada has thirteen offices for its Central Authority. The main office may be contacted at

Justice Legal Services (JUS)
Department of Foreign Affairs
Tower C, 7th Floor
Lester B. Pearson Building
125 Sussex Drive
Ottawa, Ontario K1A OG2
Fax: (613) 992-6485

Phone numbers for the other offices are as follows:

CHARLOTTETOWN, Prince
Edward Island
Telephone: (902) 892-5411

ST. JOHN'S, Newfoundland
Telephone: (709) 576-2893
Fax: (709) 576-2129

EDMONTON, Alberta
Telephone: (403) 422-3715
Fax: (403) 297-6381

TORONTO, Ontario
Telephone: (416) 326-4160

FREDERICTON, New Brunswick
Telephone: (503) 453-2784
Fax: (506) 453-5364

HALIFAX, Nova Scotia
Telephone: (902) 424-4044

REGINA, Saskatchewan
Telephone: (306) 787-8954
Fax: (306) 787-9111

SAINT-FOY, Quebec
Telephone: (418) 644-7152
Fax: (418) 646-1696
Fax: (416) 326-4181

VANCOUVER, British Columbia
Telephone: (604) 660-3093

WHITEHORSE, Yukon Territory
Telephone: (403) 667-5412

WINNIPEG, Manitoba
Telephone: (204) 945-2841
Fax: (204) 945-0053

YELLOWKNIFE, Northwest
  Territories
Telephone: (403) 873-7466
Fax: (403) 873-0106

CHILE

Member of The Hague since July 1, 1994. A passport is required for entry into the country. Visas are not required for stays up to three months.

Located on the southwestern coast of South America, Chile is officially known as the Republic of Chile. Its capital is Santiago, while Vina del Mar and Concepcion are its other major cities.

Embassy of Chile
1732 Massachusetts Ave. NW
Washington DC 20036
Telephone: (202) 785-1746
Fax: (202) 887-5579

Central Authority
La Corporación de Asistencia
  Judicial de la Región
Metropolitana
Agustunas 1419
Santiago de Chile

Consulate Phone Numbers:

CA (213) 624-6357
   (415) 982-7662
FL (305) 373-8623
PA (215) 829-9520

NY (212) 980-3366
TX (713) 621-5853
PR (809) 725-6365

CROATIA

Member of The Hague since December 1, 1991. Passport and visa are required for entry into the country. Travelers are advised to contact the embassy and state department for travel advisories due to civil war conditions.

Croatia's capital is Zagreb.

Embassy of the Republic of Croatia
236 Massachusetts Ave. NW
Washington DC 20002
Telephone: (202) 543-5580

Central Authority
Ministry of Labour and Welfare
Prisavlje 14
41000 Zagreb

CYPRUS

Member of The Hague since March 1, 1995. Passport required for entry; visa required for stays longer than three months. The common points of entry into this island nation are Larnoca and Paphos international airports located in the southern part of the island. Legal entry can also be made through the seaports of Limassol, Larnaca and Paphos. All entries are from the southern part of the island. Although it is possible to enter in the northern section of the island, travel from the northern to the southern portion may not be permitted. Those entering the island from the south may enter the north for short periods. Travelers should contact the embassy for travel requirements.

Located in the Eastern Mediterranean, Cyprus is divided into two areas. The Turks operate the northern section, while the Greeks operate the southern section. The capital of Cyprus is Nicosia, and Limassol is a major city.

**Embassy of the Republic
   of Cyprus**
2211 R Street NW
Washington DC 20008
Telephone: (202) 462-5772

Central Authority
Minister of Justice and Public Order
12 Helioupoleos Street
Nicosia

Consulate Phone Numbers:

CA (415) 893-1661
IL (312) 677-9068

St. Louis (314) 781-7040
NY (212) 686-6016

DENMARK

Member of The Hague since July 1, 1991. While a passport is required for entry, a stay for up to three months does not require a visa. A traveler's stay begins upon entry into the Scandinavian area (Finland, Iceland, Norway and Sweden as well as Denmark).

The Kingdom of Denmark is located in northwest Europe. Copenhagen is the capital. Major cities include Arhus and Odense.

Royal Danish Embassy
3200 Whitehaven St. NW
Washington DC 20008
Telephone: (202) 234-4300
Fax: (202) 328-1470

Central Authority
Ministry of Justice
Department of Private Law
(Civilretsdirektoratet)
Æbeløgade 1
2100 Copenhagen 0

Consulate Phone Numbers:

CA (213) 387-4277
IL (312) 329-9644

NY (212) 223-4545

ECUADOR

Member of The Hague since April 1, 1992. Passport required for entry along with return/onward ticket. No visa is required for entry along with return/onward ticket. No visa is required for stays up to three months. Dual nationality may not be recognized in some Central and South American countries; therefore, an individual with United States citizenship may not be afforded the rights someone without the dual nationality has. Travelers concerned about dual nationality should contact the Office of Citizens Consular Services, Room 4817, Department of State, Washington DC 20520, (202) 647-3712.

The Republic of Ecuador is located in northwest South America. The capital is Quito. Other major cities include Guayaquil and Cuenca.

Embassy of Ecuador
2535 15th St. NW
Washington DC 20009
Telephone: (202) 234-7200

Central Authority
National Court of Minors
Gonzalas Suarez #1555
Edificio El Peñon
Departamento 6 N
Quito

Consulate Phone Numbers:

CA (213) 628-3014   LA (504) 523-3229
   (415) 391-4148   MA (617) 227-7200
FL (305) 539-8214   NY (212) 683-7555
IL (312) 642-8579   TX (214) 747-6329

ENGLAND AND WALES

Member of The Hague since July 1, 1988. An American citizen entering England or Wales must have a passport. No visa is required if staying less than 90 days. Scotland Yard has assisted in successful recovery by searching parents. England and Wales are part of the United Kingdom, which also includes Northern Ireland and Scotland. All are members of The Hague.

Embassy of the United Kingdom of
Great Britain and Northern Ireland
3100 Massachusetts Ave. NW
Washington DC 20008
Telephone: (202) 462-1430
Fax: (202) 898-4255

Central Authority
Northern Ireland Court Service
Windsor House
9-15 Bedford Street
Belfast
BT2 7LT

Central Authority for
England & Wales
Child Abduction Unit
81 Chancery Lane, 4th Floor
London WC2A 1DD
Telephone: [071]-(911)-7047 or 7094
Fax: [071]-(911) 7248

Central Authority for Scotland
Office of the Secretary of State
for Scotland
Scottish Courts Administration
Hayweight House
23 Lauriston Street
Edinburgh
EH3 9DQ United Kingdom

Consulate Phone Numbers:

CA (213) 385-7381   MA (617) 437-7160
   (415) 981-3030   NY (212) 752-8400
GA (404) 524-5856   OH (216) 621-7674
IL (312) 346-1810   TX (214) 637-3600

Legal aid is available. Contact:

London Office of the Legal Aid Board
29/37 Red Lion Street
London WC1R, England

FINLAND

A member of The Hague since August 1, 1994. A passport is required for entry into the country. A visa is not required for stays up to 90 days. The 90-day period begins once one has entered the Scandinavian area (Sweden, Denmark, Norway, and Iceland as well as Finland).

The Republic of Finland is located in northern Europe. Its capital is Helsinki. Other major cities include Espoo and Tampere.

Embassy of Finland
3216 New Mexico Ave NW
Washington, DC 20016
Telephone: (202) 363-2430
Fax: (202) 363-8233

Central Authority
Ministry of Justice
Eteläesplanadi 10
P.O. Box 1
00131 Helsinki

Consulate Phone Numbers:

CA (213) 203-9903   NY (212) 573-6007

FORMER YUGOSLAV REPUBLIC OF MACEDONIA

The former Yugoslav Republic of Macedonia became a member of The Hague on December 1, 1991. It has not been recognized as a country by the United States. A passport is needed to enter the country, and permission to enter can be obtained at border points.

For more information, travelers should contact the Department of State's Bureau of Consular Affairs.

FRANCE

Member of The Hague since July 1, 1988. Passports are required to enter the country; however, a visa is not required for stays up to three months. The French embassy can also provide information on travel requirements for Andorra, Monaco, Corsica and French Polynesia. Dual nationality status may not be recognized by France. Tourists are requested to contact the U.S. embassy for further information.

Travelers flying on certain Air France flights may stop in Syria, Jordan, or Lebanon. Check travel advisories.

The French Republic is located in western Europe. The capital of France is Paris.

Embassy of France
4101 Reservoir Road NW
Washington DC 20007
Telephone: (202) 944-6000
Fax: (202) 944-6166

Central Authority
Bureau du droit international
    et de L'entraide judiciare
    internationale en matière
    civile et commerciale
Ministère de la Justice
13 Place Vendôme
75042 Paris Cedex 01

Consulate Phone Numbers:

CA (310) 479-4426
    (415) 397-4330
FL (305) 372-9798
GA (404) 522-4226
IL (312) 787-5359

LA (504) 523-5774
ME (617) 482-3650
MI (313) 568-0990
HI (808) 599-4458
NY (212) 606-3688

GERMANY

Member of The Hague since December 1, 1990. A passport is required for entry into the country; however, a visa is not required for stays up to three months. Travelers are required to show proof of health insurance.

The Federal Republic of Germany is located in North Central Europe. The capital is Berlin. Other major cities include Hamburg and Munich. Children have been successfully recovered from Germany.

**Embassy of the Federal Republic
of Germany**
4645 Reservoir Rd. NW
Washington DC 20007
Telephone: (202) 298-4000
Fax: (202) 298-4249

Central Authority
Der Generalbundesanwalt beim
Bundesgerichtshof-Zentrale
Behörde nach dem
Sorgerects-Übereinkommens-
Ausführungsgesetz
Neuenburgerstrasse 15
10969 Berlin

Consulate Phone Numbers

CA (415) 775-1061

FL (305) 358-0290

GREECE

Member of The Hague since June 1, 1993. A passport is required for entry. Visas not required for stays up to three months. Greece may not recognize dual nationality status. Tourists are advised to consult with the embassy for further information.

The Hellenic Republic (the official name of Greece) is located in southeastern Europe and its capital is Athens. Other major cities include Salonika and Piraeus.

Embassy of Greece
2221 Massachusetts Ave. NW
Washington DC 20008
Telephone: (202) 686-4520
Fax: (202) 939-5824

Central Authority
Ministère de la Justice
Direction de l'élaboration des Lois
4éme Section
Athénes

Consulate Phone Numbers:

CA (415) 775-2102
GA (404) 261-3313
IL (312) 372-5356

LA (504) 523-1167
MA (617) 542-3240
NY (212) 988-5500

HONDURAS

Member of The Hague since June 1, 1994. A United States passport and return/onward ticket are required for entry. Inquire about immunization requirements.

Honduras is located in Central America. The capital is Tegucigalpa.

Embassy of Honduras
3007 Tilden St. NW
Washington DC 20008
Telephone: (202) 966-7702
Fax: (202) 966-9751

Central Authority
Junta Nacional de Bienestar Social

HUNGARY

Member of The Hague since July 1, 1988. A passport is required for entry into the country. No visa is required for stays up to 90 days. Contact embassy concerning dual nationality laws.

The Republic of Hungary is located in east central Europe. Hungary's capital is Budapest, and Debrecen and Miskolc are among the major cities.

Embassy of the Republic of Hungary
3910 Shoemaker St. NW
Washington DC 20008
Telephone: (202) 362-6730
Fax: (202) 966-8135

Consulate Phone Number:

NY (212) 879-4127

Central Authority
The Ministry of Justice
Szalay Utca 16
P.O. Box 54
1363 Budapest

IRELAND

Member of The Hague since October 1, 1991. Passports are required to enter the country. Stays up to 90 days do not require a visa; however, onward/return ticket may be required. Seek travel advisory due to terrorist activity in border area of Northern Ireland.

Ireland is an island in the eastern North Atlantic Ocean. Ireland's capital is Dublin, and other major cities include Cork and Limerick.

Embassy of Ireland
3514 International Dr. NW
Washington DC 20008
Telephone: (202) 462-3939

Central Authority
Department of Equality and Law Reform
43-49 Mespil Road
Dublin 4

Consulate Phone Numbers:

CA (415) 392-4214
IL (312) 337-1868

MA (617) 267-9330
NY (212) 319-2555

ISRAEL

Member of The Hague since December 1, 1991. A passport is required for entry as well as onward/return ticket and proof of funds. A visa is issued upon entrance into the country good for up to three months. Children have been successfully recovered from Israel. Entry into and out of Israel can be difficult. Security is heavy and confiscation of personal items is not uncommon. Individuals with Arabian last names may find it more difficult to enter Israel, even though they possess a United States passport. Israeli dual nationals as well as their children, are considered Israeli by Israel.

Travelers are advised to contact the State Department or embassy for travel advisories, and the United States Passport Agency for passport information and assistance.

The state of Israel is located in the Middle East. The capital is Jerusalem. Other major cities include Tel Aviv–Jaffa and Haifa. Extreme caution should be exercised when traveling to the Golan Heights and Gaza areas. Persons crossing over to Jordan may not be permitted to re-enter Israel. Children have been successfully recovered from Israel.

Embassy of Israel
3514 International Dr. NW
Washington DC 20008
Telephone: (202) 364-3500
Fax: (202) 364-5610

Central Authority
International Department of
   the State Attorney's Office
Ministry of Justice
P.O. Box 1087
Jerusalem 91010

Consulate Phone Numbers:

CA (213) 651-5700   IL (312) 565-3300
   (415) 398-8885   MA (617) 542-0041
FL (305) 358-8111   NY (212) 351-5200
GA (404) 875-7851   PA (215) 546-5556
TX (713) 627-3780

ITALY

Member of The Hague since May 1, 1995. Passports are required for entry into the country. Tourists may stay up to three months without a visa. Contact embassy concerning dual nationality status

Some Alitalia flights to Syria and Jordan may stop in Lebanon. Tourists should check travel advisory. The State Department warns all United States citizens to avoid all travel to Lebanon.

The Italian Republic is located in Southern Europe. Rome is its capital, and other major cities include Milan and Naples.

Embassy of Italy   **Central Authority**
1601 Fuller St. NW   Ministry of Justice
Washington DC 20009   Central Office for the Justice of Minors
Telephone: (202) 328-5500   Via Giulia 131
                               00186 Rome

Consulate Phone Numbers:

CA (310) 820-0622   MA (617) 542-0483
   (415) 931-4924   MI (313) 963-8560
FL (305) 374-6322   NY (212) 737-9100
IL (312) 467-1550   PA (215) 592-7369
LA (504) 524-2272   TX (713) 850-7520

LUXEMBOURG

Member of The Hague since July 1, 1988. A passport is required for entry into the country. Visas are not required for stays up to three months.

Luxembourg is located in western Europe. The capital is Luxembourg.

Embassy of Luxembourg
2200 Massachusetts Ave. NW
Washington DC 20008
Telephone: (202) 265-4171
Fax: (202) 328-8270

Consulate Phone Numbers:

CA (415) 788-0816
FL (305) 373-1300
GA (404) 952-1157
IL (312) 726-0355

Central Authority
Le Procureur Général d'Etat
Palais de Justice
Boîte postale 15
2010 Luxembourg

MO (816) 474-4761
NY (212) 370-9850
OH (513) 422-4697
TX (214) 746-7200

MAURITIUS

Member of The Hague since October 1, 1993. A passport is required for entry as well as onward/return ticket and sufficient funds. No visa is required for stays up to three months. Travelers should check for immunization requirements as well as travel advisories.

Mauritius is located in Sub-Saharan Africa. The capital is Port Louis.

Embassy of Mauritius
4301 Connecticut Ave. NW £441
Washington DC 20008
Telephone: (202) 244-1491
Fax: (202) 966-0983

Central Authority
Ministère du Travail et
   de la Politique
Sociale/Ministry of Labour and
   Social Policy
Rue Dame Gruev No. 14
91000 SKOPJE

Consulate Phone Number:

NY (212) 737-7780

MEXICO

Member of The Hague since October 1, 1991.

A United States citizen does not need a passport or a visa for stays up to 90 days; however, a tourist card is required as well as proof of United States citizenship and photo I.D.

A very high number of international parental abductions involve Mexico, largely due to geographic convenience. Many Mexican children are abducted to the United States and many American children to Mexico. To combat this problem, Mexican law requires that a child traveling alone or with one parent must have written notarized consent of the other parent, the other parent's death certificate, or a custody decree. Consent is not needed if the child is traveling on a United States passport.

Mexico's Central Authority in charge of International Parental Abduction is the Legal Advisor's Office of the Mexican Minister of Foreign Affairs. The function of the Central Authority is to give jurisdictional advice to the Mexican foreign ministry in the field of public and private international law and to supervise the approval of treaties signed by Mexico. It is this authority which takes applications for Hague assistance.

Mexico has extradition treaties with the United States in parental abductions (1) when a child has been abducted by a parent who has previously been deprived of parental rights by the competent family court; or (2) when a child is under 12 years of age, and taken by a relative other than the parents, without legal guardianship.

In order for Mexico to extradite an abductor, a warrant must be issued for his or her arrest.

Legal aid is available to Hague applicants.

Embassy of Mexico
1911 Pennsylvania Ave. NW
Washington DC 20006
Telephone: (202) 728-1600
Fax: (202) 728-1698

Central Authority
Consultoria Jurídica
Secretaría de Rellaciones Exteriores
Homero No 213, Piso 17
Colonia Chapultepec, Morales
11570 Mexico, Distrito Federal

Consulate Phone Numbers:

Washington DC (202) 736-1000
CA (213) 351-6800
   (415) 392-5554
   (619) 231-8414
CO (303) 830-6702
FL (305) 441-8780
IL (312) 855-1380

LA (504) 522-3596
NY (212) 689-0456
TX (214) 522-9741
   (713) 463-9426
   (512) 227-9145
   (915) 533-3644

U.S. Consulates General and Consulates in Mexico:

American Consulate General
Avenue Lopez Mateos 924-N
Ciudad Juarez, Chihuahua
Tel: [52]-(15)-134-048
Emergency: (915)-525-6066

American Consulate General
Progreso 175
Guadalajara, Jalisco
Tel: [52]-(36)-25-2998 or 25-2700

American Consulate
Calle Monterrey 141, Poniente
Tel: [52]-(621)-723-75
Emergency: [52]-(621)-725-85

American Consulate
Ave. Primera No. 2002
Matamoros, Tamaulipas
Tel: [52]-(891)-2-52-50
                    2-52-51
Emergency: (512) 546-1611

American Consulate
Paseo Montejo 453
Merida, Yucatan
Tel: [52]-(99)-25-5011
Emergency: [52]-(99)-25-5409

American Consulate Genral
Avenida Constitucion 411
Poniente
Monterrey, Nueva Leon
Tel: [52]-(83)-45-2120

American Consulate
Avenida Allende 330
Col. Jardin
Nuevo Laredo, Tamaulipas
Tel: [52]-(871)-4-0696
                4-9616
                4-0512
Emergency: (512)-727-9661

American Consulate Genral
Tapachula 96
Tijuana, Baja CA

American Consulate
Circunvalacion No. 120 Centro
Mazatian, Sinaloa
Tel: [52]-(678)-5-2205
Tel: [52]-(66)-81-7400
                (706)-681-7400
Emergency: (619)-585-2000

Resident Consular Agents in Mexico:

(Agents may be contacted through their office in preceding list or directly)

ACAPULCO, Guerrero-[52]-(748)-5-7202 ext. 273
U.S. Embassy, Mexico City

CANCUN, Quintana Roo-[52]-(988)-4-63-99
U.S. Consulate, Merida

DURANGO, Durango-[52]-(181)-1-2217
U.S. Consulate Genral, Monterrey

MULEGE, Baja California Sur-[52]-(68)-5-3-0111
U.S. Consulate General, Tijuana

OAXACA, Oaxaca-[52]-(951)-6-0654
Puerto Vallarta, Jalisco-[52]-(322)-2-0069
U.S. Consulate General, Guadalajara

SAN LUIS POTOSI, San Lui Potosi-[52]-(481)-7-2501
U.S. Consulate General, Monterrey

SAN MIGUEL DE ALLENDE, Guanajuato-[52]-(465)-2-2357
U.S. Consulate General, Guanalajara

TAMPICO, Tamaulipas-[52]-(121)-3-2217
U.S. Embassy, Mexico City

MONACO

Member of The Hague since June 1, 1993. Passports are required for entry into the country. No visa is required for stays up to three months. There is no U.S. embassy in Monaco; however, travelers can contact the U.S. Consulate General in France: (33) 93888955.

Monaco is located in southern Europe. The capital is Monaco-Ville.

Central Authority
Direction des Services Judiciares
Palais de Justice
5 rue Colonel Bellando de Castro
MC 98000 Monaco

Consulate Phone Numbers:

CA (213) 655-8970	LA (504) 522-5700
(415) 362-5050	NY (212) 759-5227
IL (312) 642-1242	PR (809) 721-4215

NETHERLANDS

Member of The Hague since August 1, 1990. Entry into the country requires a passport, possibly an onward/return ticket, and proof of sufficient funds. No visa is required for stays up to 90 days.

The Kingdom of the Netherlands is located in northwestern Europe. Its capital is Amsterdam. Other major cities include Rotterdam and The Hague.

Embassy of the Netherlands	**Central Authority**
4200 Linnean Ave. NW	Ministerie van Justitie
Washington DC 20008	Dienst Preventie,
Telephone: (202) 244-5300	Jeugdbescherming en Reclassering
Fax: (202) 362-3430	Stafbureau Juridishe Zaken
	Schedeldoekshaven 100
	Postbus 20301
	2500 EH The Hague

Consulate Phone Numbers:

CA (213) 380-3440	NY (212) 246-1429
IL (312) 856-0110	TX (713) 622-8000

NEW ZEALAND

Member of The Hague since October 1, 1991. A passport is required for entry into the country as well as onward/return ticket. No visa is required for stays up to three months.

New Zealand is located in the southeast Pacific Ocean. The capital is Wellington. Other major cities include Auckland, Christchurch, and Hamilton.

Embassy of New Zealand	**Central Authority**
37 Observatory Circle NW	Department for Courts
Washington DC 20008	Private Box 2750
Telephone: (202) 328-4800	Wellington

Consulate Phone Number:

CA (213) 477-8241

NORWAY

Member of The Hague since April 1, 1989. A passport is required for entry into the country. A visa is not required for stays up to three months.

Norway is located in northern Europe. Officially called the Kingdom of Norway, its capital is Oslo. Other major cities include Bergen, Trondheim, and Stavanger.

Royal Norwegian Embassy
2720 34th Street NW
Washington DC 20008
Telephone: (202) 333-6000
Fax: (202) 337-0870

Central Authority
Justisdepartementet
Sivilavdelingen
1 juridiske enhet
Postboks 8005 dep
0030 0510

Consulate Phone Numbers:

CA (415) 986-0766
          0767
          0768
CA (213) 933-7717

MN (612) 332-3338
NY (212) 421-7333
TX (713) 521-2900

PANAMA

Member of The Hague since June 1, 1994. Passport, visa or tourist card, and onward/return ticket required for entry into the country. U.S. citizens may not use tourist cards. Tourists should check travel advisories.

Panama is located in Central America. The capital is Panama City.

Embassy of the Republic of Panama
2862 McGill Terrace NW
Washington DC 20008
Telephone: (202) 483-1407
Fax: (202) 483-8413

Central Authority
Direccion General de Asuntos
Juridicios y tratados
Ministerio de Ralicones Exteriores
Panama 4

POLAND

Member of The Hague since November 1, 1992. Passports are required for entry into the country; however, visas are not required for stays up to 90 days. Visitors must register at a hotel or with the local authorities within 48 hours of arrival into the country. Dual nationals are requested to obtain information at the Polish embassy.

Poland is located in eastern Europe. The capital is Warsaw. Other major cities include Lodz and Krakow.

Embassy of the Republic of Poland
2640 16th Street NW
Washington DC 20009
Telephone: (202) 234-3800
Fax: (202) 328-6271

Central Authority
Ministére de la Justice
Departement juridique
Al Ujazdowskie 11
00-950 Varsovie

Consulate Phone Numbers:

CA (213) 365-7900
IL (312) 337-8166

NY (212) 889-8360

PORTUGAL

Member of The Hague since July 1, 1988. Passports are required for entry into the country; however, no visa is necessary for stays up to 60 days.

Portugal is located on the Iberian Peninsula in southwestern Europe. The capital is Lisbon. Other major cities include Oporto and Amadora.

Embassy of Portugal
2125 Vialorama Rd. NW
Washington DC 20008
Telephone: (202) 328-8610
Fax: (202) 462-3726

Central Authority
Instituto de Reinsercao Social
Avenida Almirante Reis 10', 7°
1197 Lisboa

Consulate Phone Numbers:

CA (415) 346-3400
MA (617) 536-8740
    (508) 997-6151

NJ (201) 622-7300
NY (212) 246-4580
RI (401) 272-2003

ROMANIA

Member of The Hague since June 1, 1993. Passports and visas are required for entry into the country. Customs official are strict. Dual nationals should contact the embassy regarding citizenship recognition status.

Romania is located in southeastern Europe. The capital is Bucharest. Other major cities include Constanta and Iasi.

Embassy of Romania
1607 23rd Street NW
Washington DC 20008
Telephone: (202) 332-4846
Fax: (202) 232-4748

Central Authority
Ministére de la Justice
Bd. M. Kogalniceanu 33
Setor 5
Bucarest

Consulate Phone Numbers:

NY (212) 682-9120, 9121 or 9122

ST. KITTS–NEVIS

Members of The Hague since June 1, 1995. No passport is required; however, proof of citizenship, photo I.D., and onward/return ticket are needed to enter the country.

Located in the Caribbean, this pair of islands has no U.S. embassy. Saint Kitts–Nevis is a member of the Association of Caribbean States. Its capital is Basseterre. The following U.S. agencies have been designated for the Caribbean:

American Consular Agent
51 Beller St.
Puerto Plata, Dominican Republic
Telephone: (809) 586-4204

American Consular Agent
St. James Place, 2nd FL
Glocester Ave.
Montego Bay, Jamaica
Telephone: (809) 952-0160

Central Authority
The Attorney General
P.O. Box 98
Attorney General's Office
Basseterre
St. Kitts-Nevis
West Indies

SLOVENIA

Member of The Hague since April 1, 1995. Passport and visa required. Visas may be obtained at entry point. Slovenia is located in the former Yugoslavia. Travelers are advised to seek travel advisories into the country due to civil war in the south.

**Embassy of the Republic
of Slovenia**
1300 19th St. NW #410
Washington DC 20036
Telephone: (202) 828-1650

Central Authority
Ministry of Labour, Family and Social
   Affairs of the Republic of Slovenia
Section for Social Affairs
Kotnikova 5
1000 Ljubljana

SPAIN

A member of The Hague since July 1, 1988. A passport is required for entry into the country; however, a visa is not necessary for stays up to six months.

Spain is located in the Iberian Peninsula in southwestern Europe. The capital is Madrid. Other major cities include Barcelona and Valencia.

Embassy of Spain
2700 15th Street NW
Washington DC 20009
Telephone: (202) 265-0190
Fax: (202) 332-5451

Central Authority
La Dirección General de Codificación
Juridica Internacional
Ministerio de Justicia e Interior
San Bernardo 45
28015 Madrid

Consulate Phone Numbers:

CA (415) 922-2995
   (213) 658-6050
FL (305) 446-551
IL (312) 782-4588
LA (504) 525-4951

MA (617) 536-2506
NY (212) 355-4080
PR (809) 758-6090
TX (713) 783-6200

SWEDEN

Member of The Hague since June 1, 1989. A passport is required for entry into the country. A visa is not required for stays up to three months.

The Kingdom of Sweden is located in northern Europe. The capital is Stockholm. Other major cities include Goteborg, Malmo and Uppsala.

Embassy of Sweden
600 New Hampshire Ave. NW #1200
Washington DC 20037
Telephone: (202) 944-5600
Fax: (202) 342-1319

Central Authority
Ministry for Foreign Affairs
Box 16121
10323 Stockholm

Consulate Phone Numbers:

CA (310) 575-3383   NY (212) 751-5900
IL (312) 781-6262

SWITZERLAND

Member of The Hague since July 1, 1988. Passport required for entry into country; however, a visa is not required for stays up to three months.

The Swiss Confederation is located in Central Europe. The capital is Bern, and other major cities include Zurich and Basel.

Embassy of Switzerland
2900 Cathedral Ave. NW
Washington DC 20008
Telephone: (202) 387-2564

Central Authority
Office fédéral de la justice
Autorité centrale en Matiére
    d'enlévement international
    d'enfants
Jundesrain 20
03 Berne

Consulate Phone Numbers:

CA (310) 575-1145   IL (312) 915-0061
    (415) 788-2272   NY (212) 758-2560
GA (404) 872-7874   TX (713) 650-0000

UNITED KINGDOM

Member of The Hague since July 1, 1988. Four countries make up the United Kingdom: England, Wales, Scotland, and Northern Ireland. Passports are required to enter the United Kingdom; however, a visa is not necessary for stays up to six months.

This island nation is located in western Europe. Children have been successfully recovered from the United Kingdom. The capital is London, England. Other major cities include Birmingham, Leeds, Glasgow, and Sheffield.

Embassy of the United Kingdom of Great Britain and Northern Ireland
3100 Massachusetts Ave. NW
Washington DC 20008   (See pages 204–5.)
Telephone: (202) 462-1430
Fax: (202) 898-4255

Consulate Phone Numbers:

CA (213) 385-7381   NY (212) 752-8400
　 (415) 981-3030   OH (216) 621-7674
GA (404) 524-5856   IL (312) 346-1810
MA (617) 437-7160   TX (214) 637-3600

UNITED STATES

Member of The Hague since July 1, 1988. The Central Authority in the United States is the United States Department of State. They can be contacted at:

United States Central Authority
Office of Children's Issues
Room 4800, Department of State
Washington DC 20520
Telephone: (202) 736-7000

Office hours are 8:30 A.M. to 5:00 P.M., Monday–Friday.

Consular officers serve as case workers in abduction cases. They are assigned cases according to the country to which a child is believed to have been abducted.

ZIMBABWE

Zimbabwe became a member of The Hague on August 1, 1995. A passport is required to enter the country. Travelers are advised to inquire about immunization requirements as well as visa and onward/return ticket information.

Zimbabwe is located in Sub-Saharan Africa. Some areas are off limits to tourists. The Republic of Zimbabwe's capital is Harre. Bulawayo and Chitung Wiza are major cities. Women and children are sometimes not allowed to leave the country without a husband's or father's consent.

**Embassy of the Republic
of Zimbabwe**
1608 New Hampshire Ave. NW
Washington DC 20009
Telephone: (202) 332-7100
Fax: (202) 483-9326

Central Authority
Permanent Secretary of the
    Ministry of Justice
Legal and Parliamentary Affairs
Corner House
Samora Machel Ave./
    Leopold Takawira St.
P.O. Box 7704
Harare

Index

223